IMAGES
of America

AROUND SQUAM LAKE

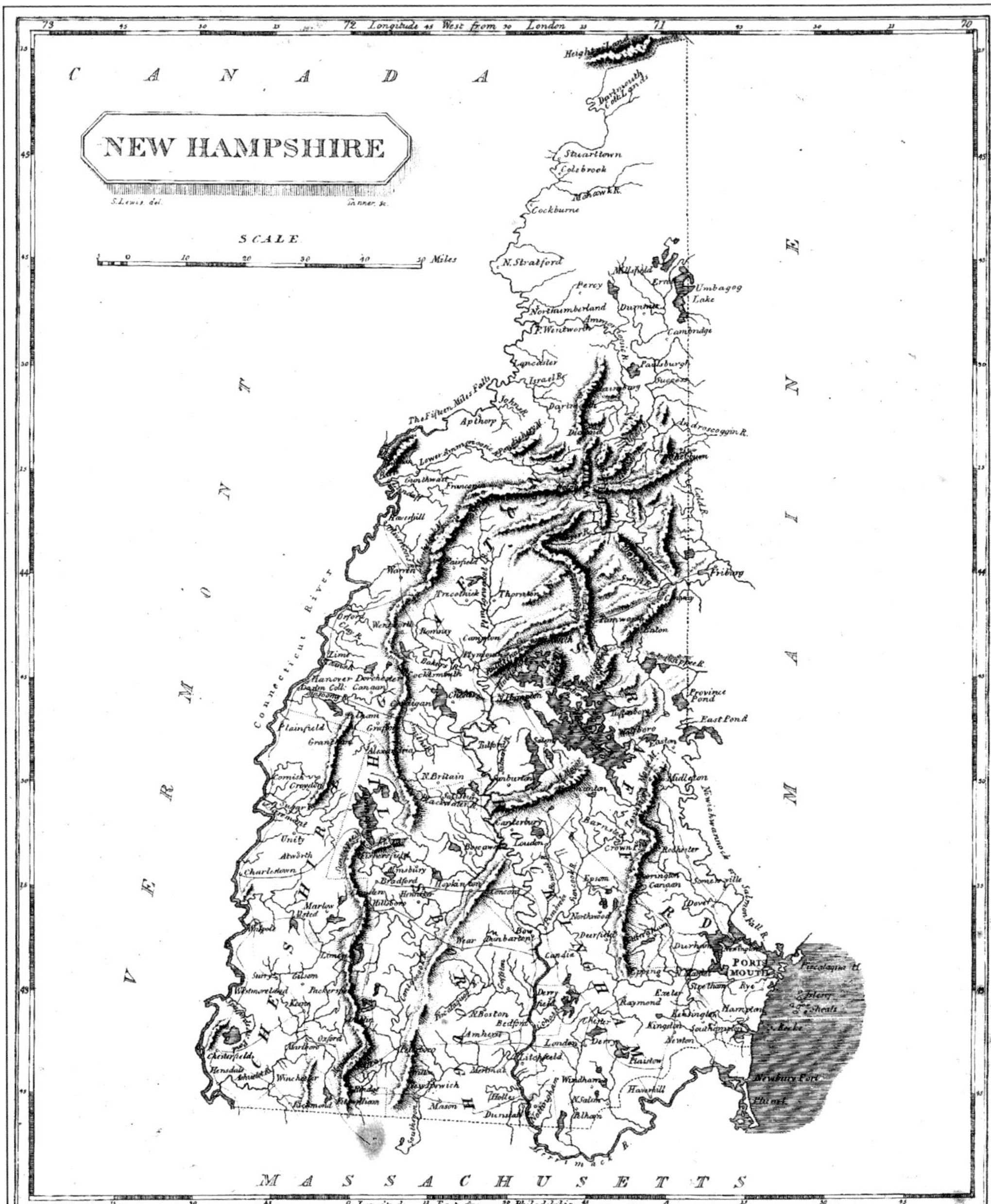

AN ACCURATE MAP OF NEW HAMPSHIRE, 1781. This map is taken from a survey for the *Universal Magazine of Knowledge & Pleasure*. The survey was conducted by John Hinton of the King's Arms in Paternoster Row, London, England.

IMAGES
of America

AROUND SQUAM LAKE

Bruce D. Heald, Ph.D.

ARCADIA
PUBLISHING

ISBN 978-0-7385-1001-9

Published by Arcadia Publishing
Charleston, South Carolina

Printed in the United States of America

Library of Congress Catalog Card Number: 2006927073

For all general information contact Arcadia Publishing at:
Telephone 843-853-2070
Fax 843-853-0044
E-mail sales@arcadiapublishing.com
For customer service and orders:
Toll-Free 1-888-313-2665

Visit us on the Internet at www.arcadiapublishing.com

Contents

ACKNOWLEDGMENTS

The author gratefully acknowledges the following individuals and organizations: Ashland Centennial Committee, Ashland Historical Society, John D. Bardwell, Robert and Barbara Bennett, Ronald P. Bergeron, Boston & Maine Railroad, Derek Brereton, Catherine H. Campbell, Centre Harbor Historical Society, Chocorua Island Chapel Association, Chisholm's White Mountain Guide, Concord & Montreal Railroad, William Depuy, Betty F. Dudley, Dorritt Fogg, Peter Francesco, Roger Gage, William H. Genne, William Greene, Gilbert M. Hewins, Holderness Historical Society, Barbara Kelley, Nancy Kelley, Roger Kelley, Helen S. Matthews, New Hampshire Farm Publication, New Hampshire Fish and Game, Osgood's White Mountain Guide, Jane Rice, David Ruell, Sandwich Historical Society, Katherine Taylor, William Twombly, Peter Van Winkle, and Dick Wakefield.

Introduction

New Hampshire is endowed with a multitude of brilliant lakes of such exquisite beauty that they have stirred the muse of poets, inspired the writings of historians, and prompted the studies of naturalists. The limpid purity of Squam Lake and Little Squam Lake reflects the grandeur of the adjacent mountains, creating an enchanted valley.

Thousands of years ago, a glacial ice sheet worked its way across the state, softening the mass of mountain peaks, grinding its way over the lowland, and leaving hundreds of basins to form the lakes and valleys of New Hampshire. Today, the state has many miles of wooded shores; roads lined with pines, maples, and birches; sloping grassy hillsides strewn with buttercups and Queen Anne's lace; and pasture pools with white and yellow water lilies.

Long inhabited by the Abenaki Nation of the Algonquin Federation, the Squam Lake area was not discovered by English settlers until the mid-1700s. The Native American name for Squam Lake is said to have been either Kees-ee-hunk-nip-ee (the goose-lake of the highlands) or Wonn-as-squam-auke (the beautiful, surrounded-by-water place). The lake is officially known as Asquam (the Native American word for water) and is popularly known as Big Squam.

The shaggy slopes of the Squam and the Sandwich Mountain ranges frame the northern half of the Squam Lake area; Red Hill commands the southern exposure. Beyond, the bald cone of Mount Chocorua, the lofty heights of Passaconaway Mountain, and the ledges of Whiteface Mountain form a backdrop for Squam. To the east is Ossipee Lake and to the west are Newfound Lake and Mount Cardigan.

Squam Lake, with an area of 6,767 acres, a length of over six miles, and a breadth of approximately three miles, contains countless inlets, bays, coves, and long peninsulas. Its waters flow into the Pemigewasset River. The lake is nearly divided into two sections, between which are several long islands parallel to one another. There are 16 islands in the lake. Several that are habitable today were originally used for pasturing horses and sheep.

Surrounded by lofty green hills and forested shores, Squam Lake is considered to be one of New Hampshire's most beautiful bodies of water. Visitors, who come from all over the world, often select a favorite view: a landmark such as the open ledge on Rattlesnake Mountain, Shepard Hill, Bennett Cove, Webster Cove, the chapel on Chocorua (Church) Island, the beaches in Sandwich, or the vista from the summit of Red Hill.

Since 1882, camps for boys and camps for girls have sprung up along the lakeshore. Along with the camps came public beaches, marinas, cabins, motels, hotels, and private summer homes. However, those who live in the towns bordering the lake have made it a priority to preserve the simplicity and vitality of the natural habitat.

The images and narrative that follow offer a glimpse of the romance and charm of bygone days in and around Squam and Little Squam Lakes and the surrounding towns of Ashland, Center Harbor, Holderness, Moultonborough, and Sandwich.

One

SQUAM LAKE AND LITTLE SQUAM LAKE

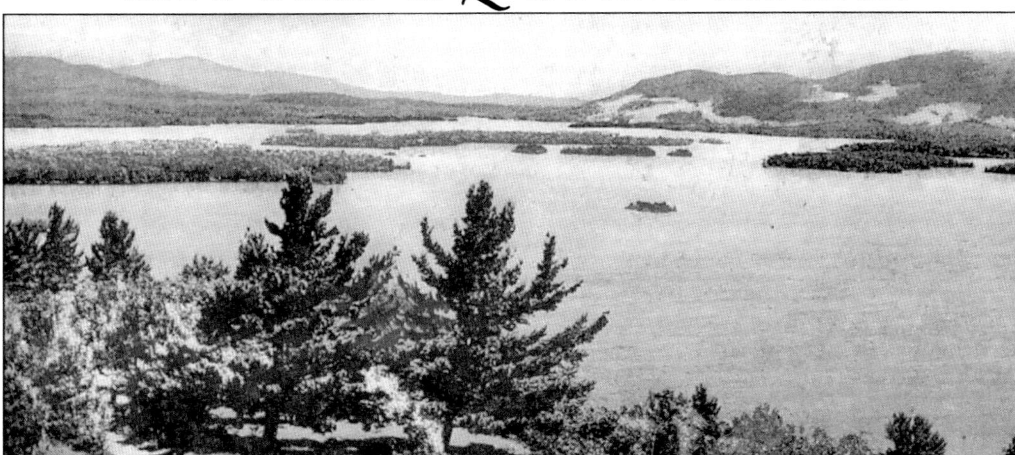

SQUAM LAKE FROM SHEPARD HILL. Native American folklore flourished throughout the Lakes Region. At the far end of Squam Lake, in the town of Sandwich, is a secluded arm of the lake called Squaw Cove. The cove took its name from a block of granite that on one side of its ledge bears the resemblance of a woman. The block has been removed, but the legend associated with it lingers. A Native American leader called Waunega had long been widowed when he fell in love with the young and graceful Suneta. Suneta lived across the lake with her father, who was a powerful sachem of an allied tribe. She loved a young man called Anonis, but her father favored his friend and ally Waunega. After the marriage feast, Waunega and Suneta paddled across the lake to the bride's new home. Anonis was not at the marriage ceremony, but during a fearful storm in the night, Suneta suddenly felt the touch of a hand on her face and heard Anonis whisper to come with him. Awakened by the storm, the old Waunega missed his bride and went in search of her. A flash of lightning revealed the lovers in a canoe. Waunega discharged an arrow at his rival, who fell into the water. Suneta swam to a ledge where she called out for help from the Great Spirit. Waunega cried out, "May the lightning blast her! Let the Manitou make of her an example to coming time." Hardly were the words out of his mouth when a crash thunder and a bolt of lightning caused the mountains and rocks to tremble. Terrified at the effect of his words, Waunega plunged into the water and perished. When morning dawned, the figure of a woman was visible on the rock where Suneta had clung.

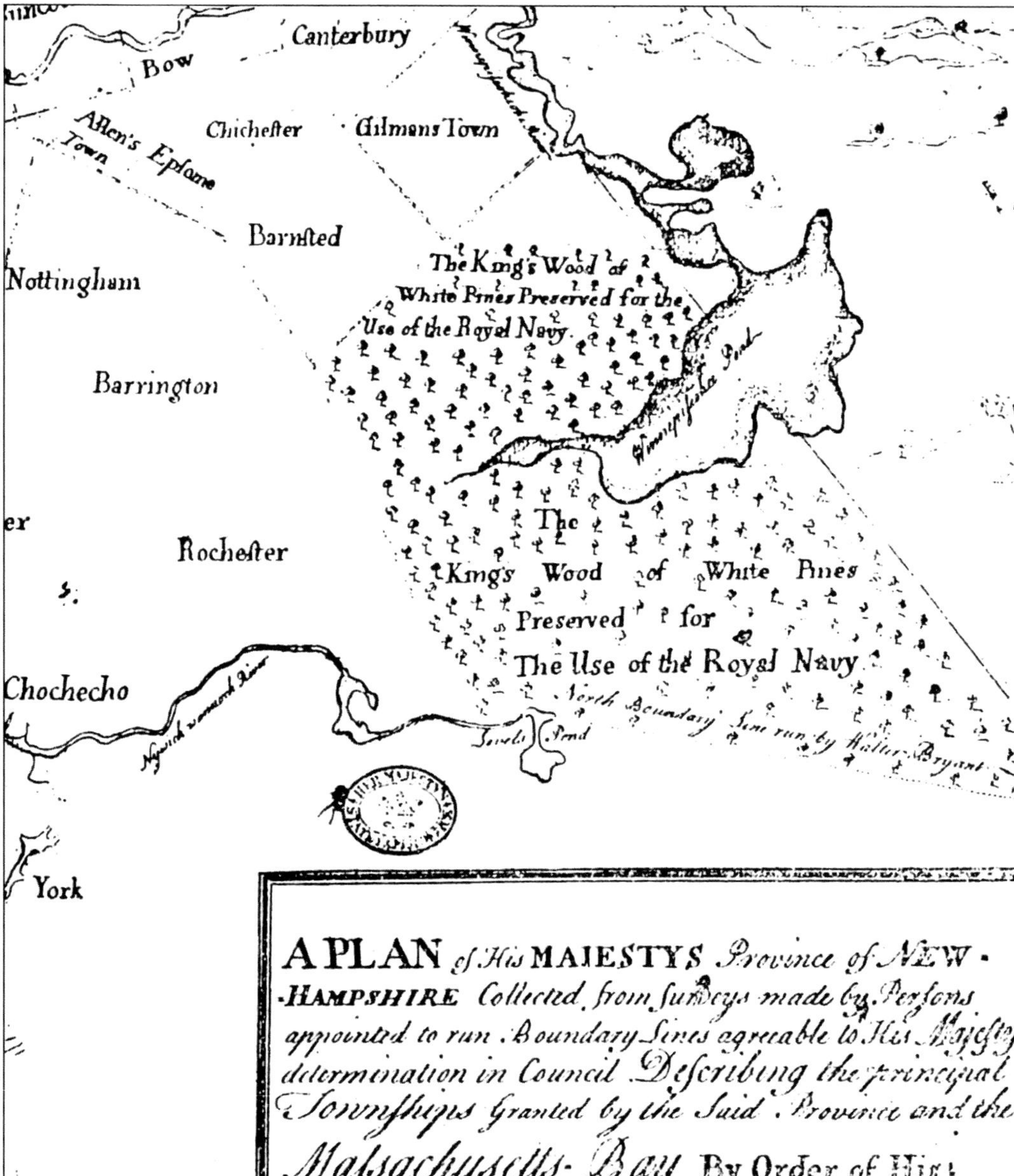

A Plan of His Majesty's Province of New Hampshire. This plan was "collected from surveys made by persons appointed to run the boundary lines agreeable to His Majesty's determination in Council of Describing the principal townships granted by the said Province and the Massachusetts Bay by order of His Excellence Benning Wentworth, Esq., Captain General and Commander-in-Chief in and over His Majesty's Province of New Hampshire. By Geo. Mitchell." The map was taken from the Crown Collection in the British Museum, Series III, No. 232; it is from a photograph that is currently in the Harvard College Library.

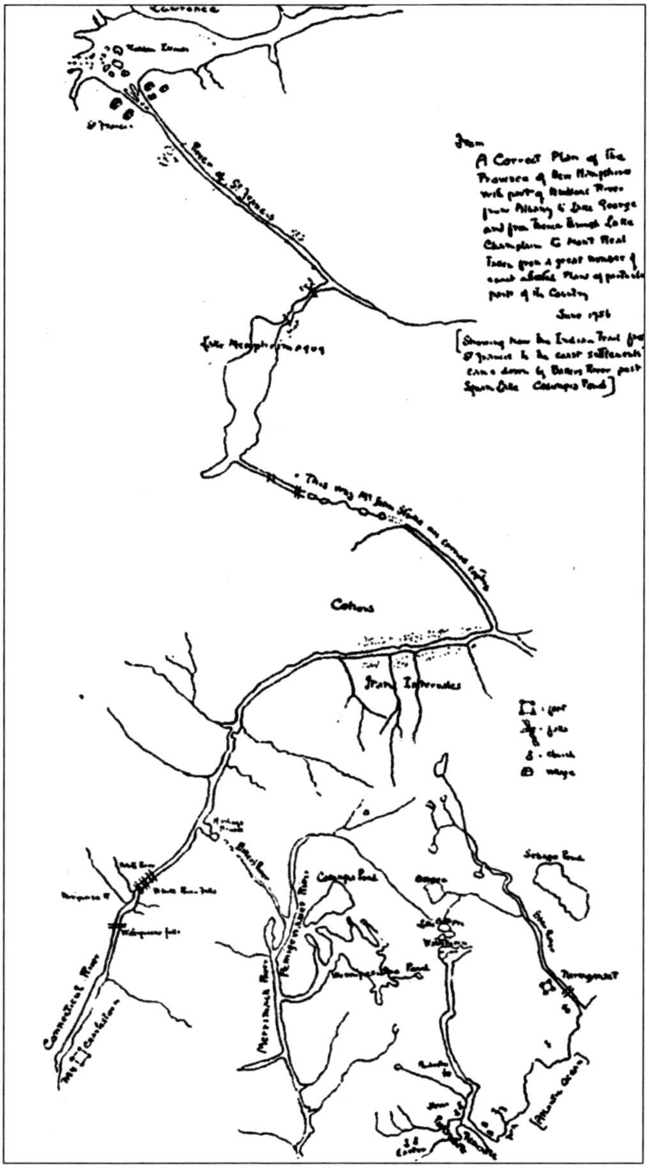

THE INDIAN TRAIL, 1756. Seen here is a correct plan of the Province of New Hampshire, with part of the Hudson River, Lake George, and Lake Champlain, from June 1756. This map indicates how the Native American trails from St. Francis to the settlement came down the Baker River, part of the Squam Lake region (Cosumpy Pond). Originally, the Abenaki Nation of the Algonquin Federation inhabited northern New England and the Province of Quebec. The dominant tribe in the Squam Lake area was the Penacook. The origin of the Indian name Squam was Kees-ee-hunk-nip-ee, meaning "the goose lake in the highlands." However, the name was shortened by European settlers to Kusumy or Cosumpe, as it appeared on a map as late as 1781. It was also known as Asquam, meaning "water." This name was again shortened to Squam and came into general use as first appeared on Philip Carrigain's map of New Hampshire in 1816. Native American trails followed river and lake valleys. Squam and Little Squam Lakes were used for passage from the Pemigewasset River Valley to Lake Winnipesaukee via Lake Long Pond (Lake Kanasatka) via the Indian Carry.

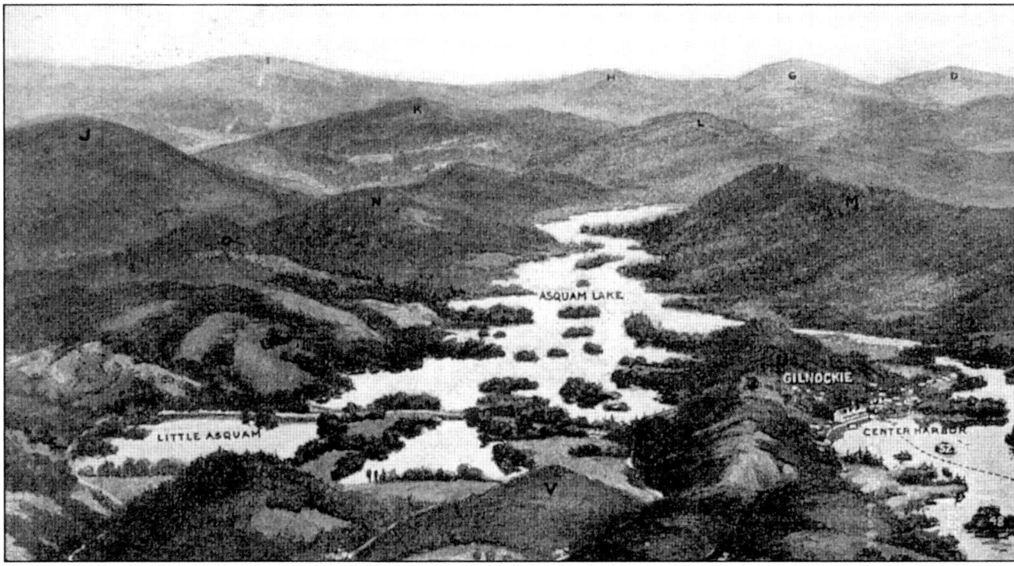

A BIRD'S-EYE VIEW OF THE SQUAM LAKE REGION, 1910. Squam Lake is a splendid sheet of water, finely engraved with arched coves, studded with a succession of beautiful islands, and surrounded by lofty mountains.

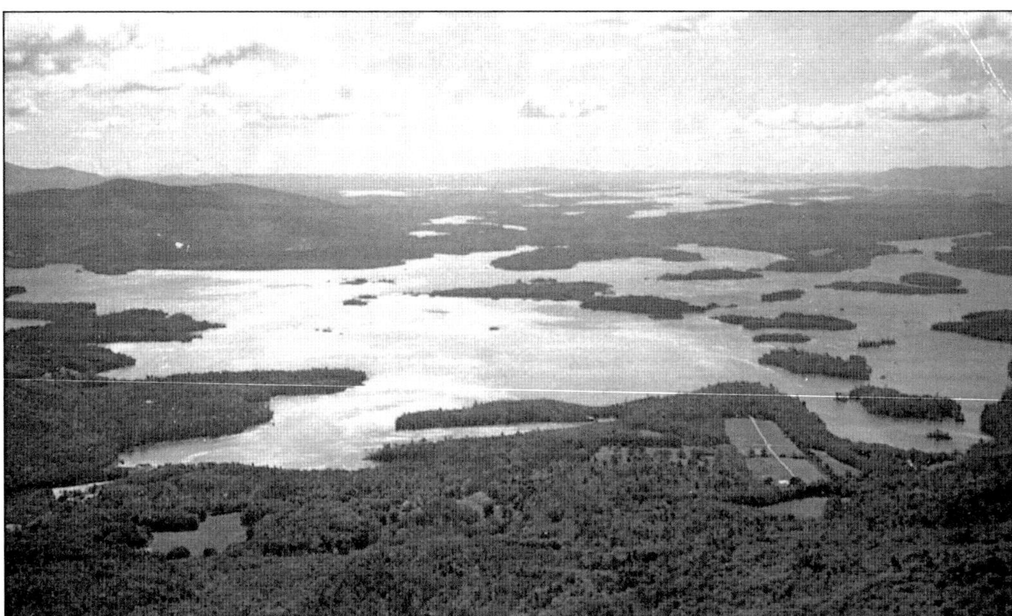

AN AERIAL VIEW OF THE SQUAM LAKE REGION, 1867. It is no wonder that the Native Americans were so strongly attached to this neighborhood, and that they fought so desperately before yielding the possession to the early settlers. The lower hills tempted them with abundance of game, and the calm water supplied them with unfailing stores of fish. The surpassing loveliness of the landscape served as a golden thread in the cord that bound them to this peaceful New England valley.

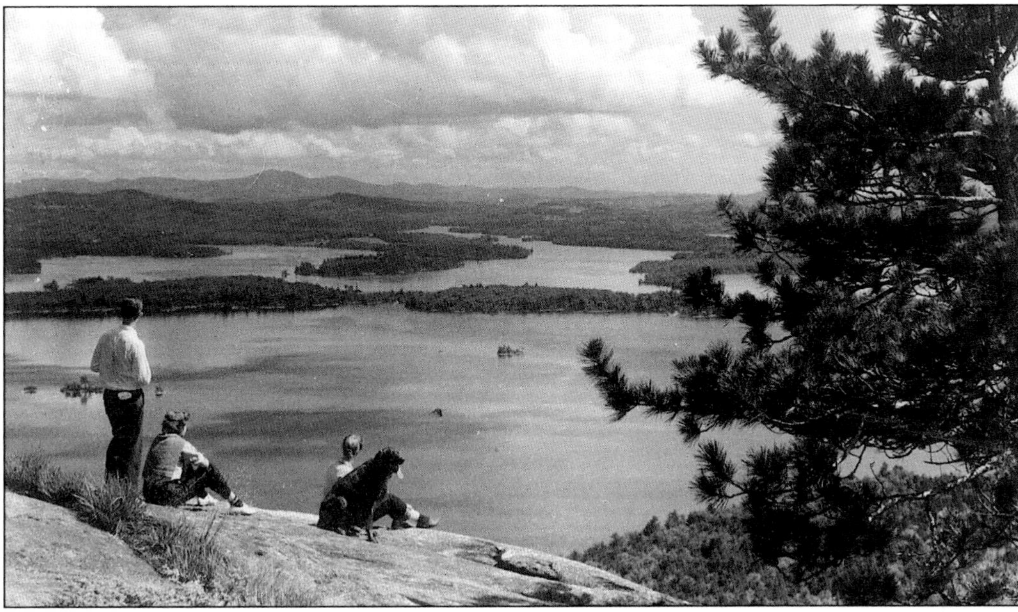

A View of Squam Lake from Rattlesnake Mountain, Rockywold-Deephaven Camps, Holderness. One of the finest views of the vastness of this lake, and its many islands and surrounding mountain ranges, is seen from this mountain. Rattlesnake Mountain (Peaked Hill) is a double-headed spur of the Squam Range, which runs out nearly to the lake, with far-viewing ledges on its low, wooded crests.

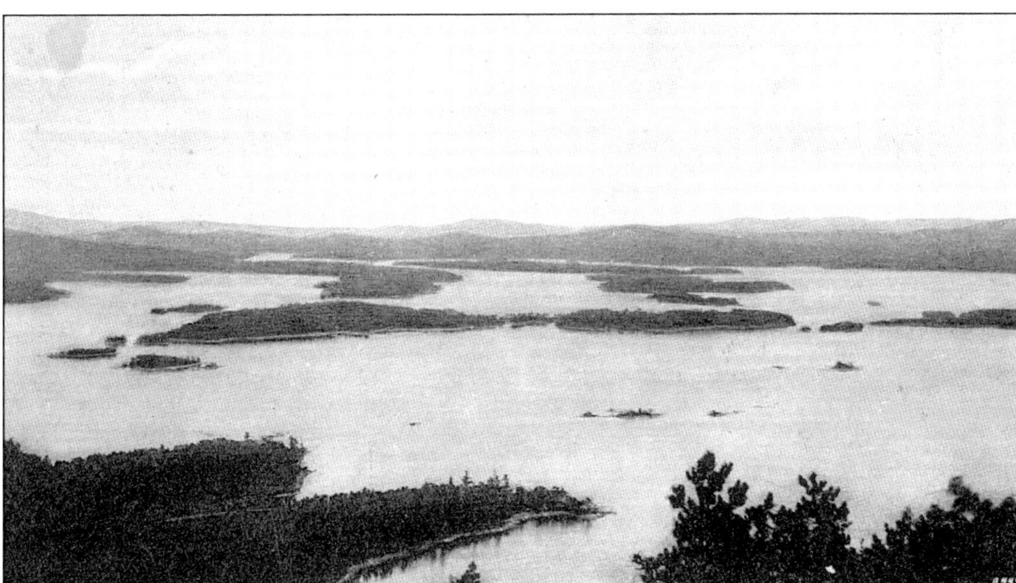

Squam Lake Looking South from East Rattlesnake Mountain. Seen in the center of the lake is Long Island. Most of the island is owned by the Coolidge family of Sandwich.

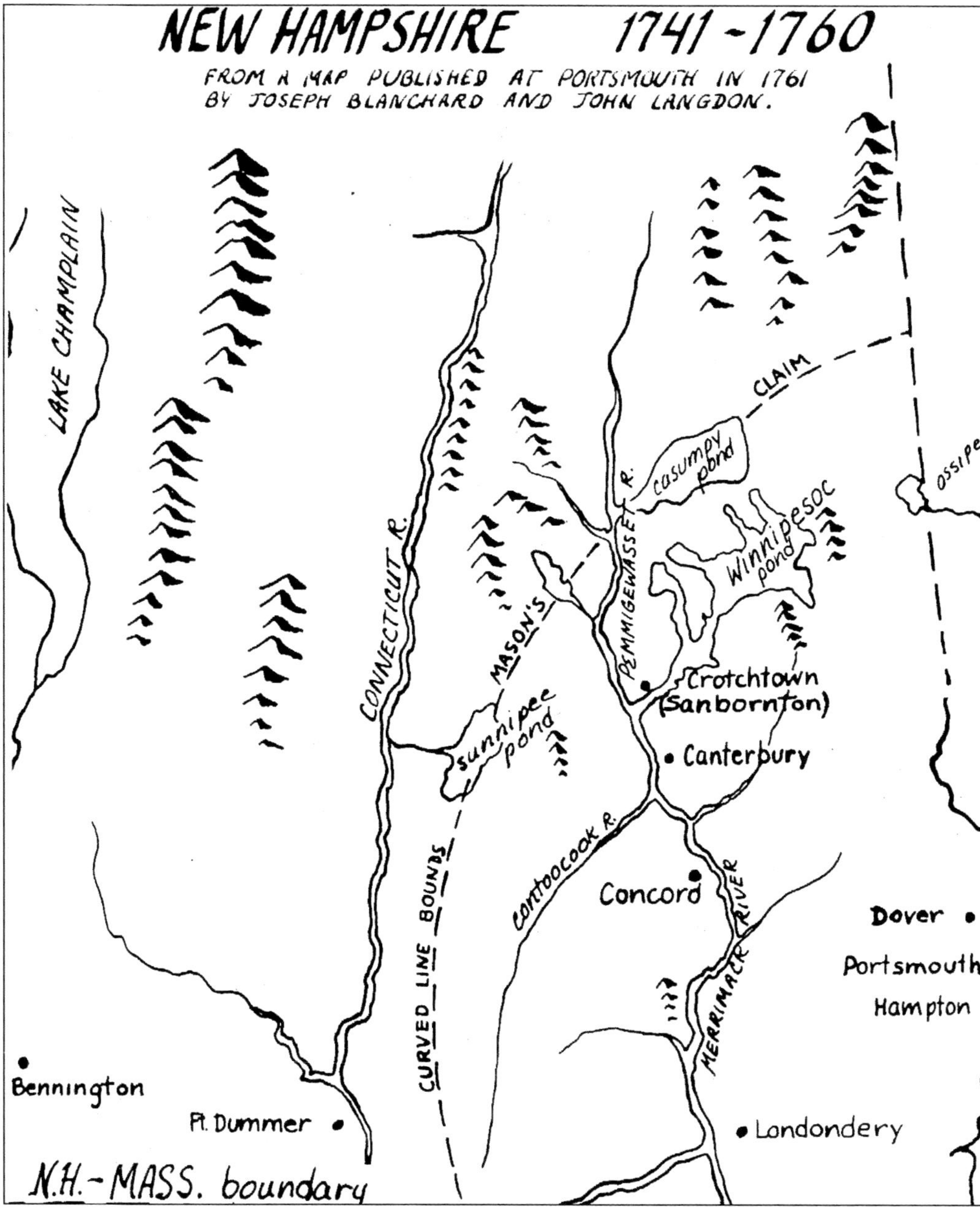

A Map of New Hampshire, 1741–1760. This image was taken from a 1761 map that was published in Portsmouth by Joseph Blanchard and John Langdon. Note the curved line which indicates Capt. John Mason's claim as it passes through Cosumpy Pond, today's Squam Lake. As late as 1784, the lake was known as Cosumpy. The earliest map showing the Holderness region dates as far back as 1756. By 1781, the spelling of the lake's name appears to have changed to Kusumpe. By 1784, the "Surveyor General of Lands for the Northern District of North America" named this body of water Squam. In 1813, when Timothy Dwight, president of Yale, came through the Lakes Region, he decided that Squam was too barbaric and primitive a name, and he declared that "we shall take the liberty to call it by the name of 'Sullivan' from Major General Sullivan formerly president of the state." The name did not stick.

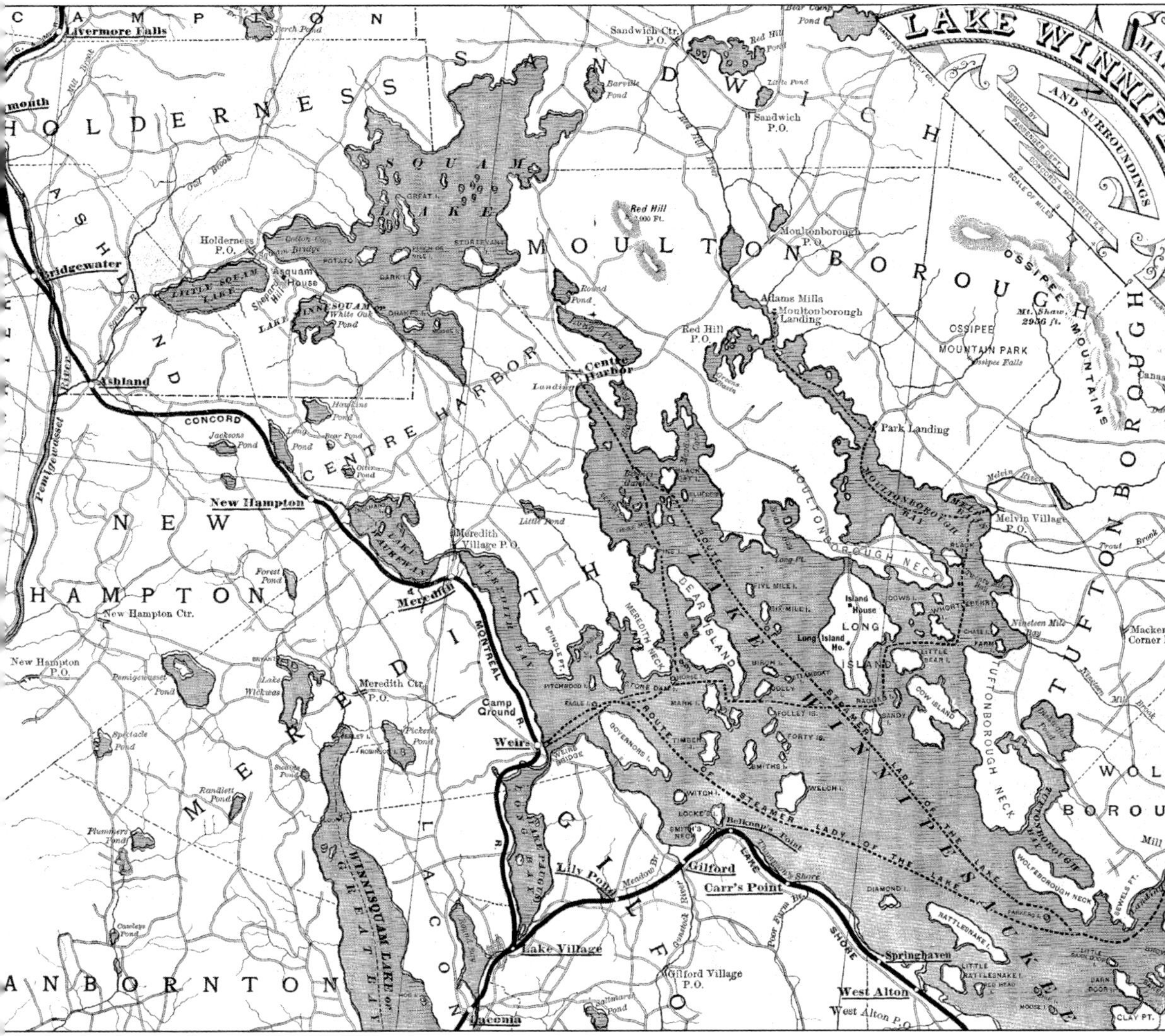

A Map of Lake Winnipesaukee and Its Surroundings, 1890s. The Passenger Service Department of the Concord & Montreal Railroad issued this map to familiarize its guests with the train routes and attractions available in central New Hampshire.

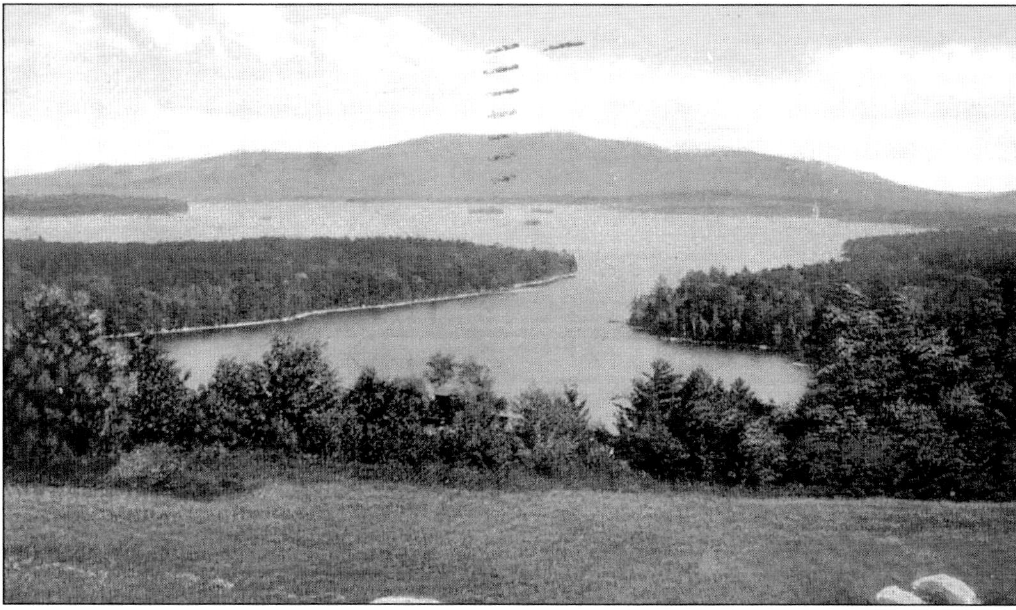

Squam Lake, Looking Southeast. From this vantage point on the Webster estate in Holderness, the visitor has a panoramic vista of the open waters of Squam Lake.

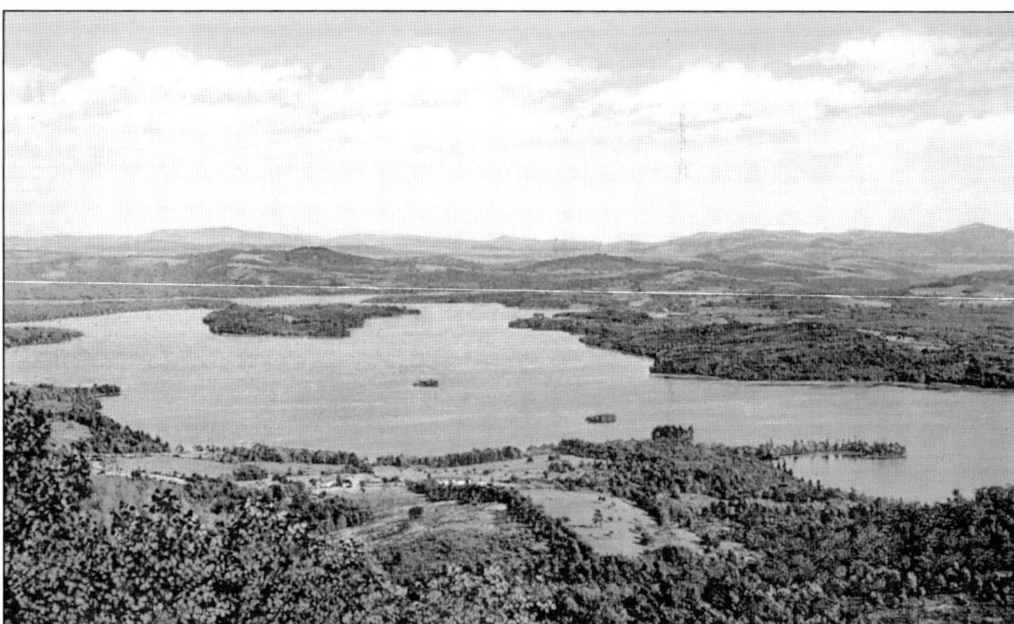

An Aerial View of Squam Lake. From Mount Livermore, the broad expanse of these mirrored waters appears placid, with few islands. In the center of the lake is Long Island, which dominates the landscape.

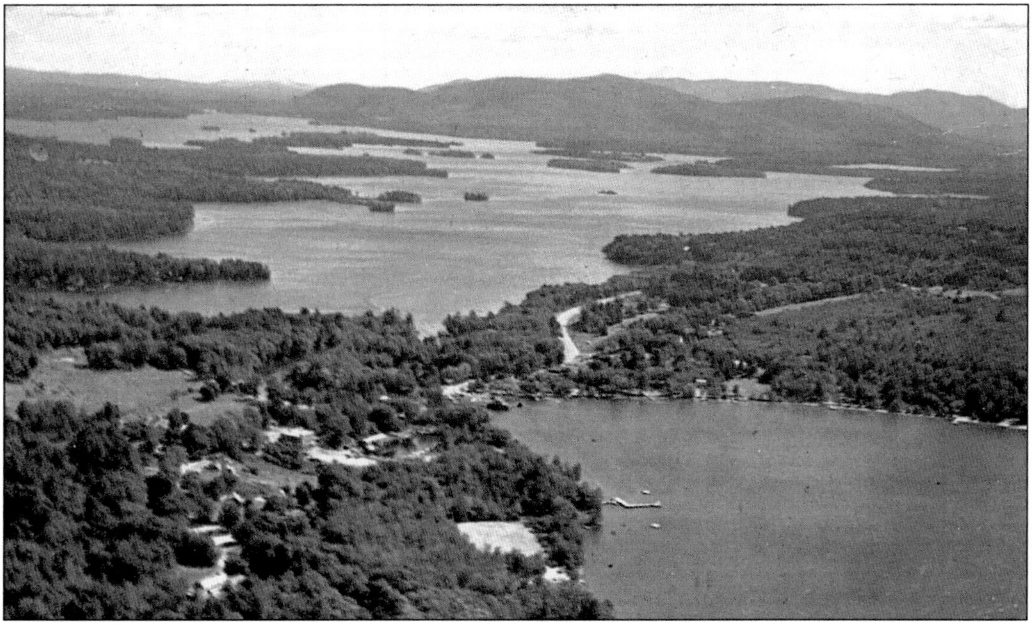

AN AERIAL VIEW OF HOLDERNESS AND THE SQUAM LAKES. In this view, facing east, the lake in the foreground is Little Squam, and the larger, distant lake is Squam—with its fleet of islands—the Queen of the Lakes. These islands, covered with evergreens, impart their hue to the mass of the lake as it stretches to the far shore in Sandwich, a distance greater than six miles.

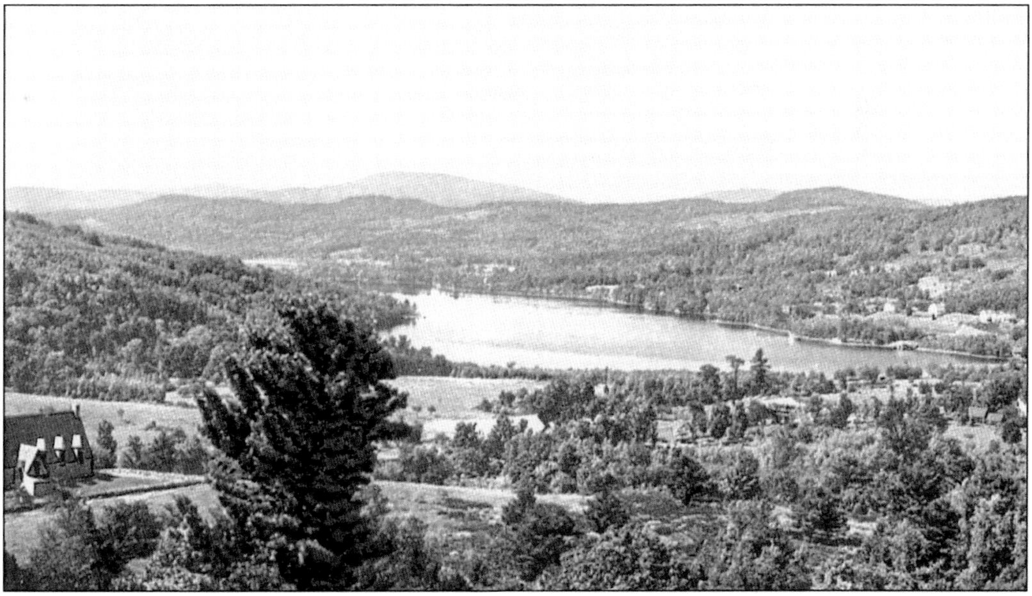

A PANORAMIC VIEW OF LITTLE SQUAM LAKE FROM SHEPARD HILL, HOLDERNESS. This vantage point offers the most comprehensive views of Little Squam Lake and its mountain ranges. A road from Ashland to Center Harbor passes over this hill. About halfway between the two towns, Shepard Hill—rising boldly in the heart of the area—overlooks the lakes as though it were a light tower for a sheltered bay.

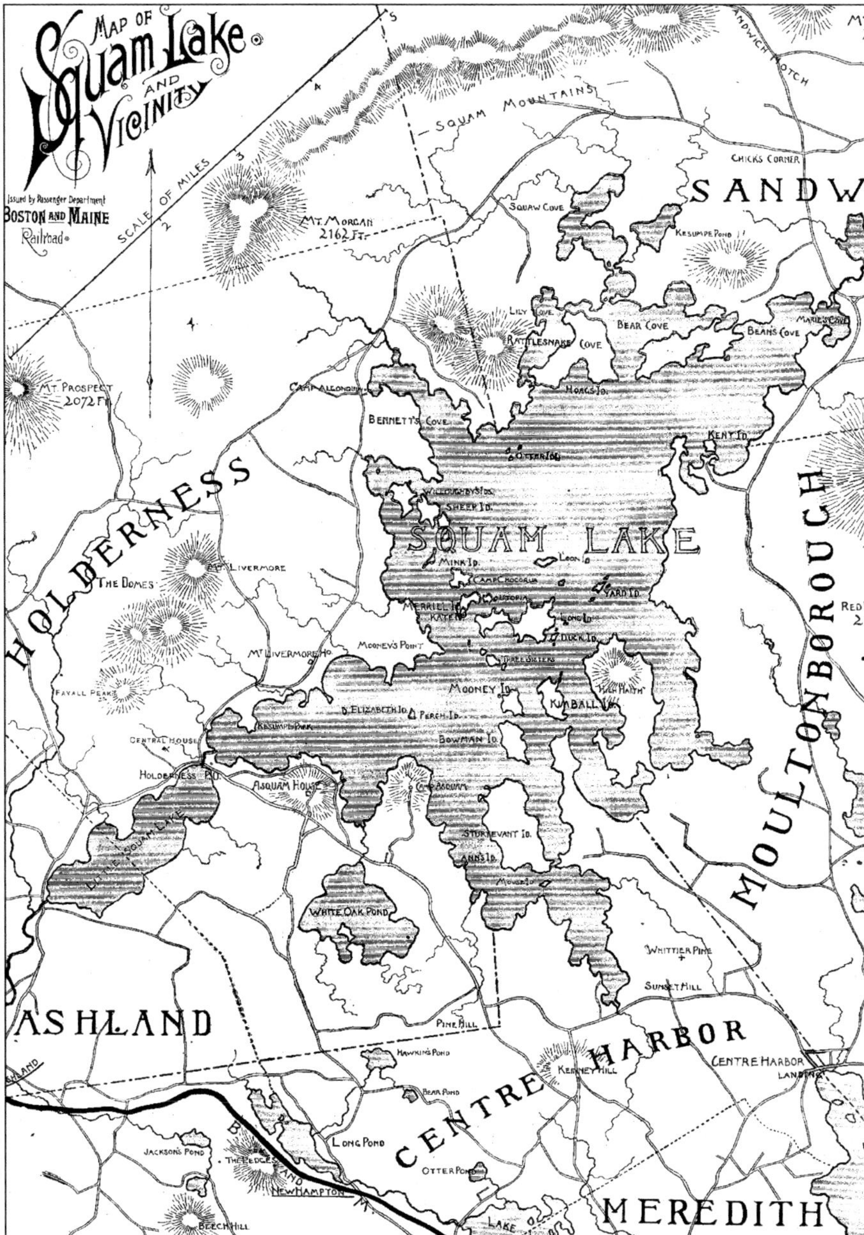

A Detailed Map of Squam Lake and Vicinity, c. 1903. This map shows the five towns that border the shore of Squam Lake and Little Squam Lake, namely Ashland, Center Harbor, Holderness, Moultonborough, and Sandwich. Squam Lake is a natural lake raised by a dam on Little Squam Lake. The lake is 562 feet above sea level with an area of 6,767 acres. Its length is more than six miles and its breadth approximately three miles. The lake holds 16 islands, several of which were originally used for pastureland for horses and sheep. The animals were made to swim out behind boats and were towed around the lake until they were very tired before they were allowed to land. It was supposed that the animals did not attempt to cross because of the prodigious distance between their islands and the mainland. The lake is nearly divided into two sections, between which are several long islands parallel to one another.

Two

ASHLAND

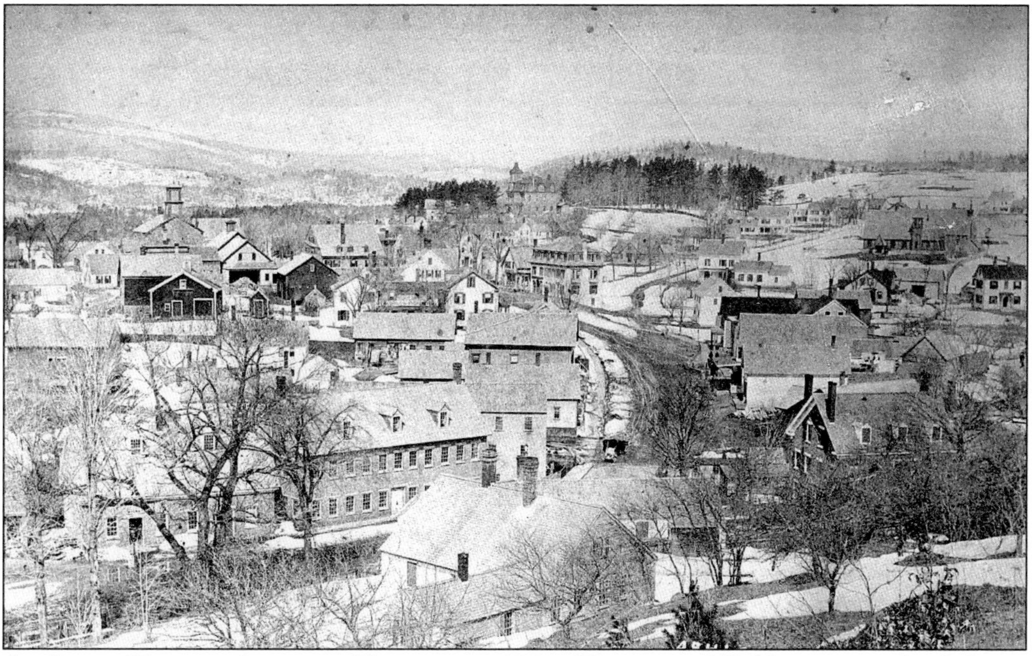

AN EARLY VIEW OF ASHLAND VILLAGE, C. 1870. The town of Holderness was divided into distinct sections: the water areas, the rock-ridged hills, and the business, or flatiron, area of Holderness Village. The citizens of the village area wished to separate and divide from Holderness for a variety of reasons. Today, the village is called Ashland.

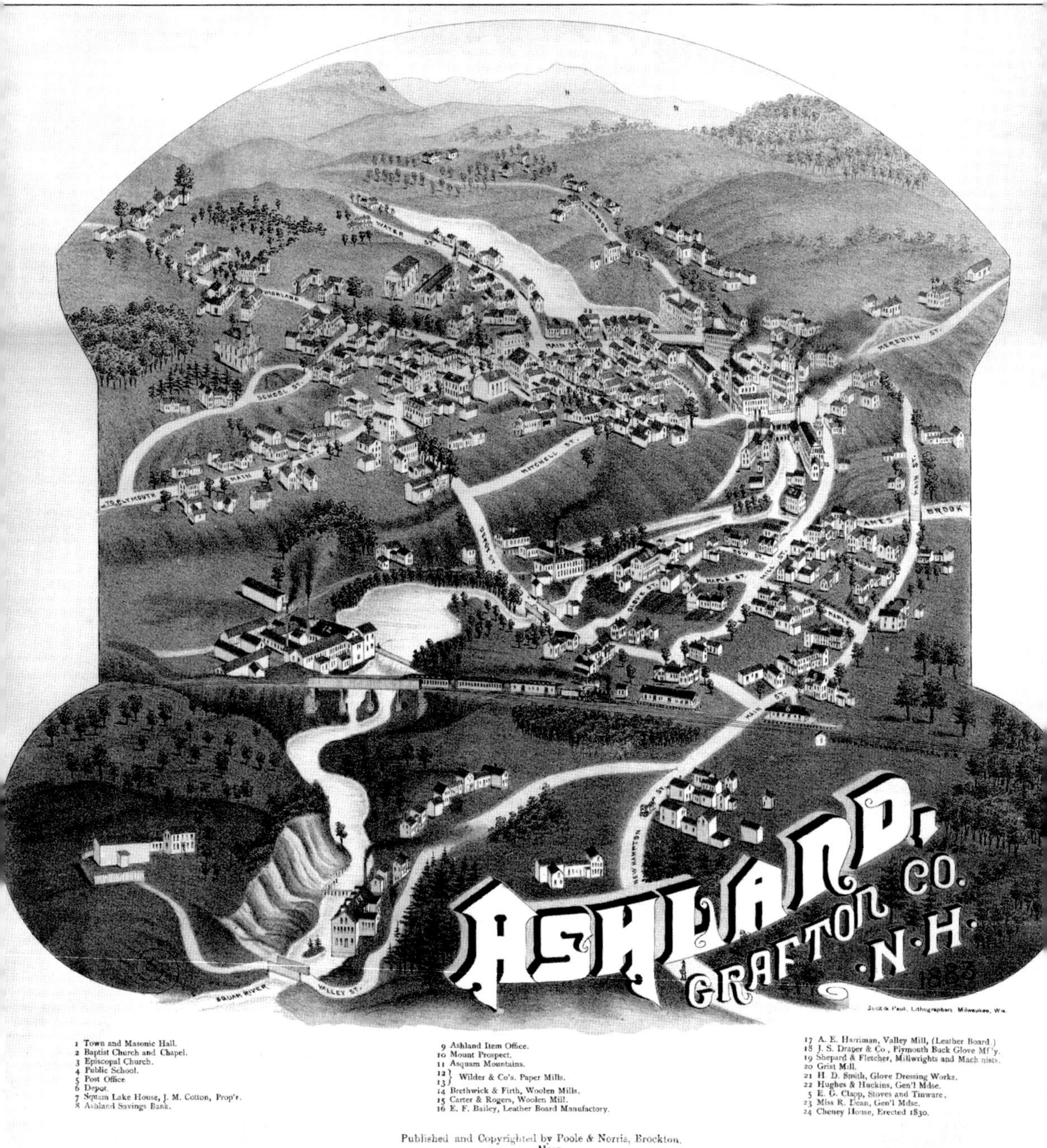

ASHLAND, GRAFTON COUNTY, 1883. This bird's-eye illustration alludes to the town's physical arrangement. The town's history is interwoven with that of Holderness. Holderness had its first charter in 1751 and was laid out by Samuel Lane, a surveyor. At this time, the town's boundaries included Ashland.

A MAP OF ASHLAND, C. 1892. Prior to 1868, a citizens group from the village section met and formulated plans to request a separation from Holderness. Col. Thomas P. Cheney had the foresight to acquire many parcels of land in this section, later to be called Ashland, and has since been credited as being the originator in the founding of Ashland. After much debate, the village section was officially set apart from Holderness. Ashland became a town of its own on July 1, 1868.

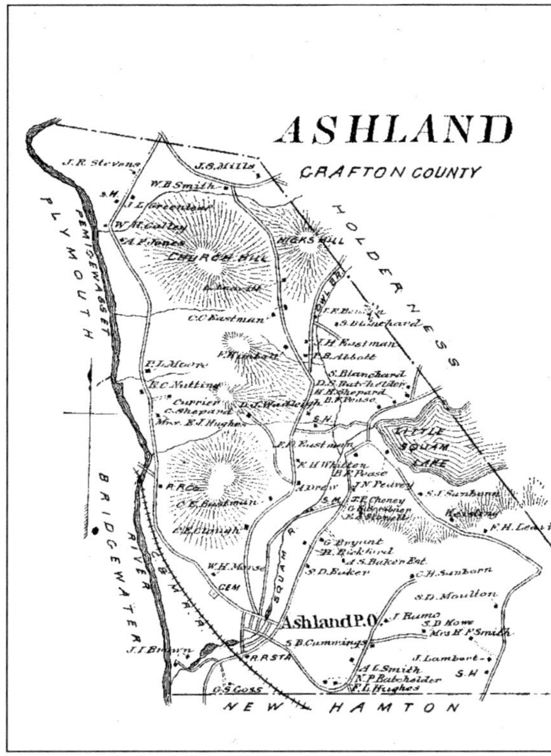

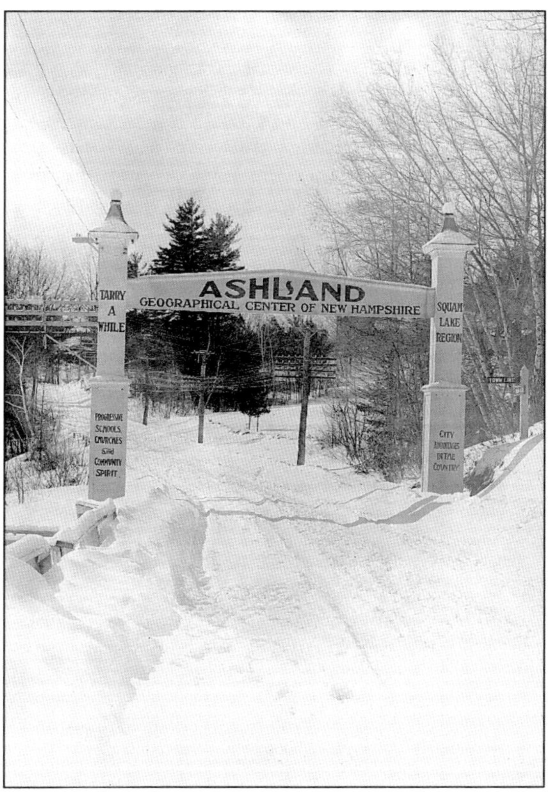

THE ASHLAND ARCHES. The arches were erected in 1923 and stood until 1934, when the town meeting voted to take them down. The town of Ashland is considered the geographical center of New Hampshire. According to the Master Plan for 1984, prepared by the Lakes Region Planning Commission, the town has a total of 7,552 acres, of which 7,296 are land and 256 are water. Located in the Pemigewasset Valley, surrounded by hills, Ashland lies in Grafton County at the southwest bounds of Holderness and is also bounded by Plymouth, Bridgewater, Center Harbor, and New Hampton.

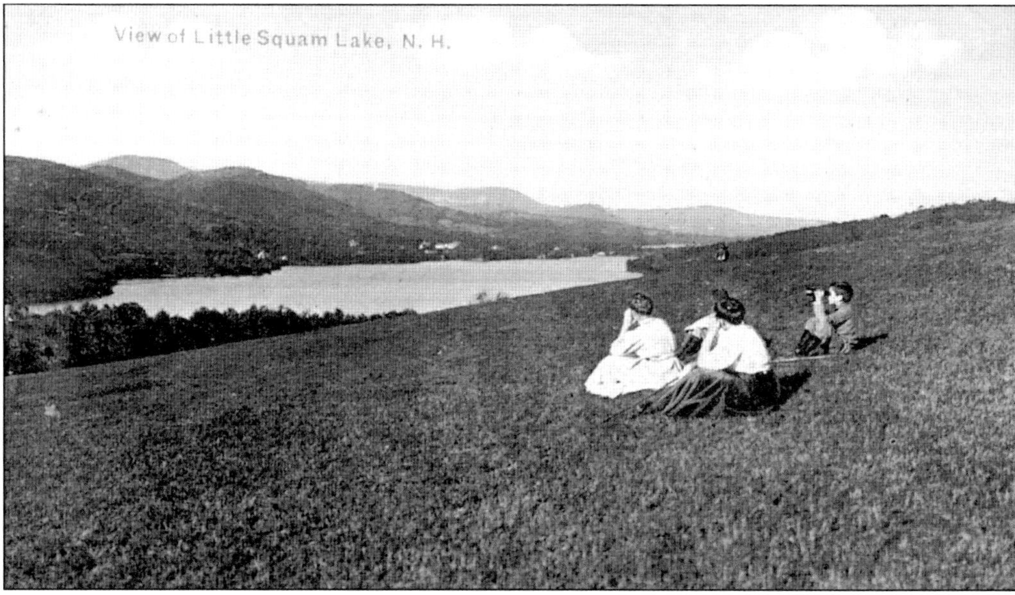

LITTLE SQUAM LAKE. Looking to the Squam Mountains and the White Mountains, these summer visitors enjoy a panoramic view of the countryside from a pasture south of Little Squam Lake. Half of Little Squam Lake lies within the township; the shores of this lovely body of water are lined with the cottages of summer residents. This is a typical country view as seen from any hillside that frames the lake and the village. Clustered about the landscape are many old farms and lovely spots to relax and enjoy the splendor of the region.

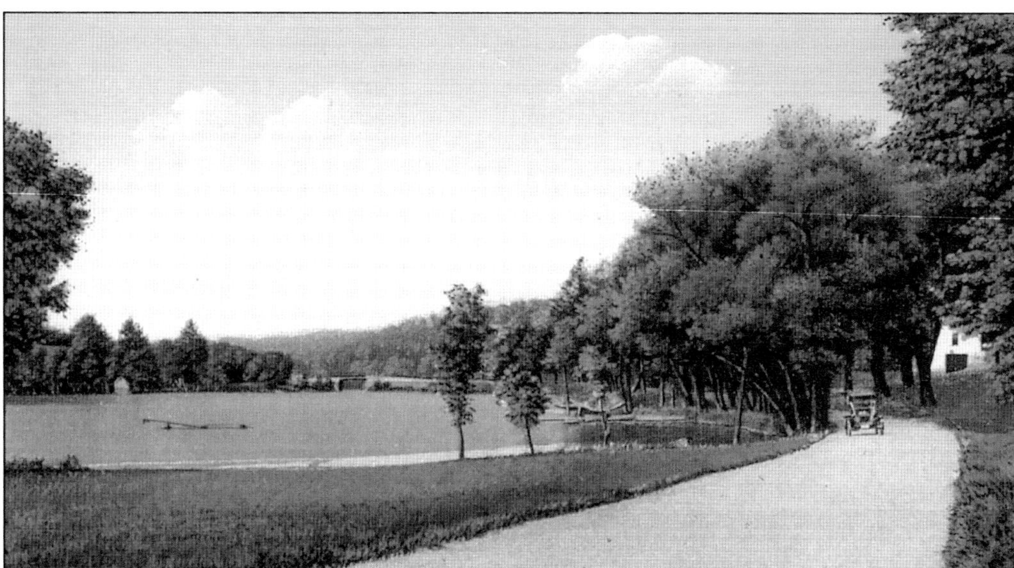

STATE ROAD AND LITTLE SQUAM LAKE. This major road, once known as River Road, connects Holderness on Squam Lake with Ashland on Little Squam Lake.

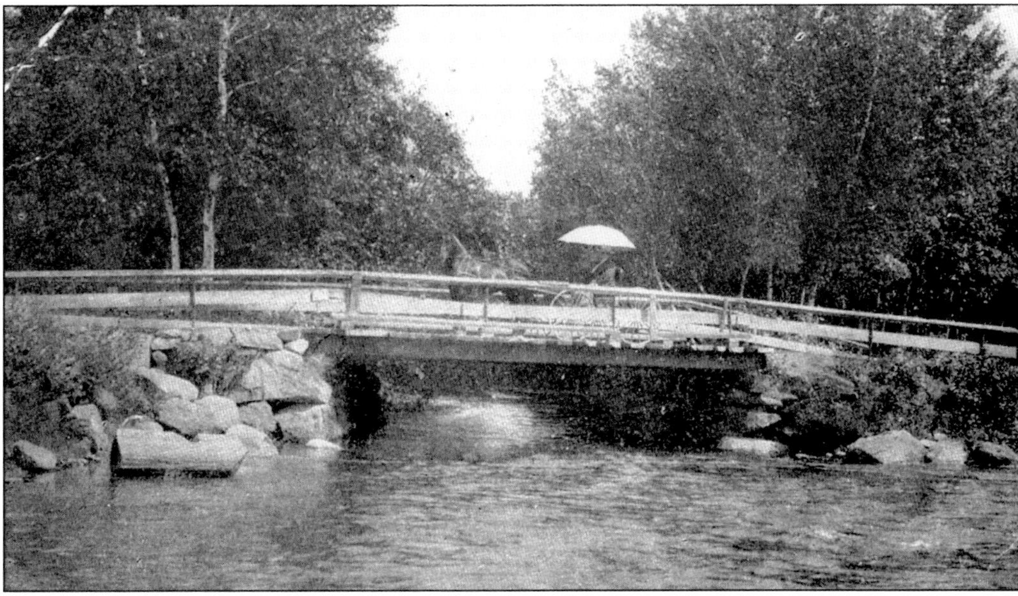

ON THE ROAD TO SQUAM LAKE FROM ASHLAND. In the summer months, Squam River was used by boats to haul logs to the sawmills on the river, where they were turned into lumber. After the first solid freeze on the lake and river, roads were created to cross the Squam and Pemigewasset Rivers.

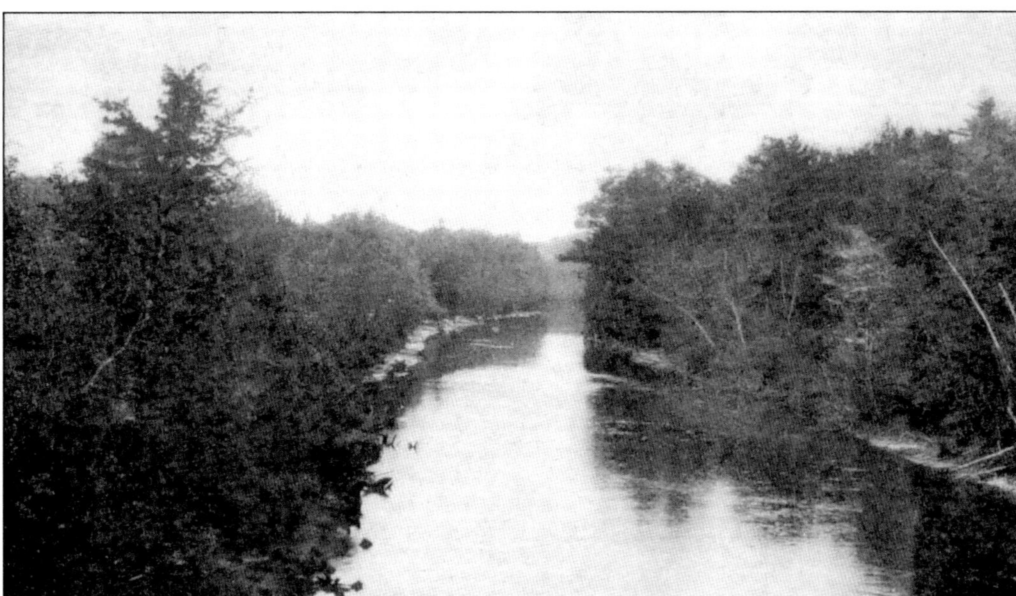

SQUAM RIVER, FROM LITTLE SQUAM BRIDGE. Squam River in Ashland provides several dam sites for waterpower. From this lake level of the river to the Pemigewasset River, there is a gradual fall of 112 feet along the entire length. On Squam River are numerous mills and boathouses. In years past, there used to be a towing service up and down the river.

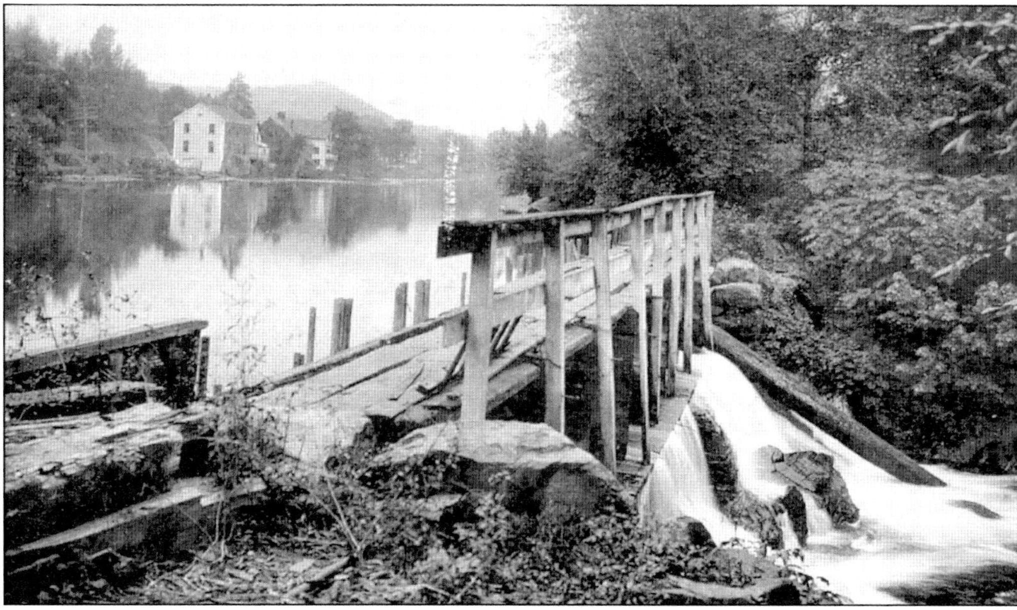

A Dam on Squam River. According to David Ruell, Ashland historian, "There were seven dams, all located in Ashland along the three-mile course of Squam River. The falls of the Squam River, in what is now the village of Ashland, have been the site of a gristmill since c. 1770, when Nathaniel Thompson, encouraged by a grant from the town proprietors, erected a sawmill and a gristmill on them. His mill was succeeded by others, as the farmers of the area needed a mill to grind their grain. In the first years of the 20th century, John H. Morrill owned and operated a one-and-a-half-story gristmill on the site of the present mill. Adjoining the gristmill to the north was the Shepard sawmill."

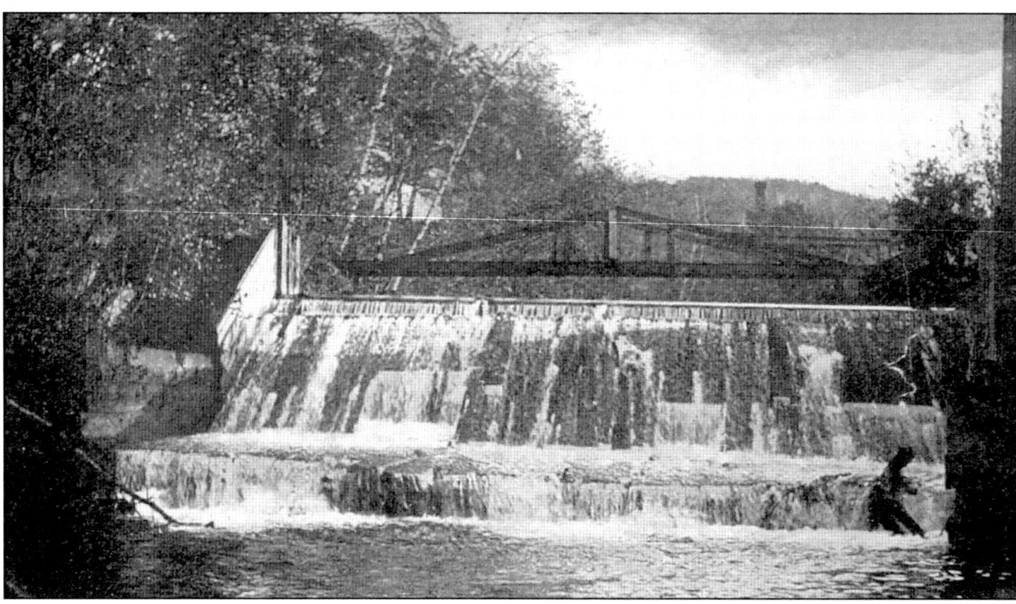

The Glove Factory Power Falls, c. 1910. It is easy to see that waterpower played a natural part in the establishment of Ashland's early industry.

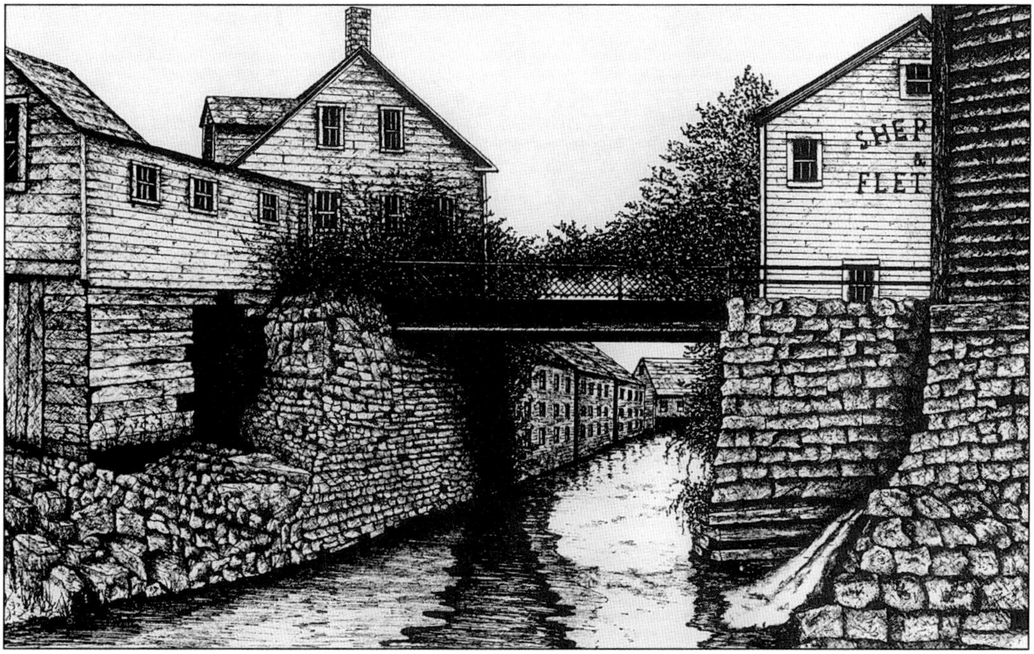

A View of Squam River, Ashland, 1881. This view, looking south from the gristmill in the village, shows the corner of the gristmill. Across the street was located the Shepard and Fletcher Shop. Many businesses operated from the river—gristmills, lumber mills, woolen mills, leather-board mills, hosiery mills, paper mills, and the Glove Factory.

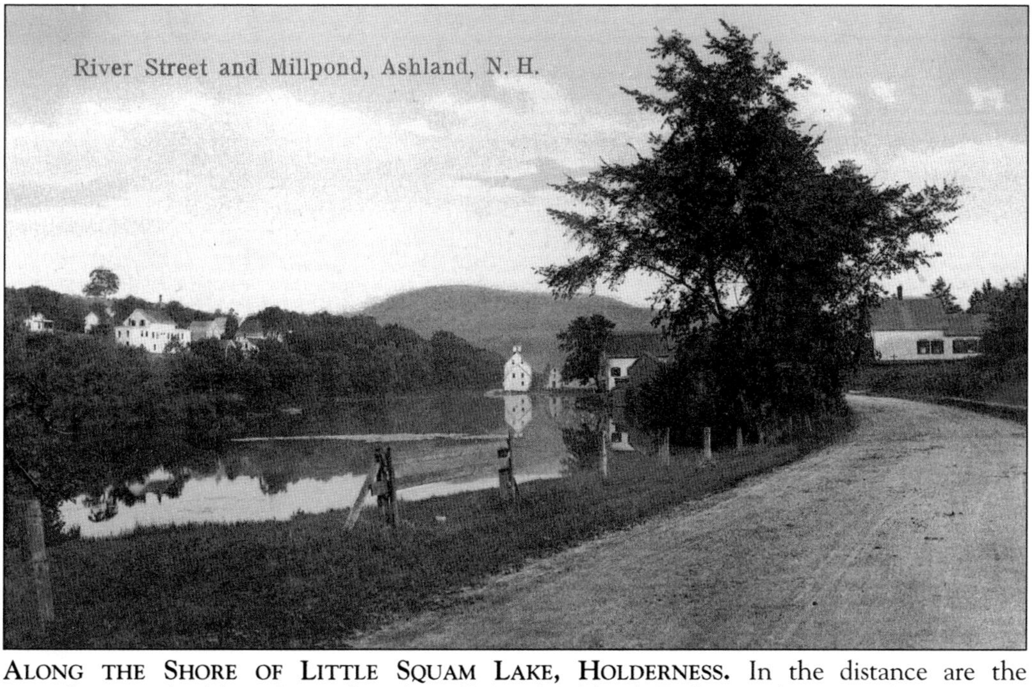

Along the Shore of Little Squam Lake, Holderness. In the distance are the manufacturing buildings located in the village of Ashland. Earlier in the town's history, grist, lumber, woolen, leather-board, hosiery, and paper mills had been located there.

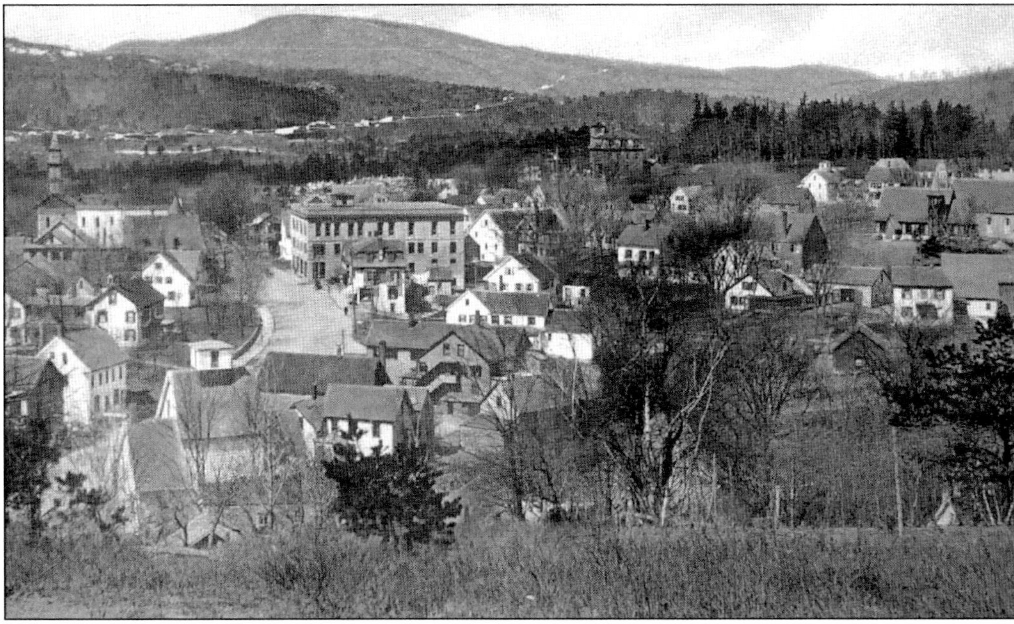

ASHLAND VILLAGE. The new town adopted the name of Ashland in honor of the home of Henry Clay. Much of its popularity as a summer resort is due to Little Squam Lake and the consequent opportunities for boating, fishing, and bathing.

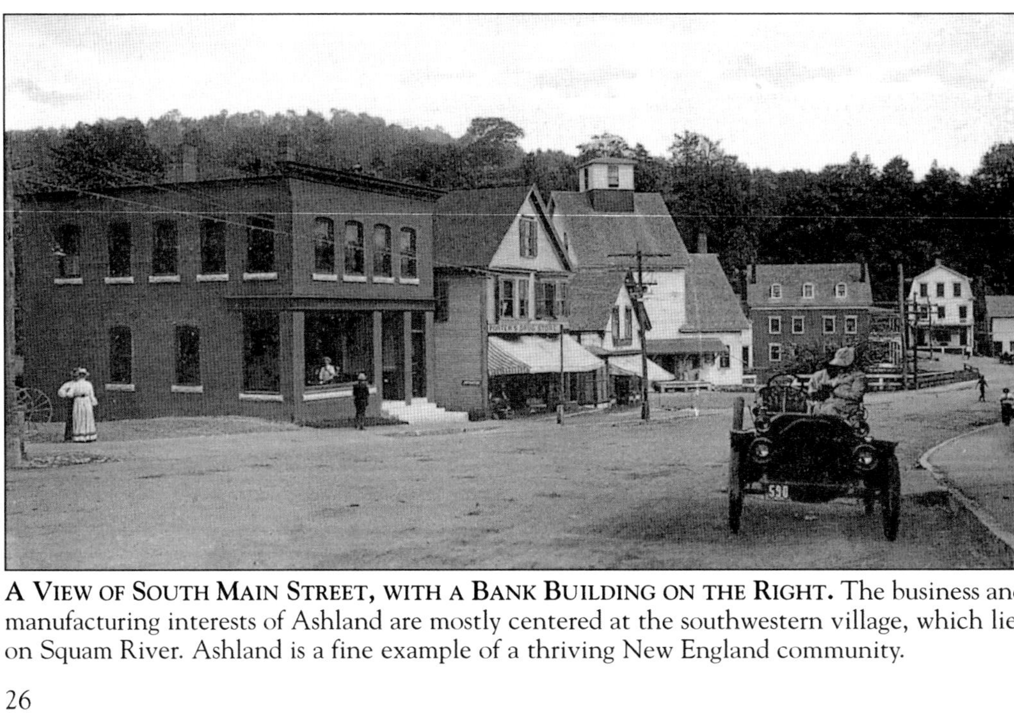

A VIEW OF SOUTH MAIN STREET, WITH A BANK BUILDING ON THE RIGHT. The business and manufacturing interests of Ashland are mostly centered at the southwestern village, which lies on Squam River. Ashland is a fine example of a thriving New England community.

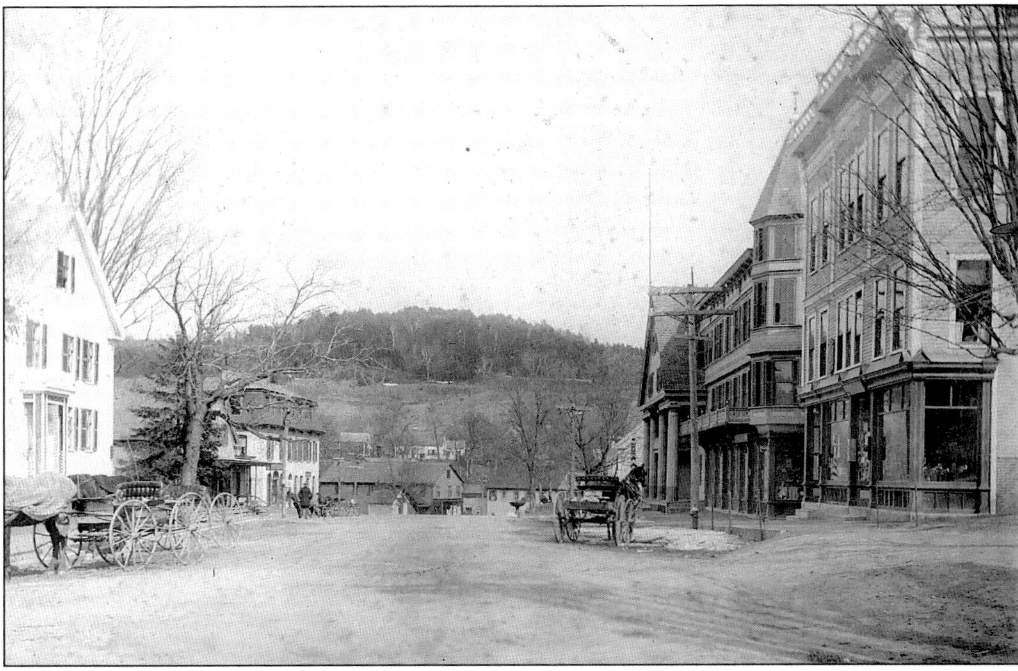

LOOKING EAST ON MAIN STREET. During the last half of the 19th century, the village experienced a boom of activity. The creation of some of the finest boardinghouses, hotels, and inns, together with well-equipped livery stables for drives around the area, made Ashland a popular stop.

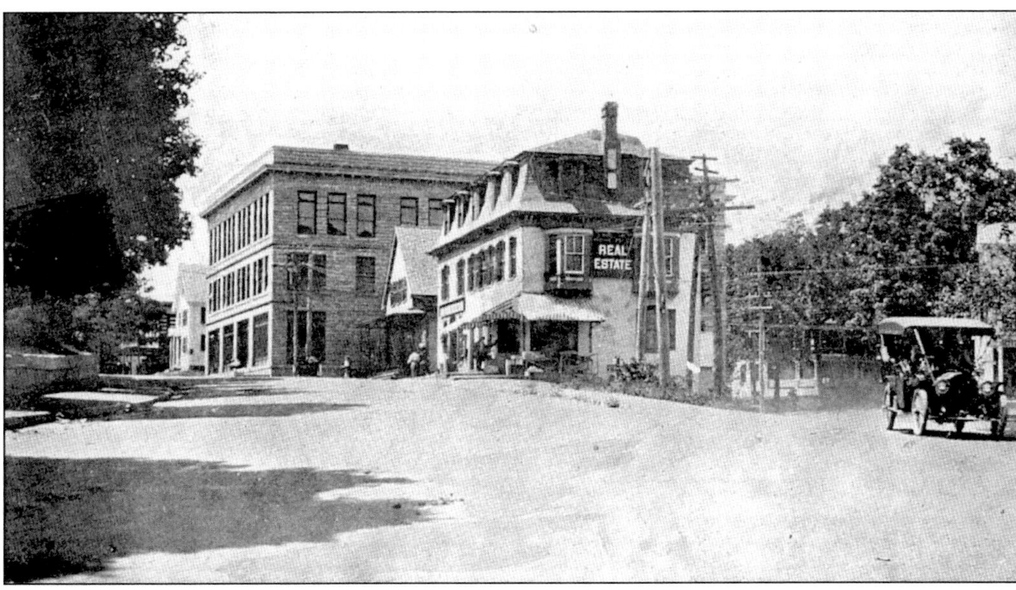

THE SHEPARD BLOCK, THE OLD POST OFFICE BLOCK, AND HIGHLAND STREET, 1908. In this view, looking west, Main Street swings to the left through the business district. To the right is Highland Street, a residential area of the town.

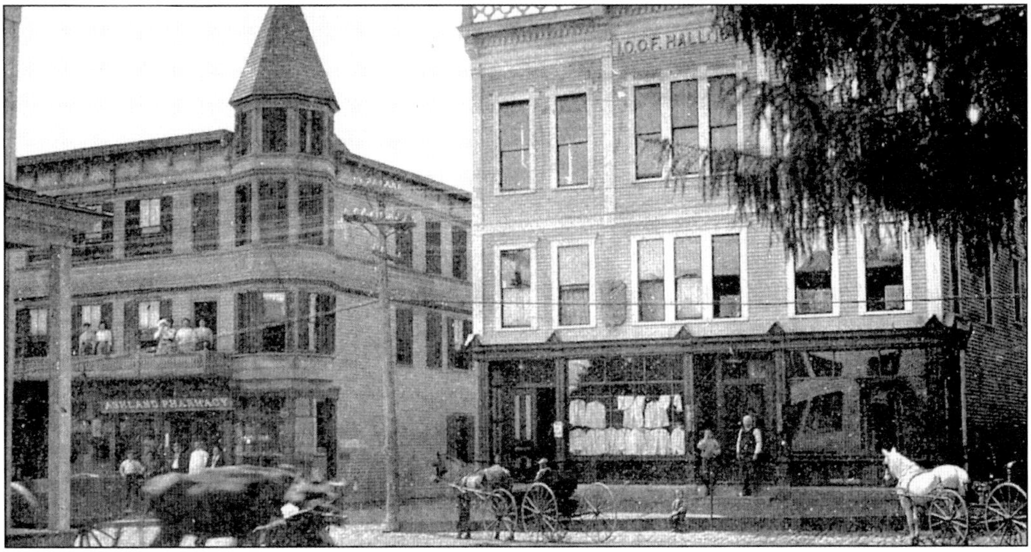

THE SQUAM LAKE HOTEL AND THE ODD FELLOWS BLOCK. The hub of commerce for the Squam Valley, the village was often be seen with many carriages and oxcarts lined up in front of the Squam House and throughout the business district.

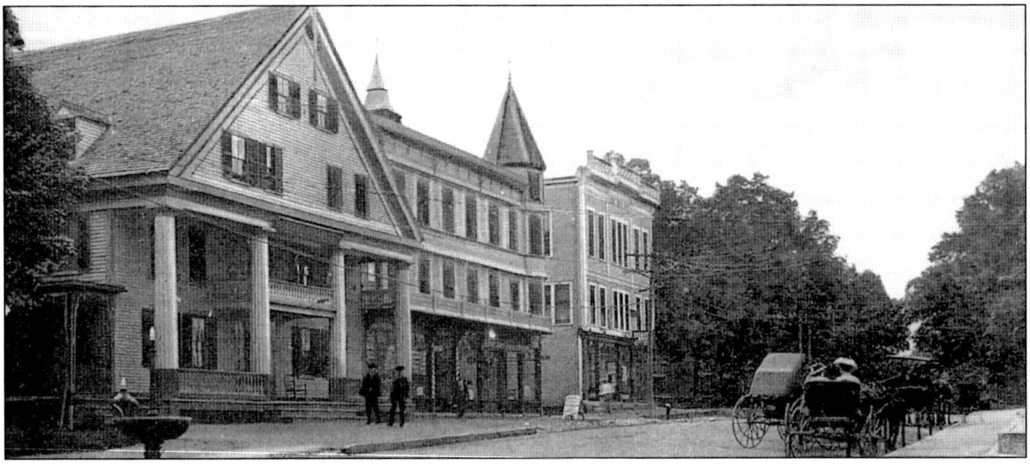

THE SQUAM LAKE HOUSE AND THE ODD FELLOWS BLOCK, C. 1900S. According to the records of the 1968 Ashland Centennial Committee, "In 1843, the hotel was owned and managed by Noah Cate and called 'Cate's Tavern.' In 1843, Daniel Sawyer took over the hotel from Mr. Cate and the Cates moved into the Whitten House, just back of the hotel." Sawyer operated the hotel for six years and then went into the lumber business. Cate again managed the hotel and operated it until his death; his wife then took it over. In 1874, James Melville Cotton purchased the hotel. It was advertised that the hotel had "30 steam heated sleeping-rooms, a bridal suite, and the cooking and dining facilities are first class in every respect, while the bill of fare is varied and abundant, the service prompt, the bed comfortable and 'neat as a pin.'" The rate was $2 a day. On December 27, 1934, fire swept through the center of Ashland, which, according to the *Meredith Examiner,* "started in the garage of the Ednor Hotel, formerly the Squam Lake House, forcing fifteen or twenty guests into the street with practically all of their belongings. Five automobiles which were in the hotel garage were destroyed as well as a small garage owned by John Cotton. The hotel, then known as the Ednor Hotel, which had been operated by Mr. and Mrs. Gates Murchie, was totally destroyed."

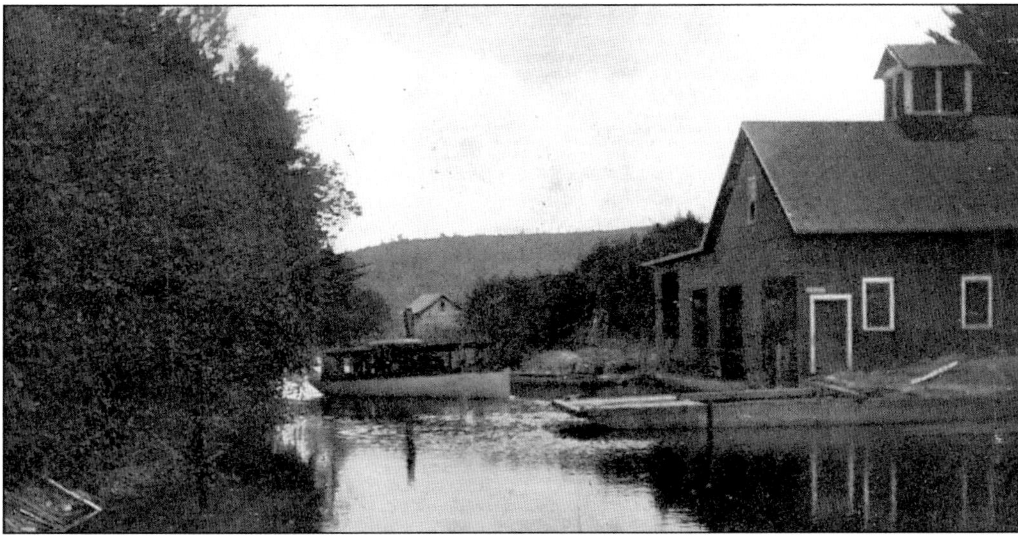

THE SQUAM TRANSPORTATION BOAT COMPANY LANDING AND STEAMER, 1901. This company began regular steamer service in the summer of 1902, having had its first meeting of incorporation on October 30, 1901. The company was a thriving enterprise on the local lakes and rivers for more than 15 years. It hauled fruits and vegetables, ice, furniture, and building materials for the camps on the lakes. It even provided mail service to the summer island residents. However, as visitors started to travel by automobile and had their own boats for lake travel, few needed commercial boat services. Finally, the old gave way to the new, and the once-flourishing transportation company ceased operation.

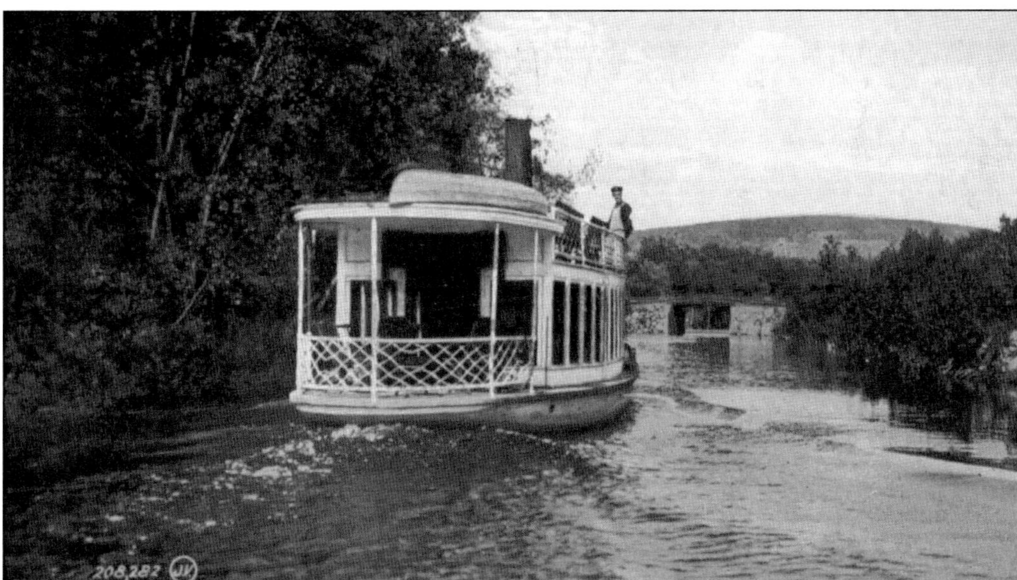

THE *HALCYON* APPROACHING SQUAM BRIDGE IN HOLDERNESS, 1916. Steamboats were very popular on Squam Lake. Pictured is the 50-foot *Halcyon*, which became the mail boat for the many island and summer residents around the lake. Other popular boats on the lake were the *Zylpha*, *Chocorua*, *Ashland*, *Venture*, *Sandwich*, *Mandelay*, *Asquam*, and *Nellie J*. Most of these vessels came from the Squam Transportation Boat Company in Ashland.

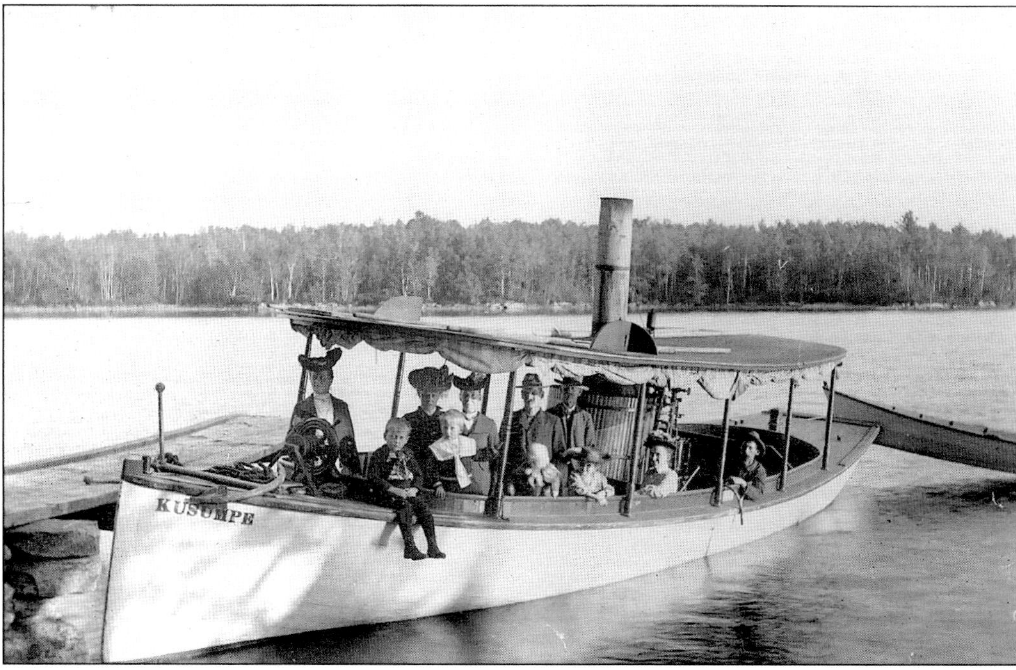

THE STEAMER *KUSUMPE*. This craft was built at the sawmill slip by Charles Eastman and was operated by Simeon Eastman and Bill St. Clair. Summer visitors frequently enjoyed an afternoon sail on Little Squam Lake.

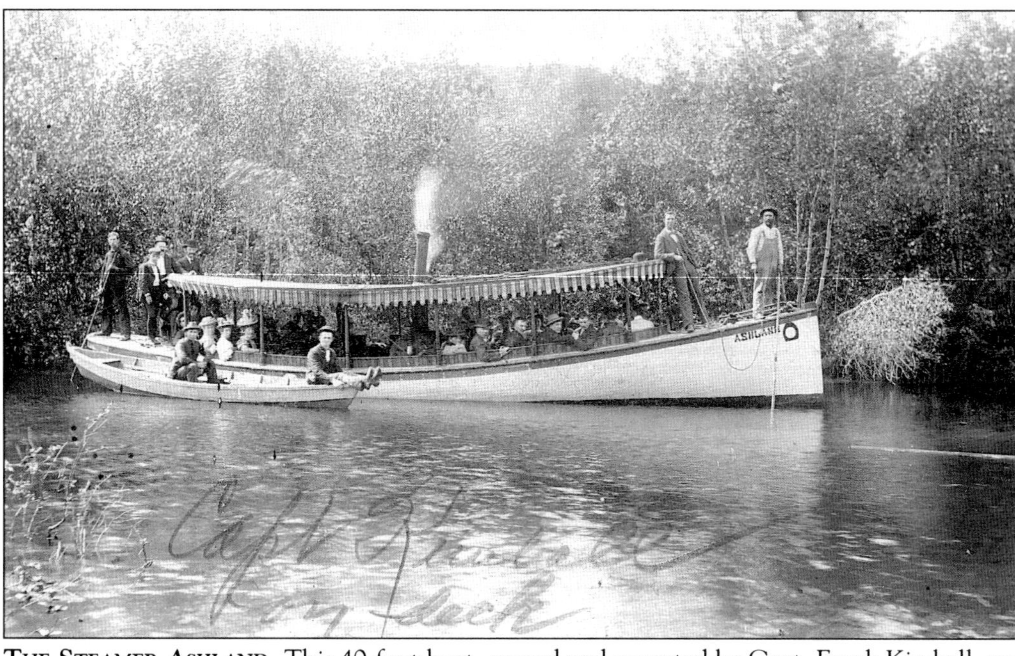

THE STEAMER *ASHLAND*. This 40-foot boat, owned and operated by Capt. Frank Kimball, was the first known steamboat on the lake. Pictured are Kimball and a group of tourists taking a summer sail up the Squam River to Squam Lake.

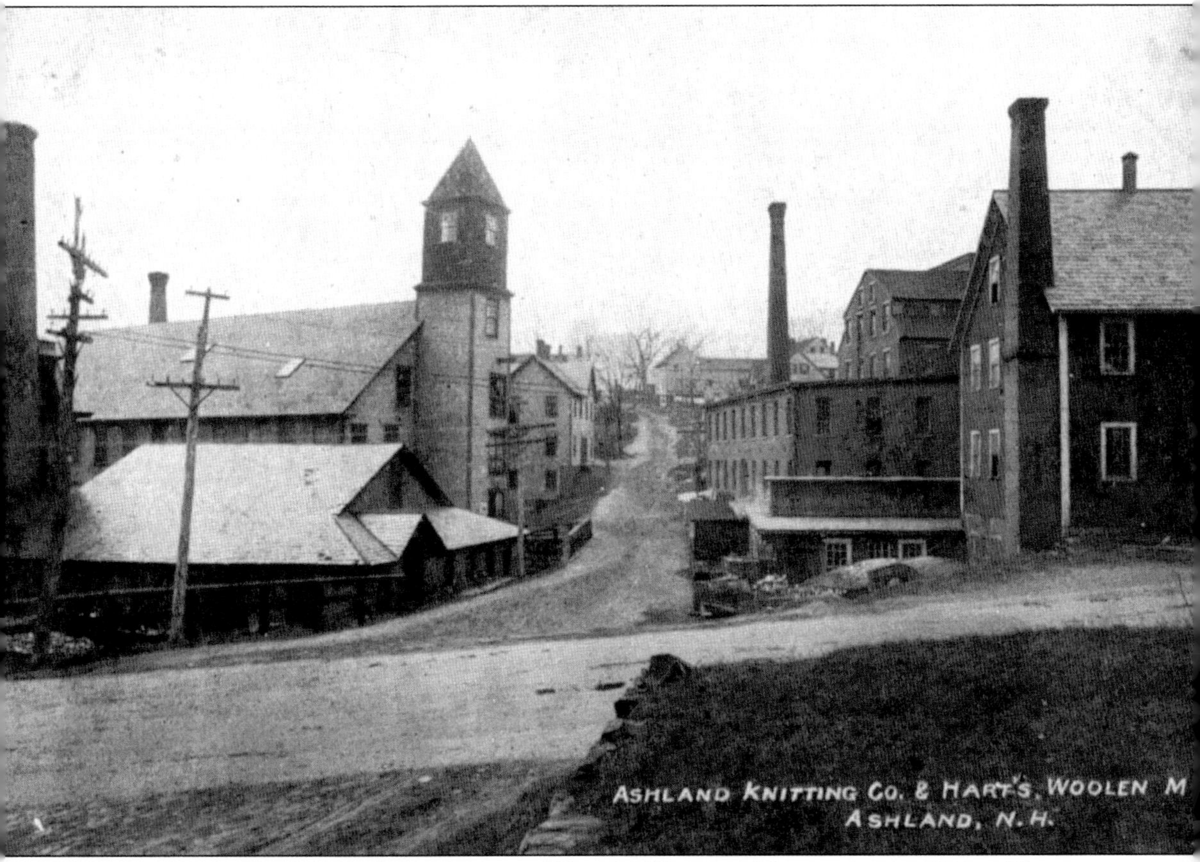

THE ASHLAND KNITTING COMPANY AND HART'S WOOLEN MILL, C. THE 1880S. The set of buildings on the left belong to the Ashland Knitting Company. In 1886, the company was formed by Thomas P. Cheney, George E. Scribner, N.P. Batchelder, and Hiram Hodgdon. The men purchased the Baker Mill, with its water rights, and built a three-story structure. The mill turned out 12,000 pairs of ladies' hose per day and employed 300 people. On the right is the Squam Lake Woolen Company Mills. The first woolen mill in Holderness Village, now Ashland, was owned by Joseph Shepard. There were two woolen mills in the town during the 1840s: the Ashland Woolen Mill and the Squam Lake Woolen Mill. James F. Briggs, a native of Leeds, England, built the Squam Lake Woolen Mills in 1840. It operated for eight years and then became idle until September 1, 1881. The mill changed hands several times before 1896. In 1908, the mill was closed, but it reopened in 1911. In 1930, Luther W. Packard of Berwick, Maine, purchased the mill, which now known as the Ashland Knitting Company.

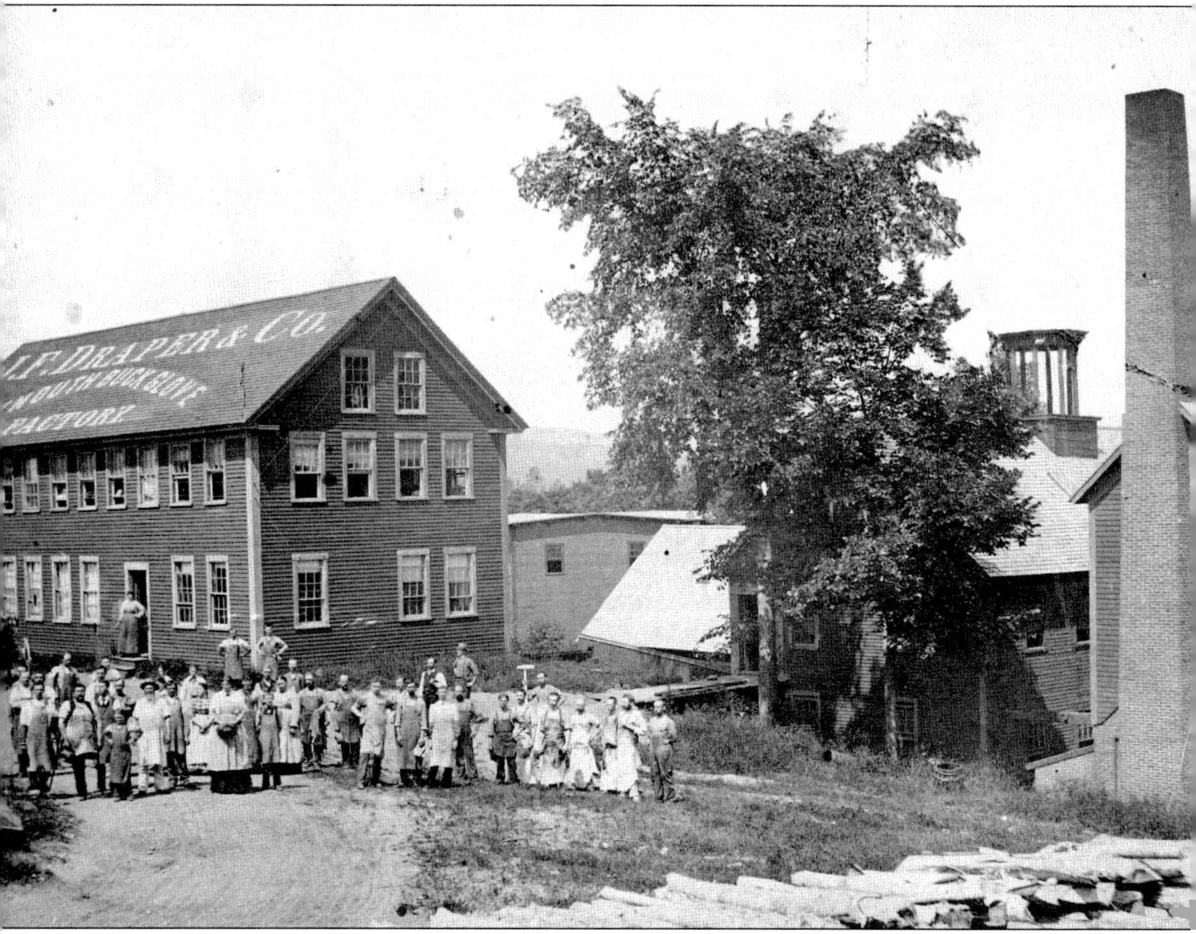

THE J.F. DRAPER & COMPANY GLOVE FACTORY, GLOVE STREET. Built between 1880 and 1881, the company moved from Ashland to Plymouth in 1900. After that, the building seems to have been vacant until 1906, when it was converted to apartments. The paper mill bought the dam and waterpower rights.

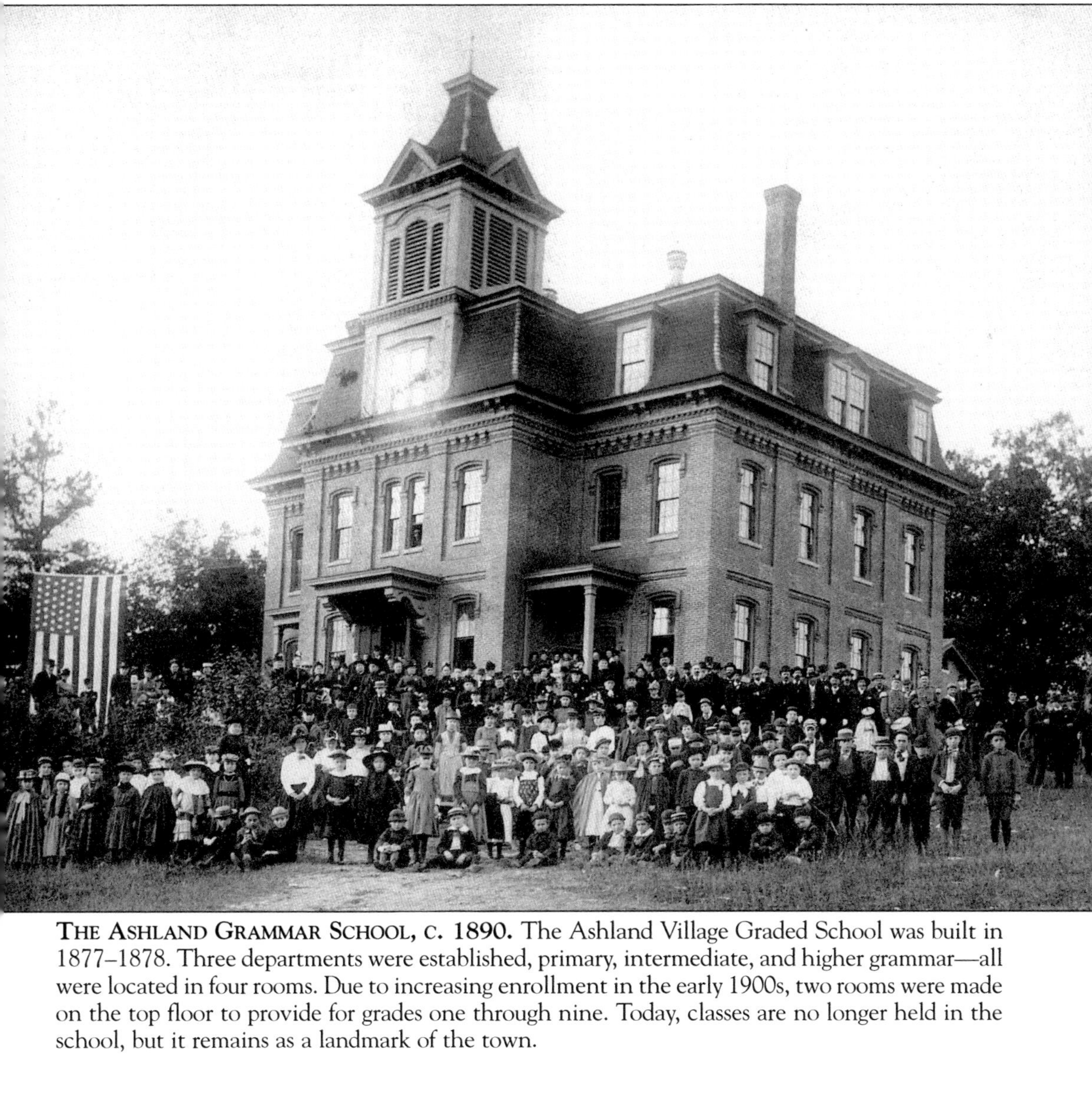

THE ASHLAND GRAMMAR SCHOOL, C. 1890. The Ashland Village Graded School was built in 1877–1878. Three departments were established, primary, intermediate, and higher grammar—all were located in four rooms. Due to increasing enrollment in the early 1900s, two rooms were made on the top floor to provide for grades one through nine. Today, classes are no longer held in the school, but it remains as a landmark of the town.

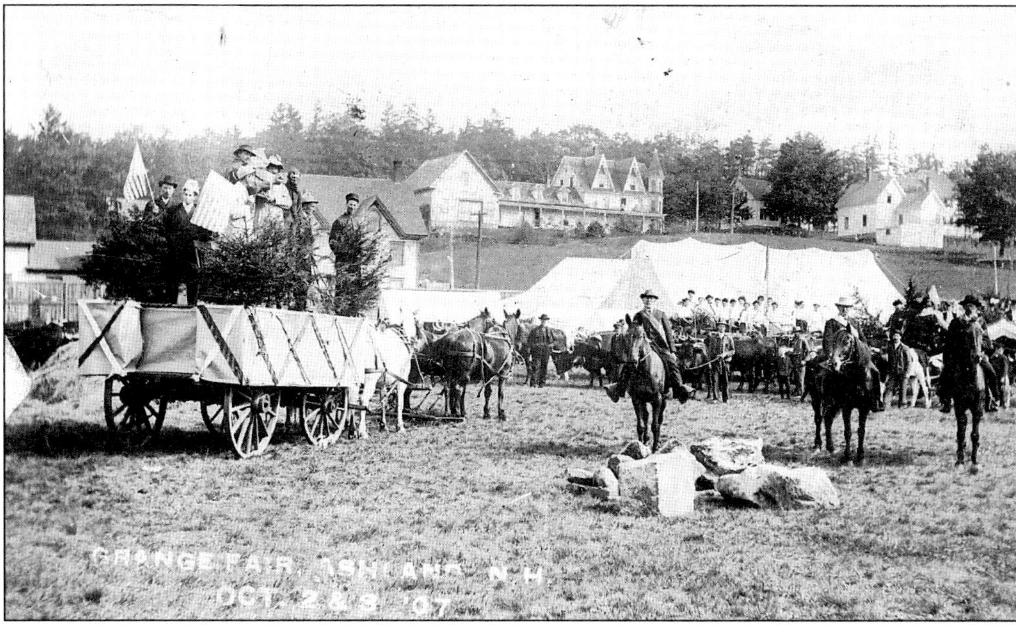

THE SQUAM LAKE GRANGE FAIR, OCTOBER 2–3, 1907. On September 14, 1897, the Squam Lake Grange No. 258 was organized to promote local agricultural projects. Starting in 1906, it sponsored and took part in agricultural fairs. Later, the Plymouth State Fair took over these activities. The Squam Lake Grange exhibited and earned many prizes in numerous departments.

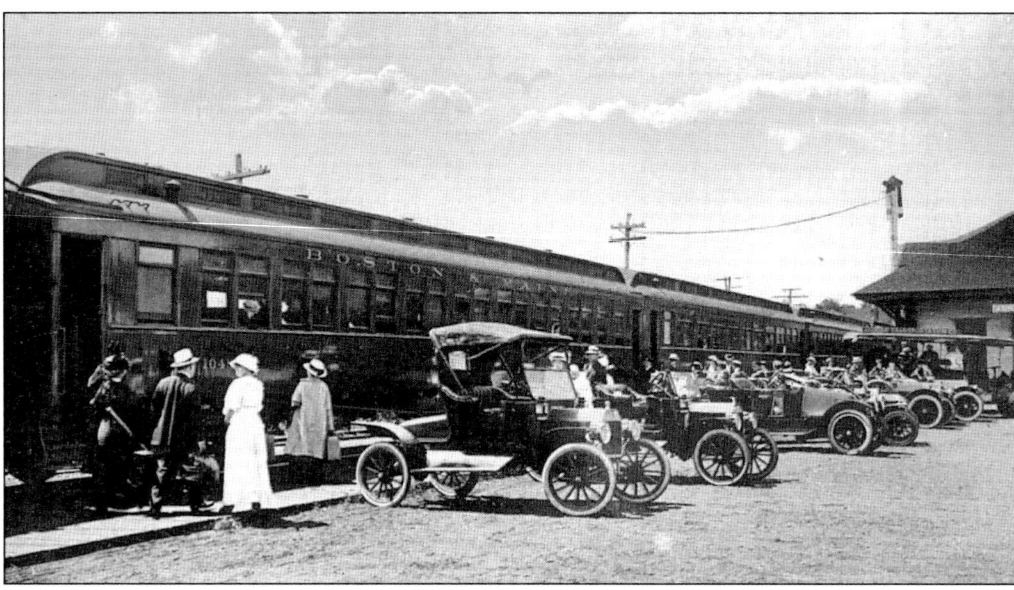

THE ARRIVAL OF THE BOSTON & MAINE EXPRESS TRAIN, ASHLAND RAILROAD STATION, C. THE 1900S. During the heyday of tourism, the grand hotels and inns around Squam Lake sent out their latest vehicles to meet guests arriving from the city.

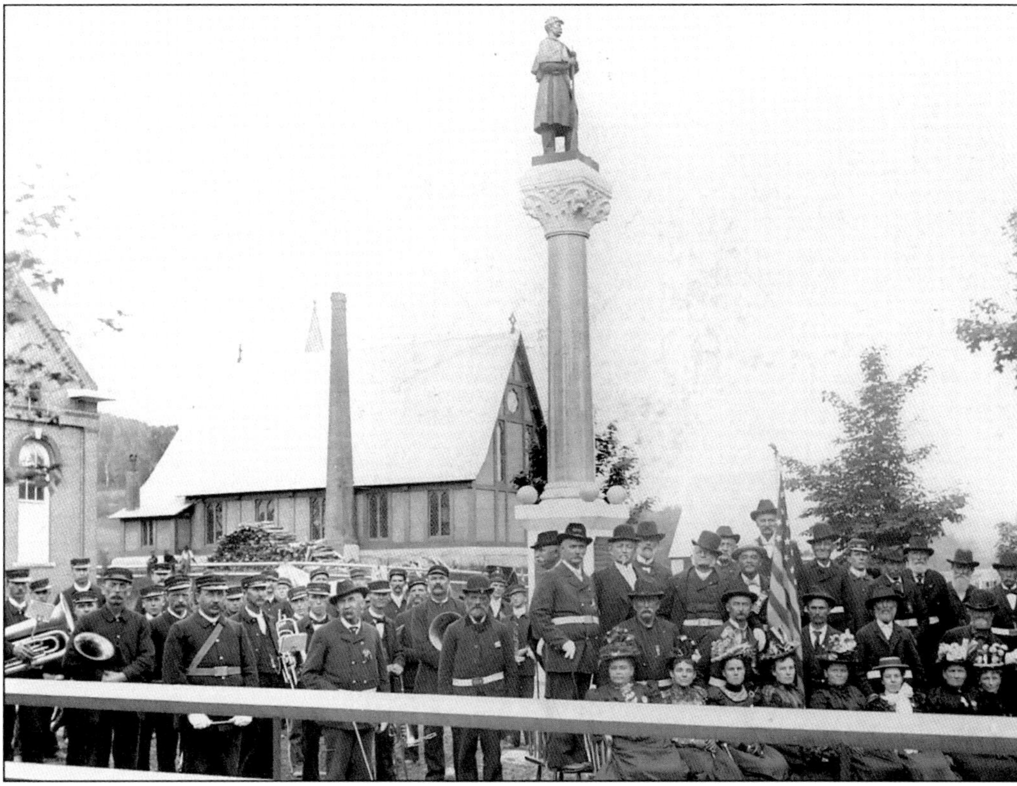

ASHLAND'S CIVIL WAR CONTRIBUTION: 83 MEN TO THE UNION. The Soldiers Monument, honoring those who served in uniform, is constructed of Concord granite with bronze tablets on four sides. On three sides are the names of all the soldiers from Ashland. The column of the monument is eleven feet high and two feet in diameter. A seven-foot bronze statue of a soldier at parade rest stands on top of the column.

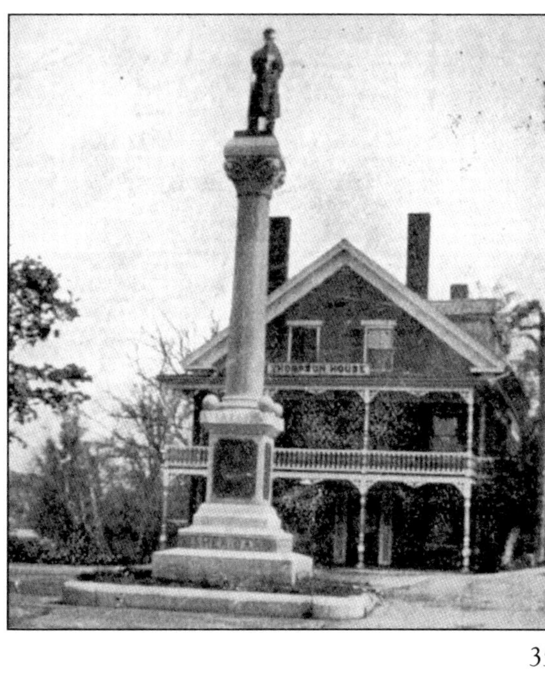

THE SOLDIERS MONUMENT, SOUTH MAIN STREET. In 1900, the town voted to move the monument to the junction of Main, Thompson, and Mill Streets. On the fourth side is the following inscription: In the memory of the Soldiers of Ashland / In the War of 1861–1865 / Erected by the town / O.W. Keyes Post GAR / And Women's Relief Corps / Dedicated May 30, 1899 / Thomas P. Cheney 6th N.H. Vols. / Frank L. Hughes 12th N.H. Vols. / Edward P. Warner, 143 Ind. Vols.

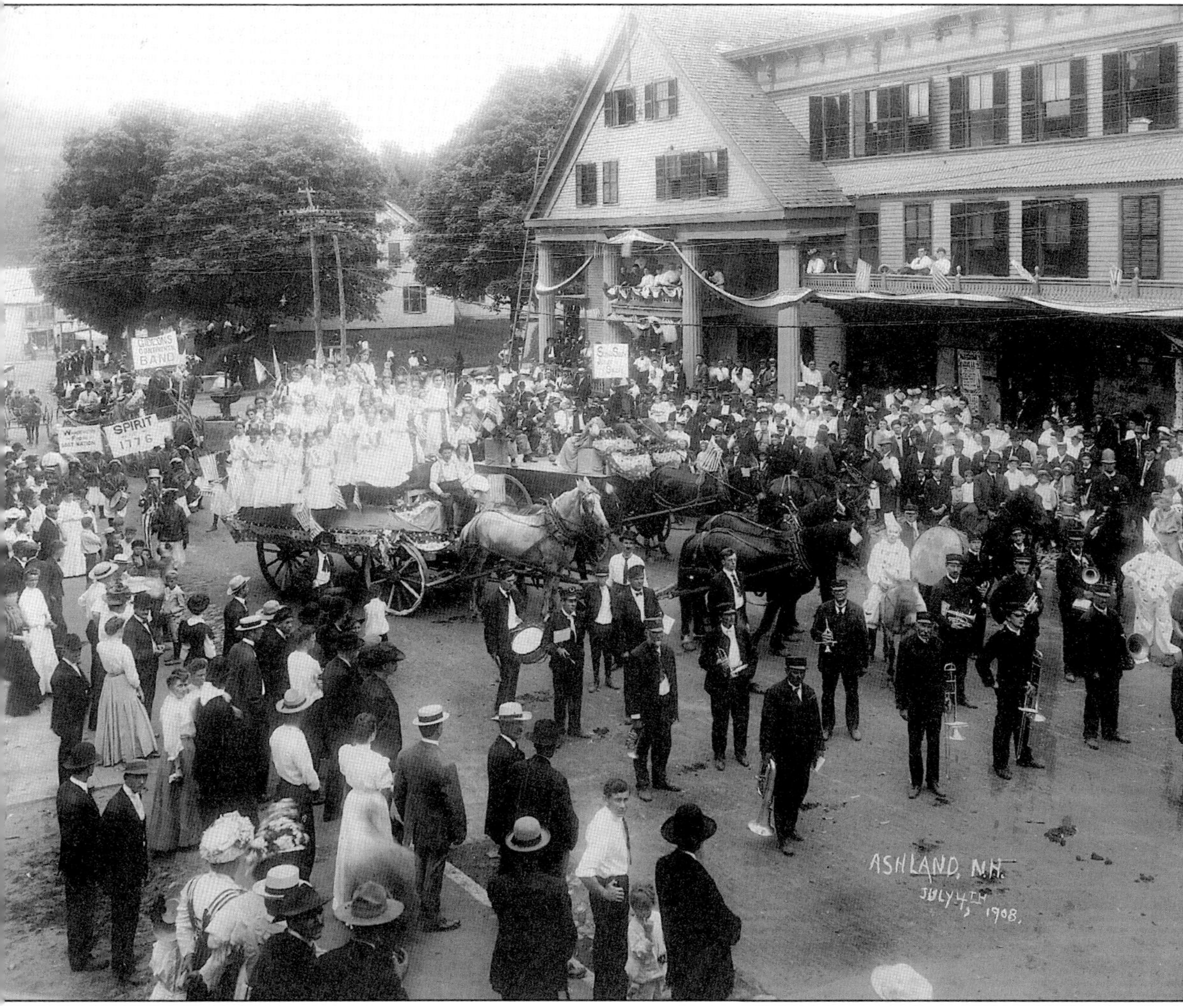

A GRAND PARADE UP MAIN STREET, JULY 4, 1908. In the background is the old Squam Lake House. The small white house in the background was bequeathed to the town by Emma Scribner, and the town library was moved there in 1939. Over the years, Ashland has taken great pride in its patriotic spirit, particularly during Memorial Day, the Fourth of July, and Veterans Day.

Three

Center Harbor

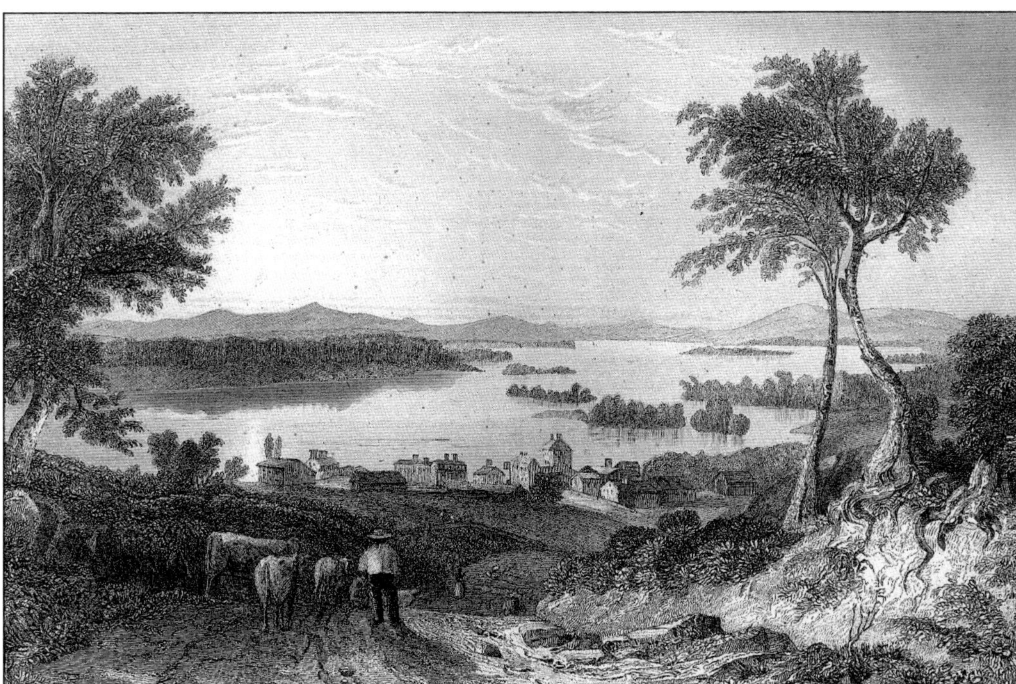

A View of Center Harbor Village from Plymouth Street, with Lake Winnipesaukee in the Background. Located on both Lake Winnipesaukee and Squam Lake, this village is a busy summer resort. Once known as Centre Harbour, it stretches from the shore of Lake Winnipesaukee and commands a panoramic view of the lakes and mountains surrounding it.

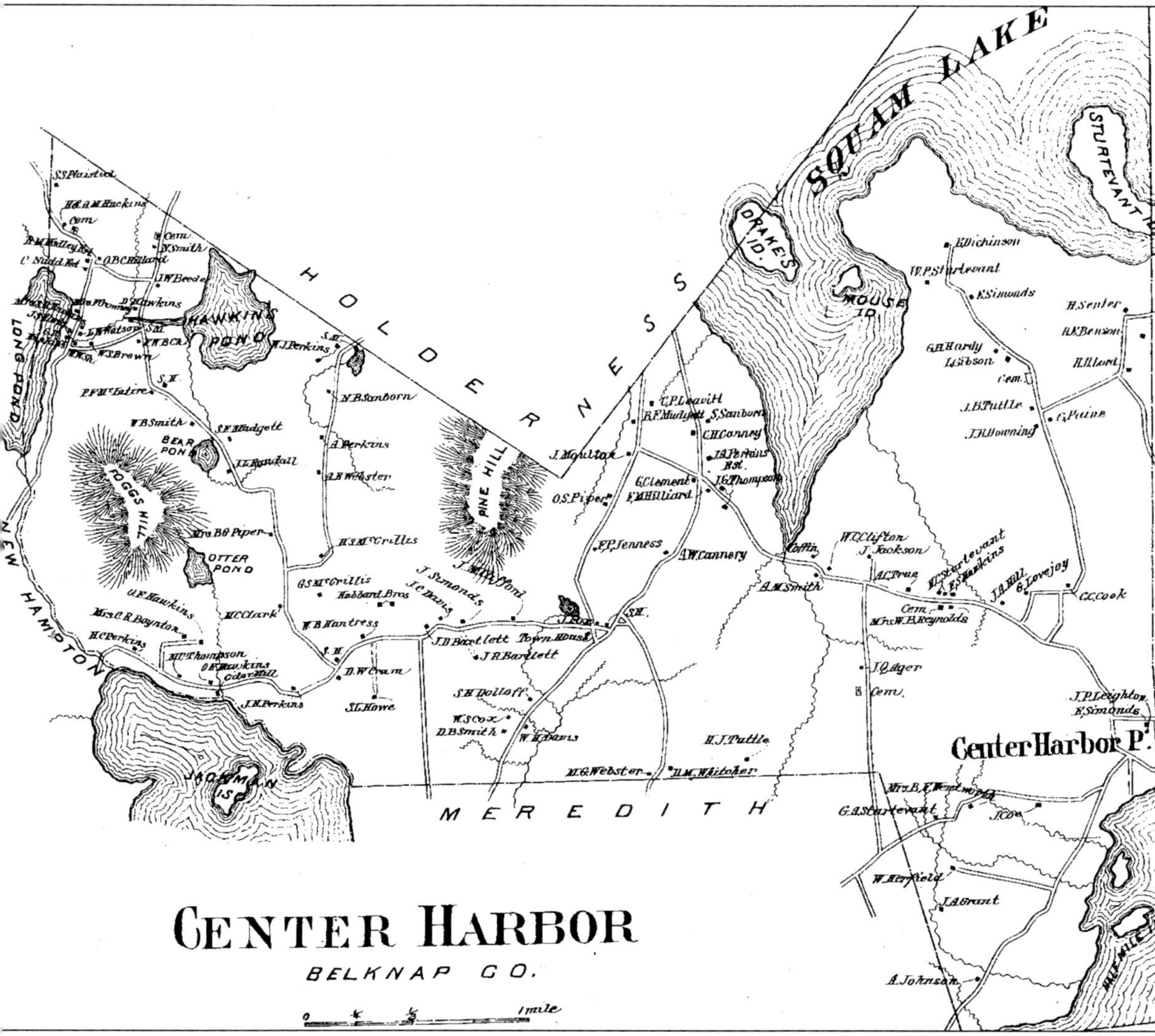

A Map of Center Harbor, Belknap County, c. 1892. According to historian Gladys S. Bickford and the Centre Harbor Historical Society, "The early history of Centre Harbor is interwoven with that of Moultonborough and a section of Meredith, which was severed from Meredith and annexed to Centre Harbor. This section in early records was known as New Salem Point. Moultonborough was granted by the Masonian Proprietors, November 17, 1763, to Colonel Jonathan Moulton and approximately 61 others. After the first survey of this region, the settlers expressed dissatisfaction with their grant because of hilly sections, lakes, swamps, ponds, etc., it was discovered that a section of land adjoining the original had been overlooked when the towns of Holderness, Sanbornton, and Meredith, formerly New Salem, had been laid out. In 1765, Gov. John Wentworth granted the above-mentioned land." Center Harbor was incorporated in 1797 and was bounded on the northeast by Moultonborough, on the southeast by Meredith, on the west by New Hampton, and on the north by Squam Lake and Holderness. The town covers a land area of 7,232 acres and a water area of 1,600 acres.

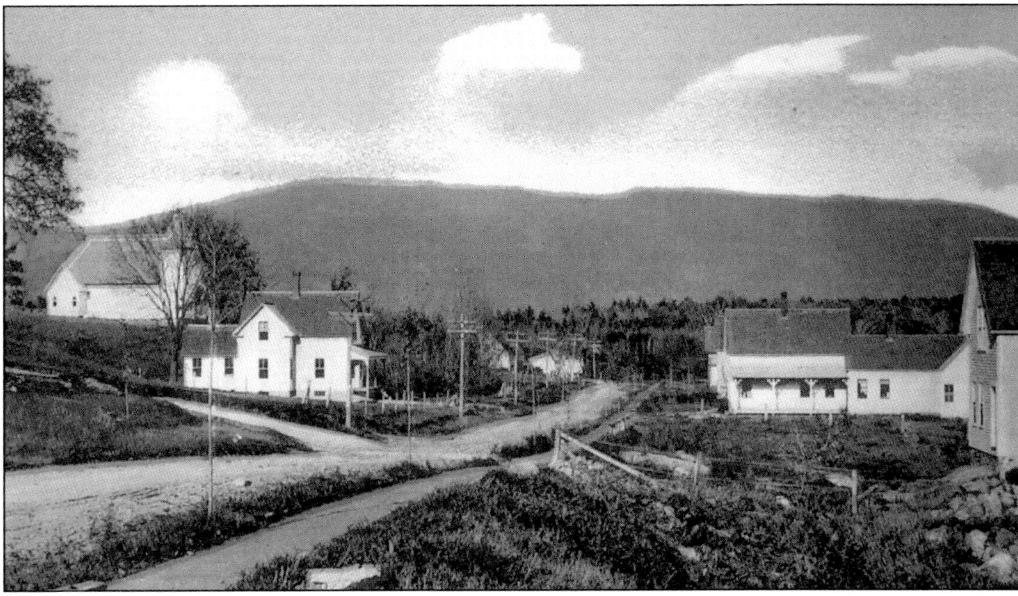

A VIEW OF RED HILL FROM THE VILLAGE OF CENTER HARBOR. For services rendered in the French and Indian War, Col. Joseph Senter secured that land which is now known as Center Harbor at the northern end of Lake Winnipesaukee. His brother Moses Senter later received grants, and came here from Londonderry *c.* 1763. He built a log cabin about a half-mile from the present Coe Mansion. It is said that, as he and his family were coming up Lake Winnipesaukee in two birch canoes, he pointed to a hill in the distance, covered with autumnal crimson, and remarked with awe, "See that red hill!" Ever since, Red Hill has been the name of the conspicuous low mountain located east of the village.

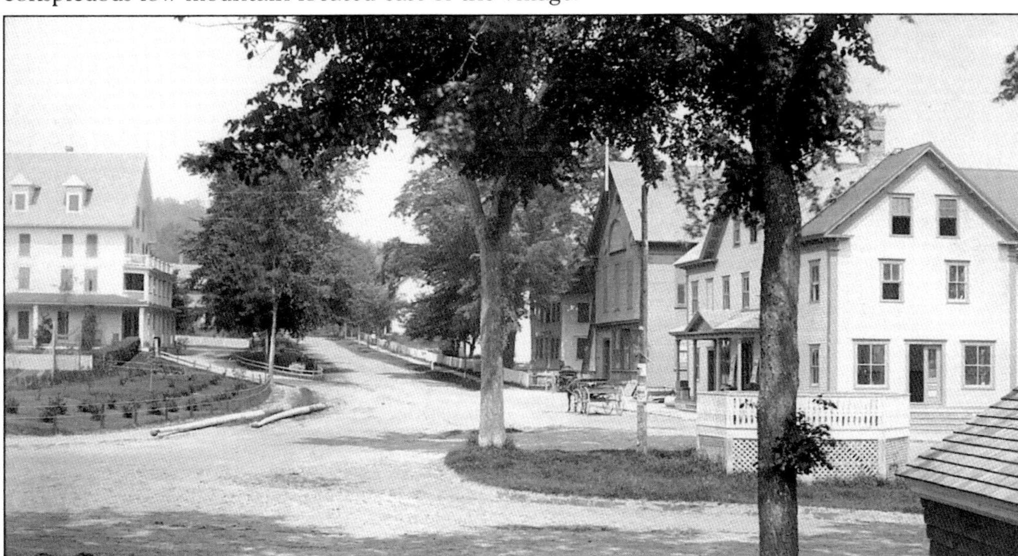

THE VILLAGE SQUARE, LOOKING WEST UP PLYMOUTH STREET. Note the early bandstand on the common green and the Moulton House on the left. At this junction is a section of the road known as the College Road, a part of the original highway Gov. John Wentworth built from his summer estate in Wolfeboro to Hanover, to attend the first commencement at Dartmouth College in 1771.

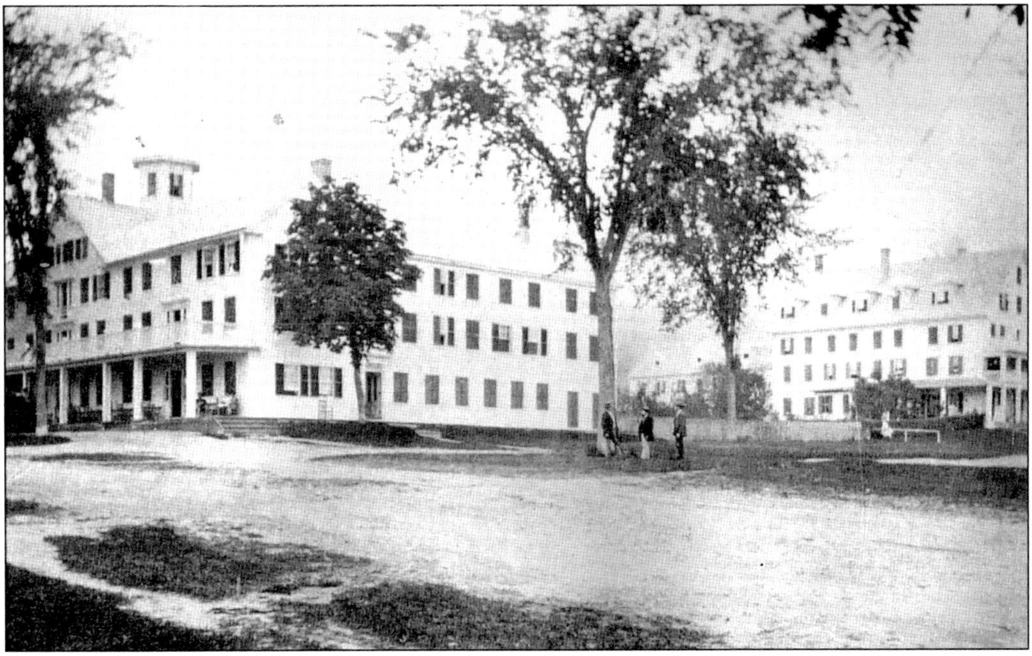

THE SENTER HOTEL (LEFT) AND MOULTON'S HOTEL (RIGHT), C. THE 1880S. During the early years, the village was an important halfway station between Concord and the Maine town of Fryeburg. The Moulton House was a popular stopping place for travelers en route to the White Mountains. In 1868, the Moulton Hotel was remodeled and enlarged to accommodate 60 to 75 guests. The hotel enjoyed prosperity during the golden age of travel.

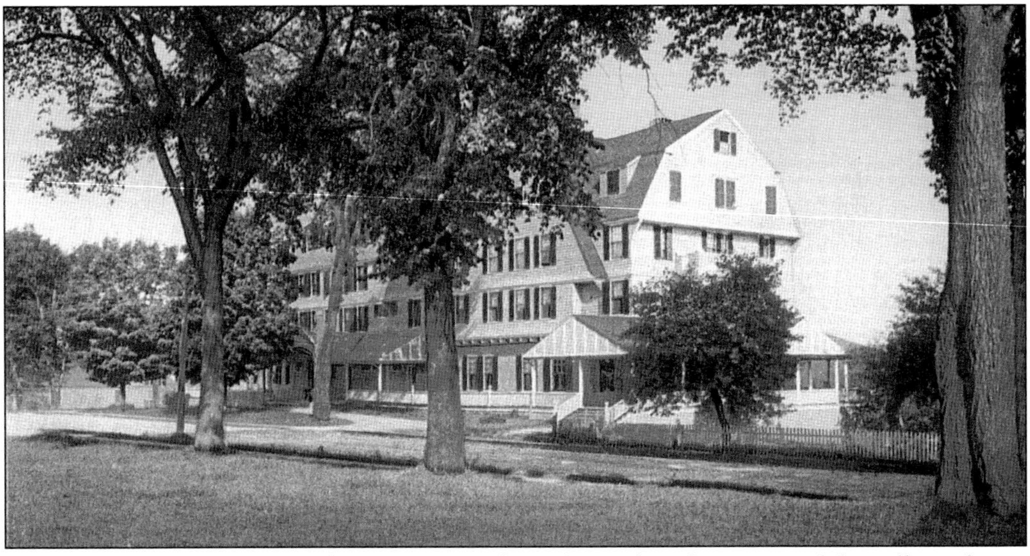

THE NEW SENTER HOUSE. The Senter Hotel was located in the center of the village, facing Lake Winnipesaukee. The old Senter House was built c. 1830 by Samuel Senter on the site of the present Nichols Memorial Library.

CENTER HARBOR HOTELS & BOARDING HOUSES
REACHED BY THE BOSTON & LOWELL RAILROAD
1885

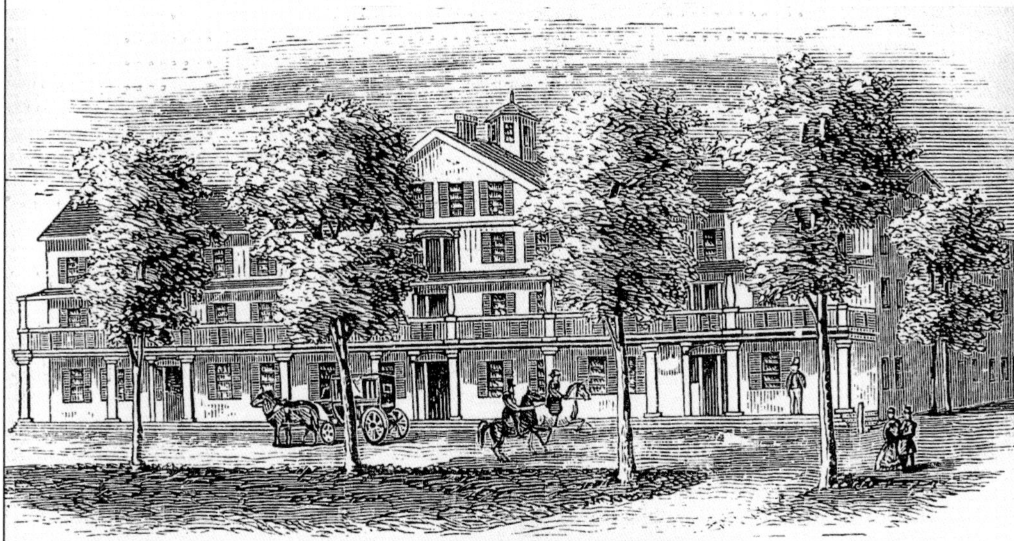

SENTER HOUSE, CENTRE HARBOR, N.H.

CENTRE HARBOR, N.H. See article on Lake Winnipesaukee.

NAME OF HOUSE	PROPRIETOR	NO. ACCOMODATE	PRICE A DAY	WEEKLY
Senter House...............	J. L. Huntress & Son...	150	$3.00	$14 to 21
Moulton House............	S. F. Emery...........	75	2.00	8 to 12
Sunset House, Pine Hill....	J. K. Kelsea...........	40	1.00	5 to 7
Lake House..................	Mrs. Almon Benson....	25	1.00	5 to 7
Locust Cottage..............	B. F. Kelsea............	25	....	6 to 10
Brown Cottage	B. F. Wentworth.......	18	....	....
Lakeside Cottage...........	Mrs. A. M. Graves......	15	....	5 to 7
Hillside Cottage............	T. C. Gordon...........	10	....	....
Willow Cottage	Stephen Wentworth....	25	1.00	7.00
Bean Farm..................	Mrs. A. M. Bean & Son.	12	....	6.00
Red Hill Cottage............	F. F. Green............	10	....	6 00
Lake View House..........	R. D. Green............	15	....	6.00
Boarding House............	W. A. Page............	25	....	7 to 10

A LIST OF HOTELS AND INNS IN CENTER HARBOR, FEATURING THE SENTER HOUSE, C. 1885. The Old Senter House brochure of 1880 read as follows: "The Hotel is situated on an eminence of the head of Lake Winnipesaukee, and from its piazzas commands a clear and unobstructed view of its entire length. As a summer resort it affords varied and delightful attractions to the tourists and sojourner. The situation of the Hotel is unequalled for picturesque beauty in New England. The drives in all directions are charming, whether skirting the shores of the beautiful lake or winding among the hills, and introduce the traveler to the marvelous scenery of the surrounding country, sung by the poet Whittier, 'The Heart of the Highlands.'"

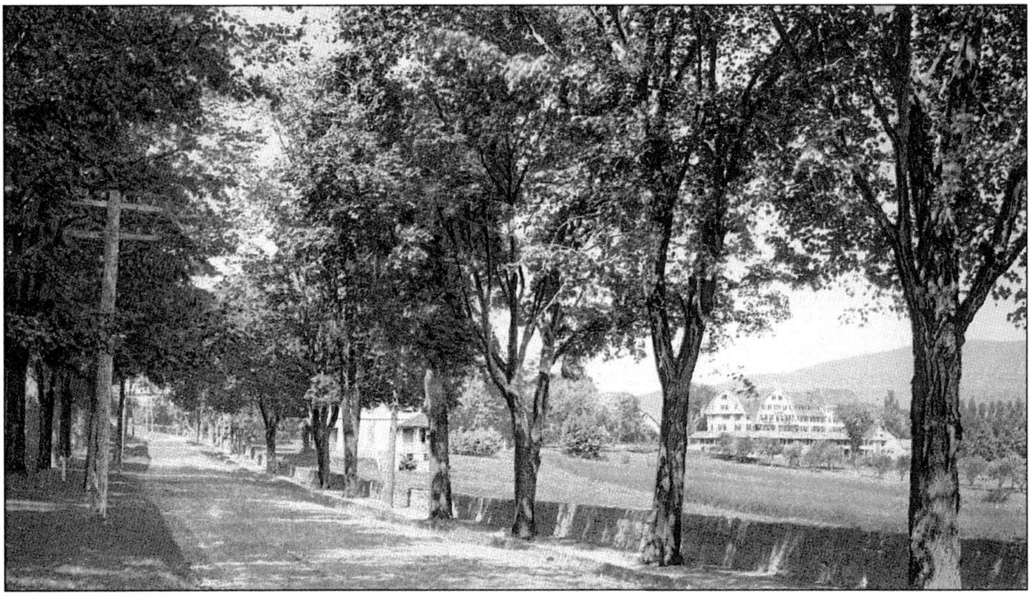

The Meredith Road, Looking North. The Senter Hotel (right) became the Colonial in later years. The hotel had 15 double fireplaces and 91 sleeping rooms. On June 20, 1919, the hotel was destroyed by fire. Today, a new bandstand dignifies the open area, and band concerts are held there in the summer.

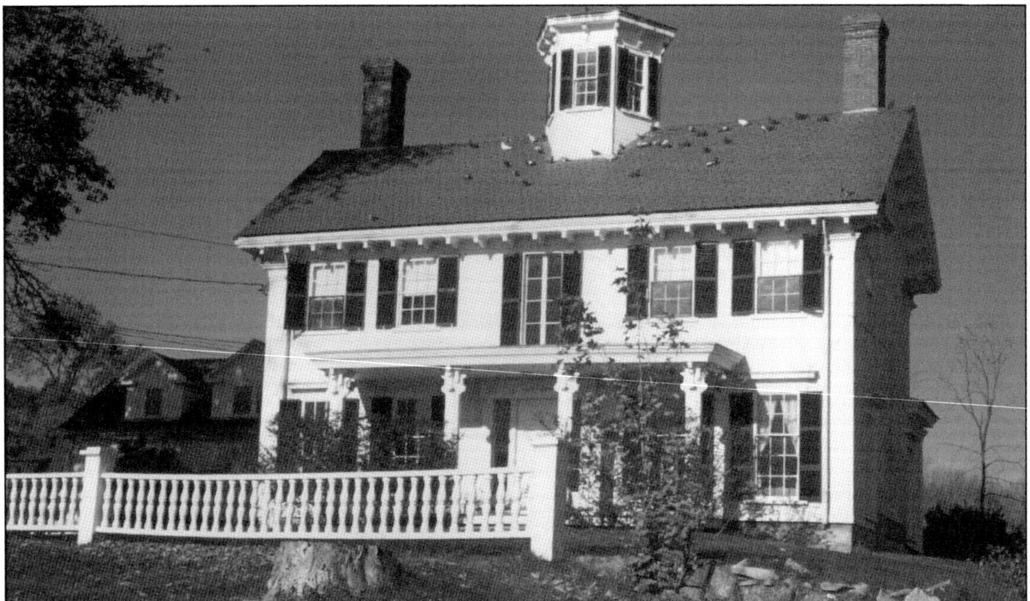

The Coe House. Located in the village of Center Harbor, this wood-framed house—surmounted by a hexagonal tower with windows—commands a southward view of Lake Winnipesaukee's northern harbor. The house was built in 1820 by John Coe Sr., who married a daughter of Samuel Senter. This home has entertained many famous visitors, including Franklin Pierce and Grover Cleveland and poets John Greenleaf Whittier and Lucy Larcom. Today, the mansion has been transformed into a gracious dining establishment worthy of its elegant heritage.

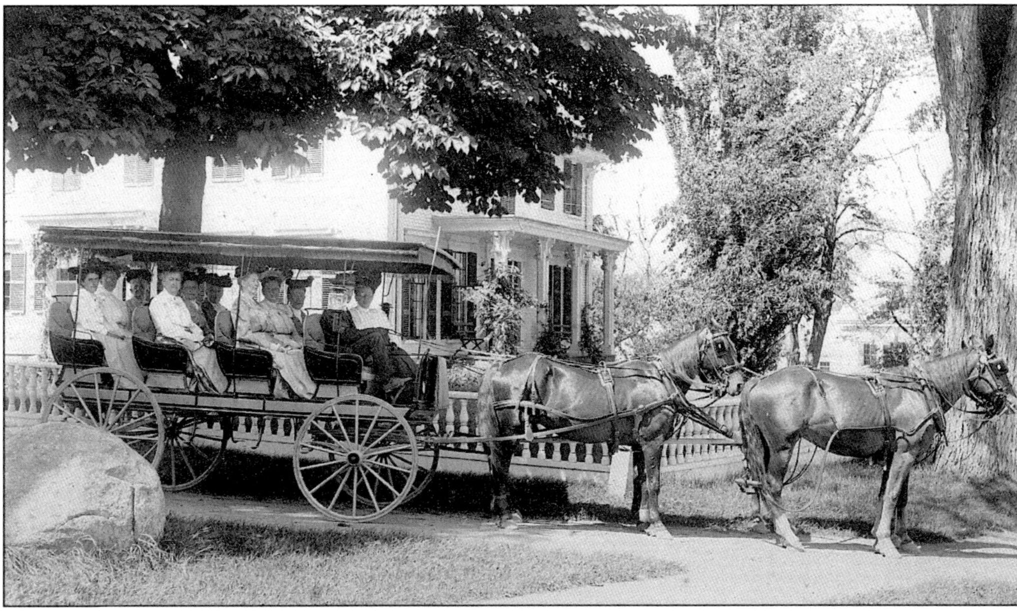

A SURRY IN FRONT OF THE COE HOUSE. The Center Harbor Women's Club, in a surrey drawn by four horses, pauses in front of the Coe House in the late 1800s.

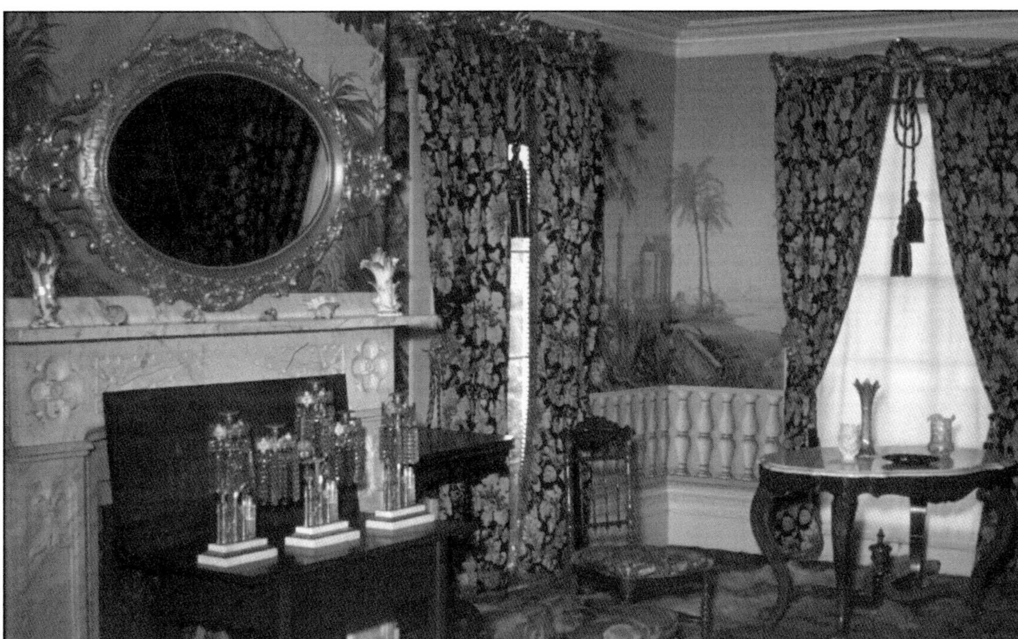

THE INTERIOR OF THE COE HOUSE. This room was furnished in the style of Boston parlors of more than a century ago. The French wallpaper was imported from Alsace-Lorraine and was decorated with a landscape in brilliant colors, portraying scenes in Italy and along the Nile River in Egypt. Below the wallpaper is a ornamental fence that runs around the whole room and matches the home's exterior fence. On the northeast side is a fireplace with a beautiful white marble mantle. Entertained in this parlor were poets and presidents: John Greenleaf Whittier and Lucy Larcom, and Franklin Pierce and Grover Cleveland.

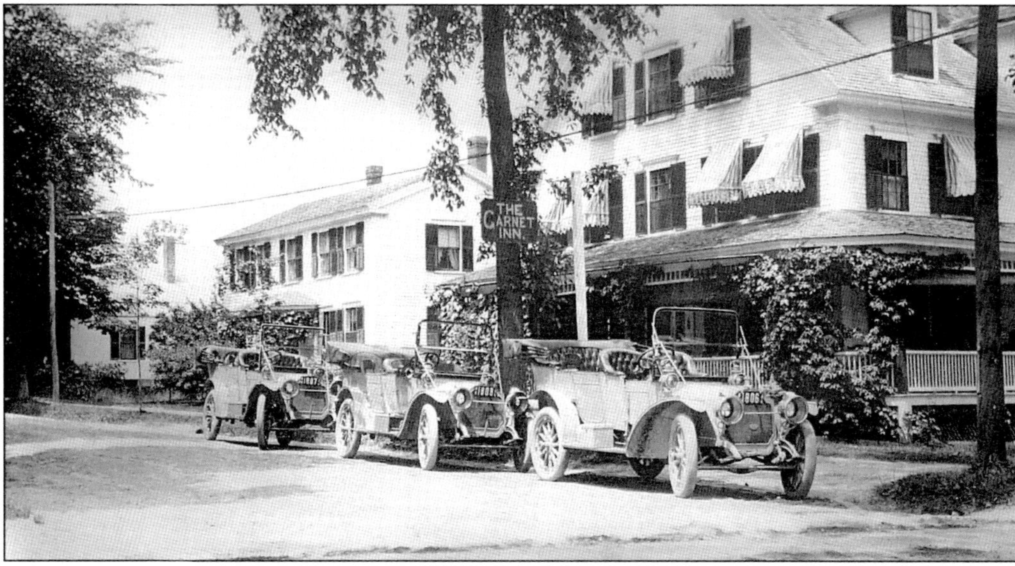

THE ROYAL GRAY LINE IN FRONT OF THE GARNET INN, PLYMOUTH STREET, C. THE 1920S. The Bennetts, who owned the Garnet Inn, had six or eight Packards, which were used to take guests on tours, especially around the White Mountains and the Lakes Region.

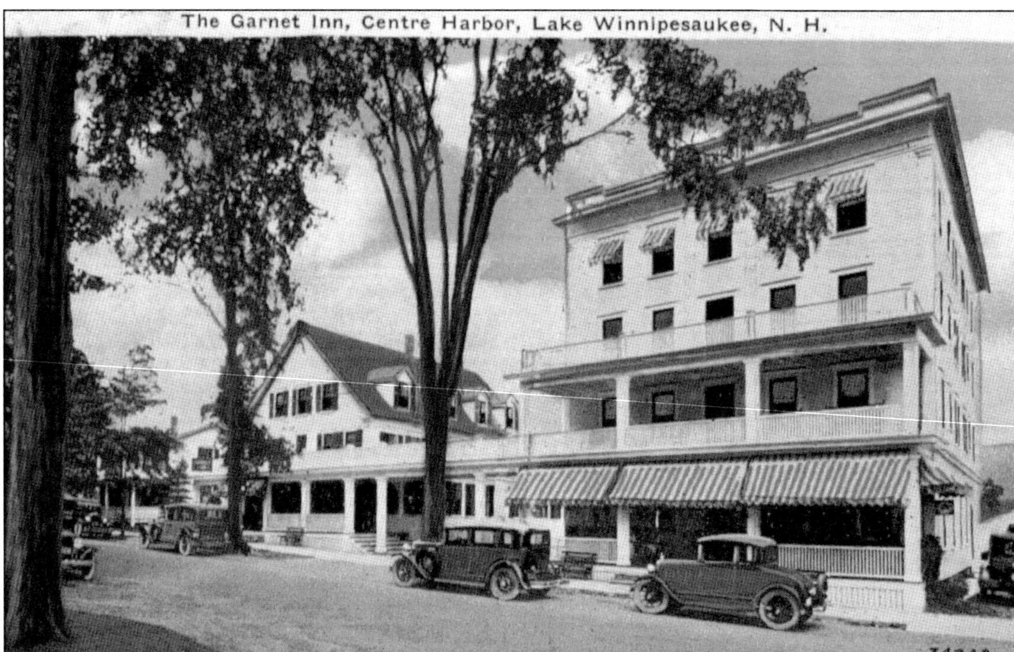

THE GARNET INN, C. THE 1920S. This hotel was quite successful during the early 1920s, and among its visitors were the Roosevelts and Duponts. The hotel brochure reads as follows: "A modern all year-round hotel at the base of Garnet Hill near the shore of Lake Winnipesaukee, a wonder view of the lake is obtained from the hotel piazza." In 1994, the inn was torn down, leaving open space in the center of the village.

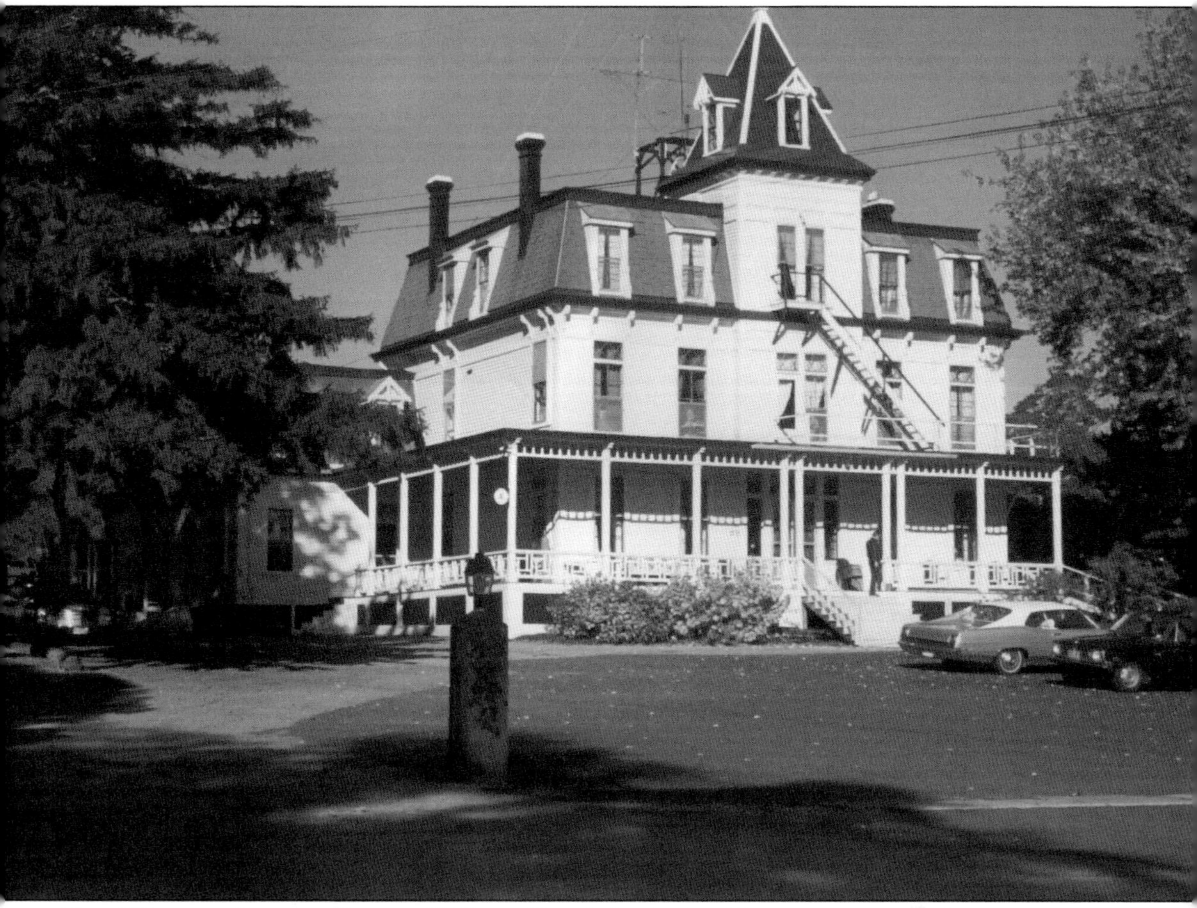

THE WILLIAM SHEAFE HOUSE. William Sheafe built this Victorian mansion for a summer home in 1881. From 1947 to 1982, the Dyer family operated this house as a nursing home. After 1983, it was made into a condominium and offices. In 1995, the Center Harbor Congregational Church purchased the property and, in 1997, the structure was moved to Bean Road, north of the village.

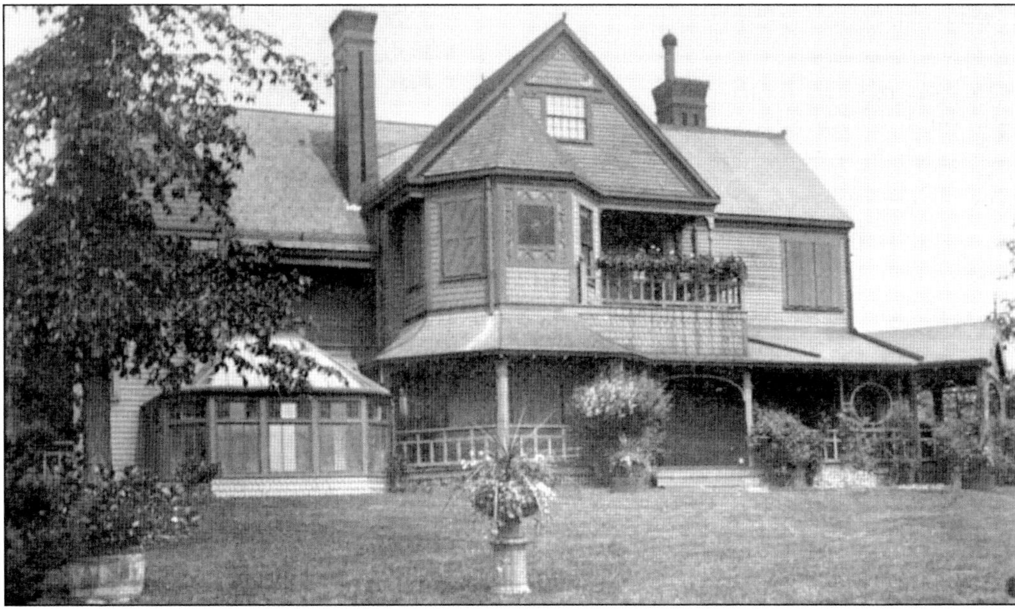

THE BRIERS. The Briers was built for a summer home by John D. Bates during the early 1800s. Bates, a wealthy Boston socialite, married his young Irish cook five years before he died. She became one of the wealthiest women in Boston and spent most of her time at the Briers, which boasted a deer park near the road. At the rear of the lot, near the wooded area, was a fish pond.

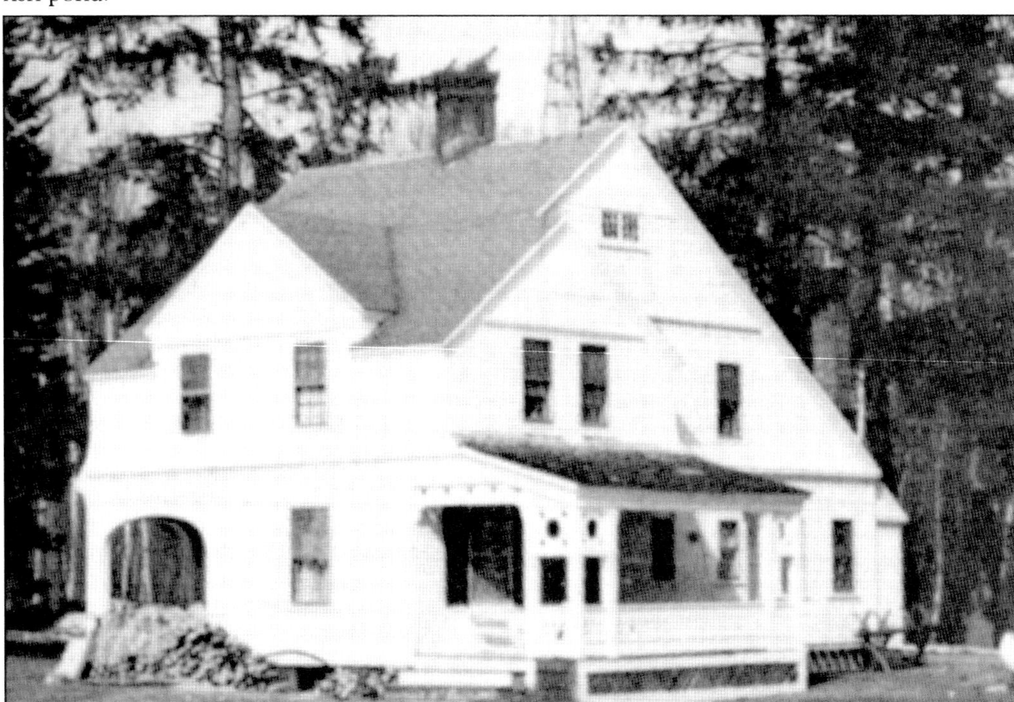

THE GATEHOUSE TO THE BRIERS. The house, barn, and several smaller buildings—including the gatehouse—were located on Route 25B and Garnet Hill.

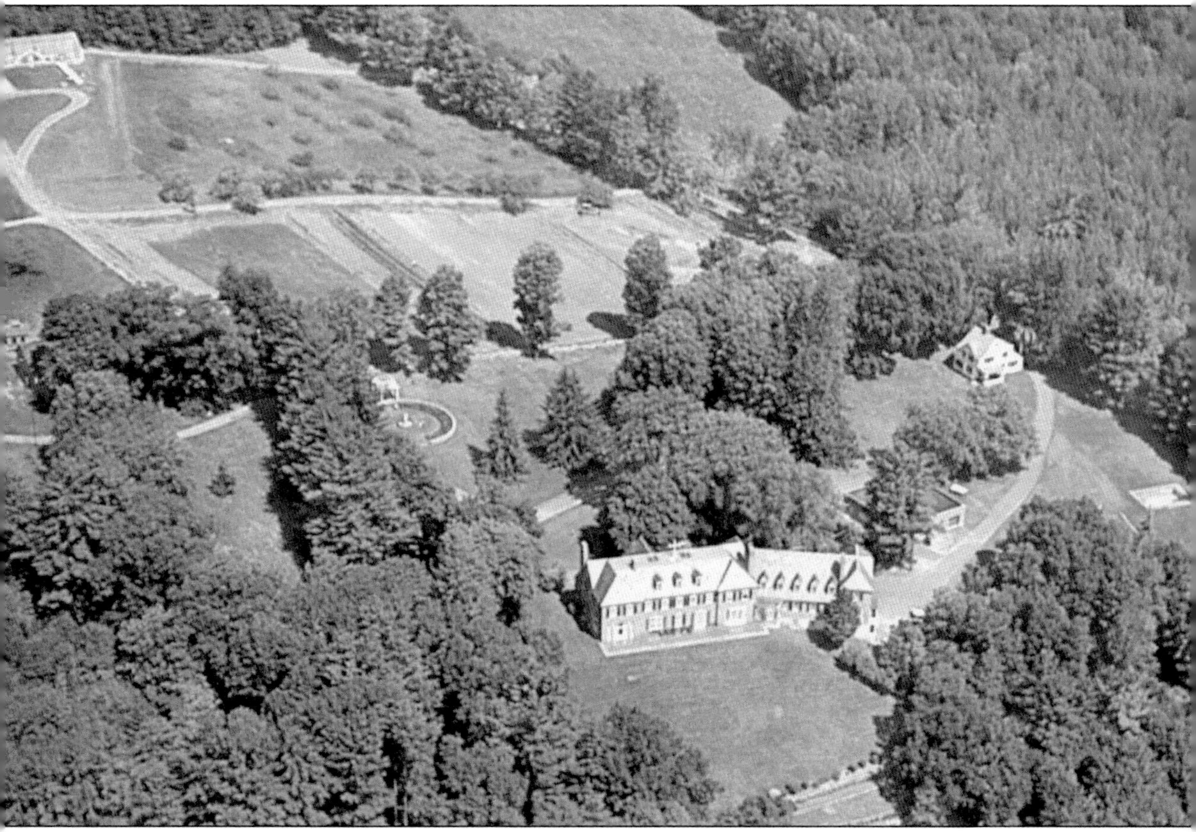

AN AERIAL VIEW OF THE DANE MANSION. In the early 1940s, this property was purchased by Ernest B. Dane, who built a new mansion on the site, replacing the older wooden estate. The original Victorian gatehouse remains. For several years, the estate was operated by the La Salette Fathers' Novitiate. Since 1982, it has been the site for the Legionaires of Christ, an Immaculate Conception apostolic school.

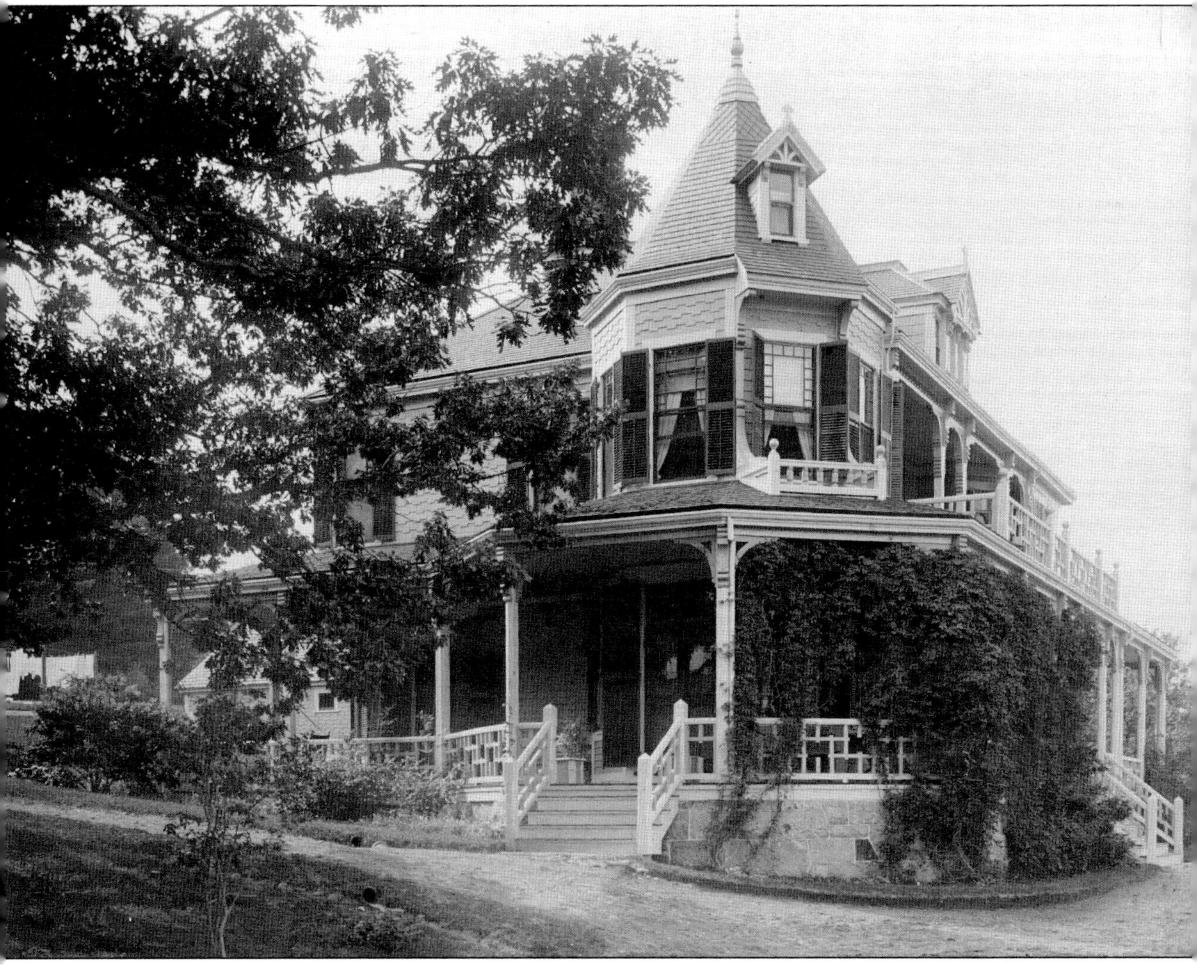

THE GILNOCKIE ESTATE. The Gilnockie estate was built in 1880 for Margaret E. Marcus, who named it Marcus Villa. Her husband was Herman Marcus, founder of the Marcus firm in New York. This elegant residence has several fireplaces, two towers, and a large veranda. In 1895, the property was sold to George W. Armstrong of Boston, Massachusetts. Several acres were purchased from Daniel Coe, Timothy Gordon, and Eliza Sutton, adding more space to the estate. Armstrong named the place Gilnockie after his ancestral home in Scotland.

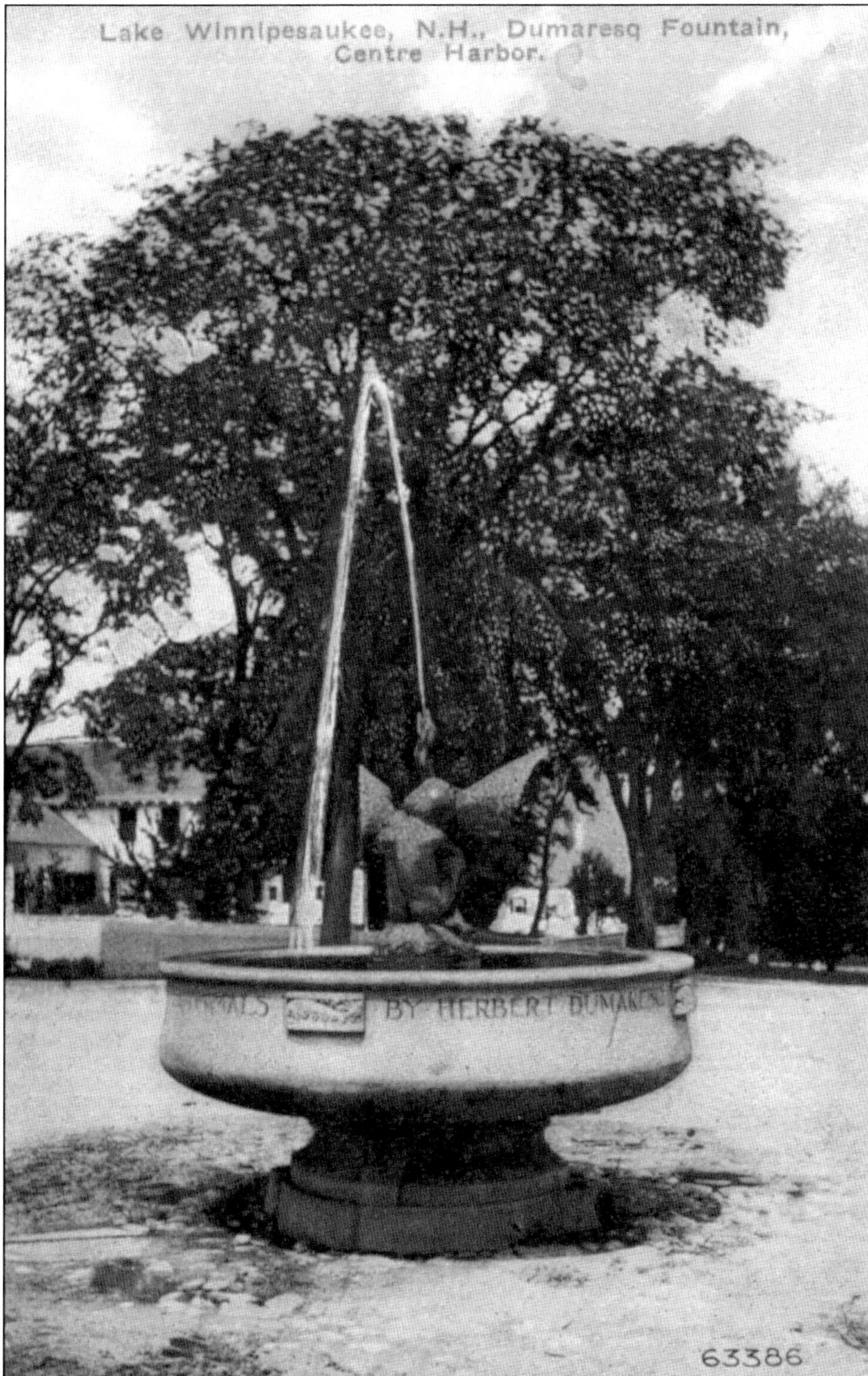

THE KONA (DUMARESQ) FOUNTAIN. On September 23, 1907, Herbert Dumaresq generously donated this beautiful drinking fountain to the town of Center Harbor. This fountain has been a source of pride for the community. The granite block from which the fountain sculpture was cut weighed 10 tons. The sculptor was Samuel Russell Gerry Cook of Lincoln, Massachusetts, a nationally known ceramic artist and protégé of Augustus Saint-Gaudens.

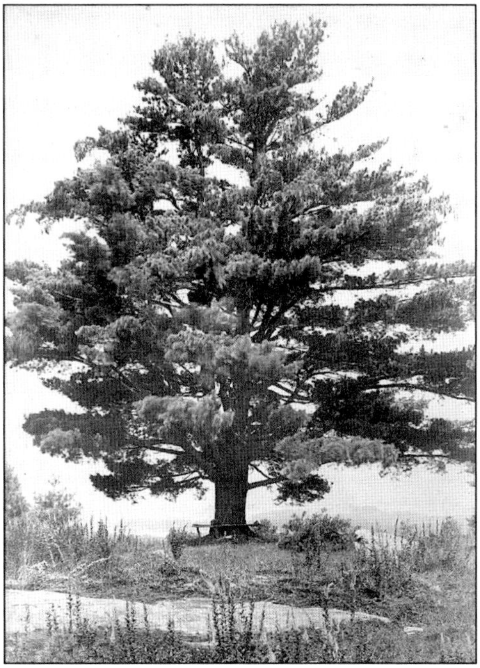

The Whittier Pine. On the grounds of Camp Pinelands stood the Whittier Pine, which is intimately associated with the gentle Quaker poet John Greenleaf Whittier, who immortalized New Hampshire. Here, sitting under its mammoth branches and looking out over the beautiful, island-dotted Squam Lakes, Whittier composed "Summer by the Lakeside," "Storm on Lake Asquam," "The Wood Giant," "The Hill-top," and many others. The Whittier Pine is believed to have been some 400 years old when it was struck by lightning in June 1950. The tree had to be cut down a few years later.

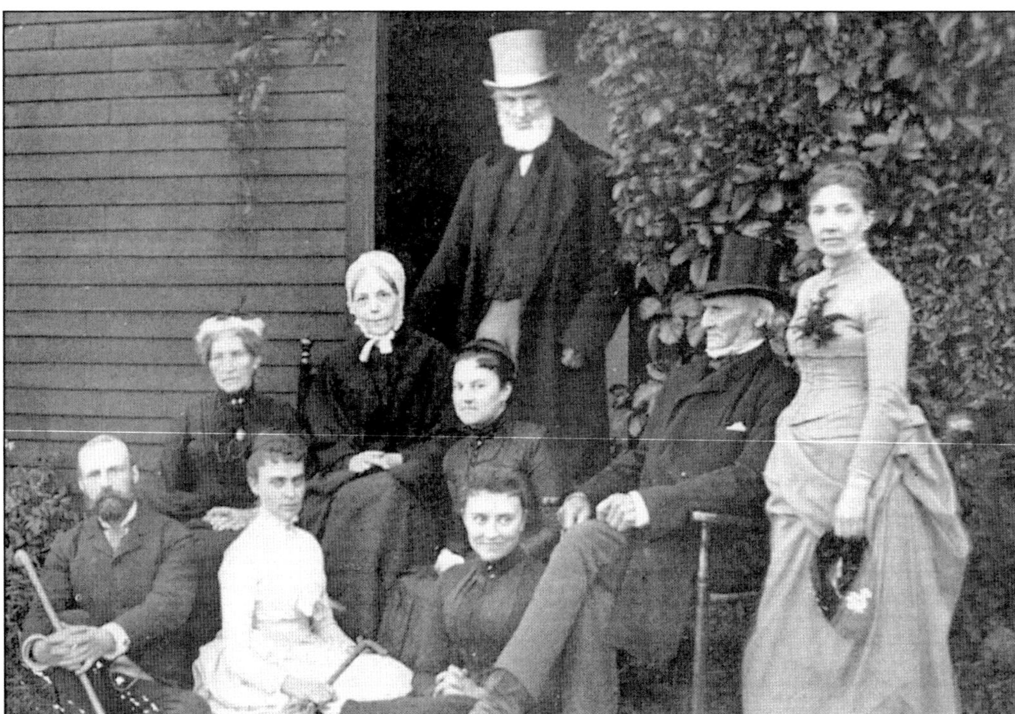

John Greenleaf Whittier and Friends at the Sturtevant Farm, 1885. This stately Colonial estate was one of Whittier's summer retreats. Both Lake Winnipesaukee and Squam Lake have felt the pull of the poet's oar as he rowed on them, fishing. Whittier is shown standing in the doorway. On the right are his cousins, Gertrude and Joseph Cartland, who were his constant companions.

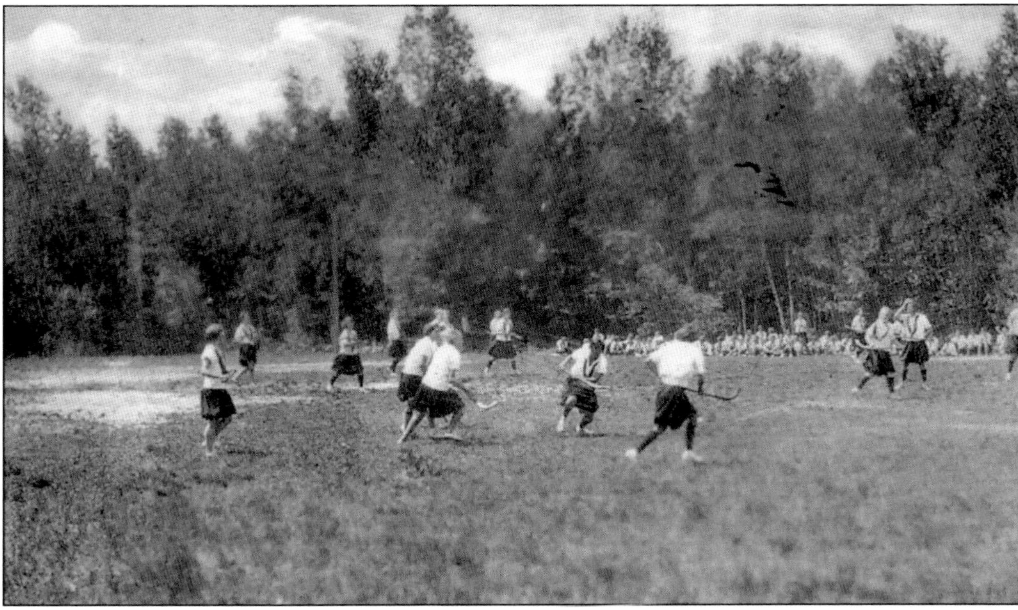

SINGING EAGLE LODGE, 1950. Singing Eagle, a summer camp for girls ages 8 to 20, was established in 1922 by Dr. Ann Tomkins Gibson. According to the camp advertisement, "Simplicity of living, a diversified program, and careful medical oversight are stressed."

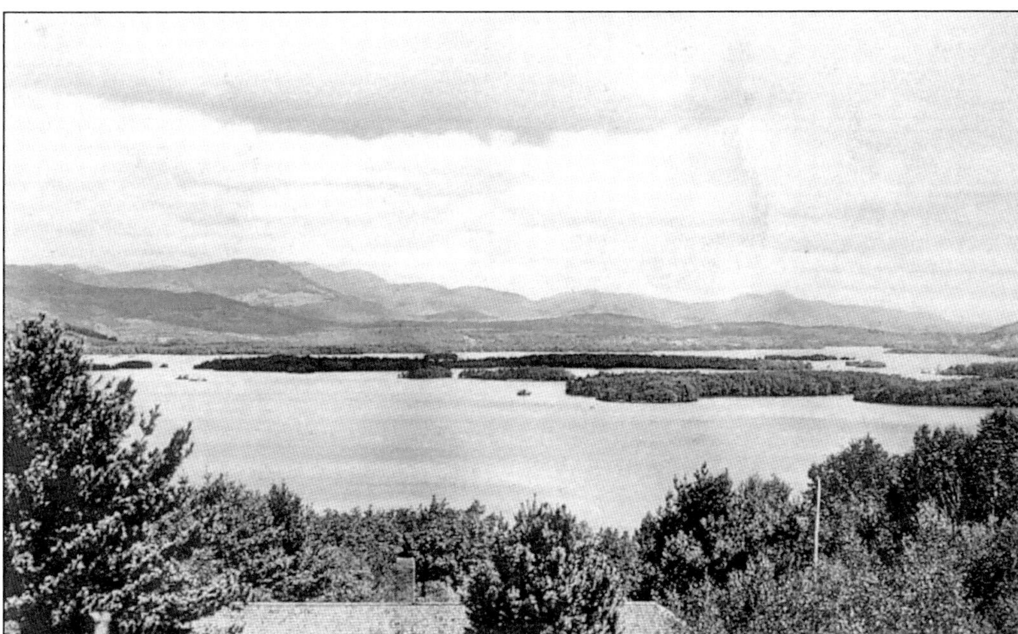

SQUAM LAKE, FROM CAMP ASQUAM, 1953. This view from High Haith is considered one of the finest on Squam Lake. Seen are the Sandwich Dome, Red Hill, and the Ossipee and Chocorua mountains.

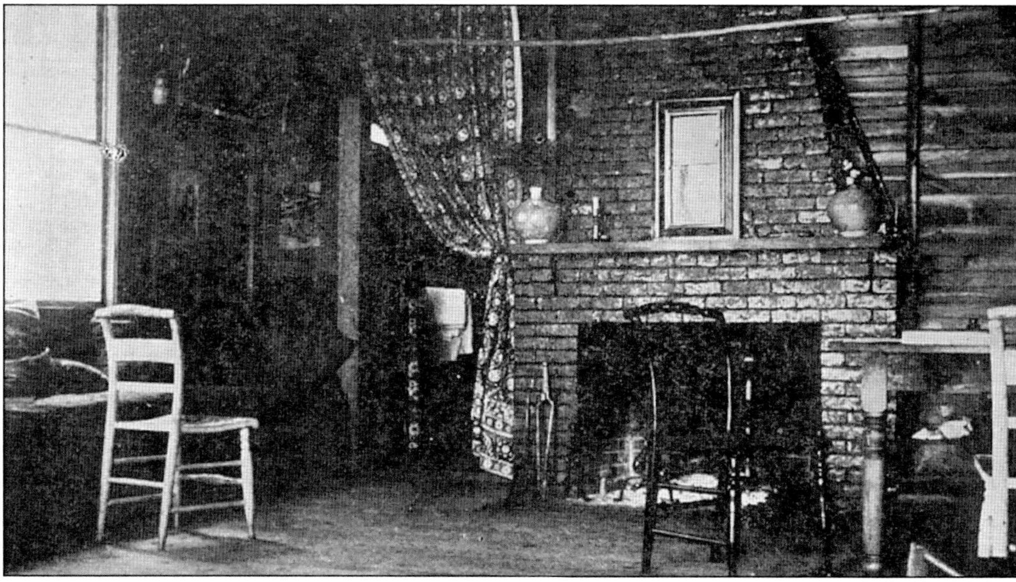

THE LIVING ROOM OF SUNSET COTTAGE, CAMP ASQUAM, CENTER HARBOR. Camp Asquam, a summer camp for girls ages 10 to 19, is situated on High Haith Peninsula, three miles from Center Harbor village and Lake Winnipesaukee. The 1952 camp brochure states that "The purpose of Camp Asquam is to develop health of body and control of mind. The out-of-door life in a beautiful mountain country with girls of their own age, should encourage in its members energy, self-reliance, and the spirit of social responsibility."

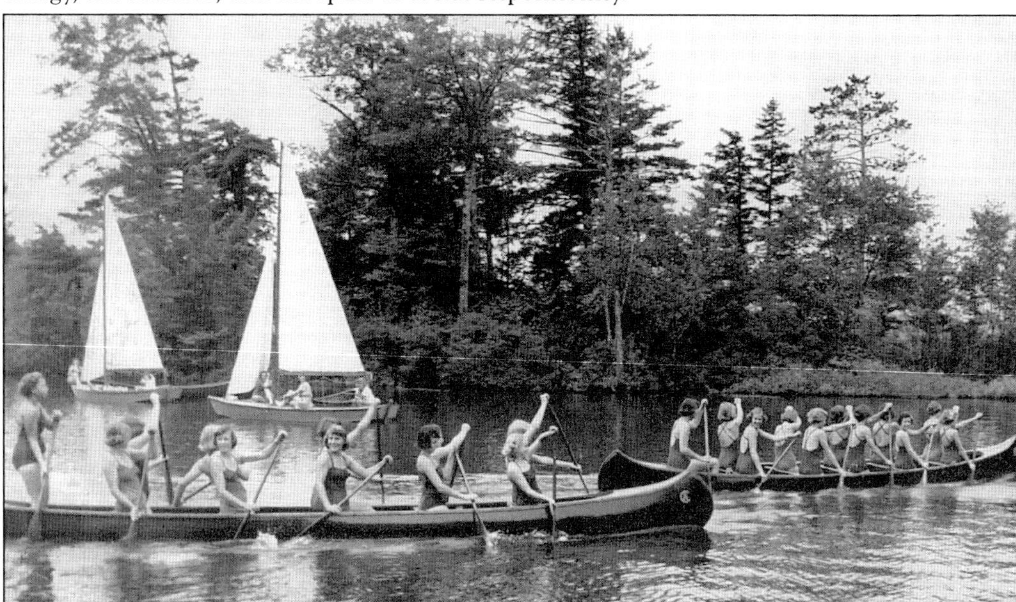

CAMP ASQUAM BEACH ON SQUAM LAKE, 1952. Mary A. Elcock established Camp Asquam in 1915. The former director of physical training at the Bryn Mawr School in Baltimore, Maryland, she also established Greenwood, a school for girls in Baltimore in 1923. Water sports, games, and informal evenings on the water or by the camp fire were highlighted activities for all who attended the camp. This camp—comprised of 30 acres of high land—is covered with pines and birches, and has an excellent sandy shore for bathing.

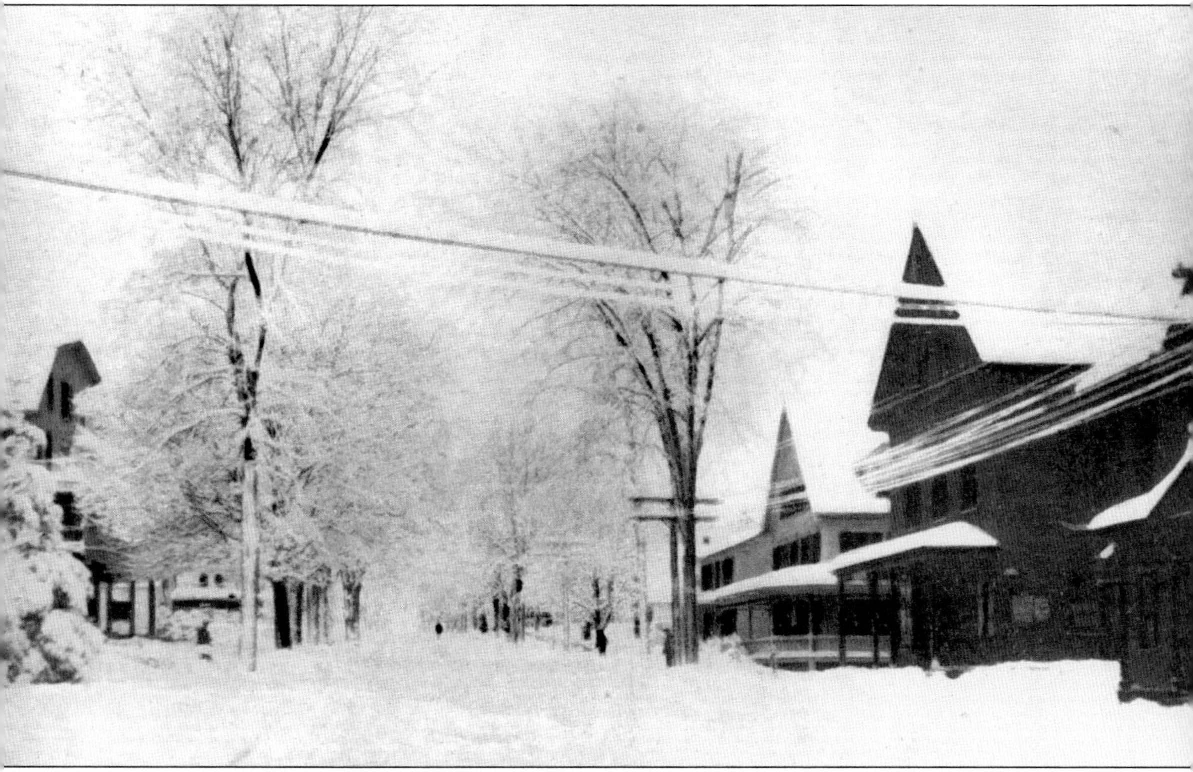

A Winter Scene of the Village, 1922. This scene shows the village of Center Harbor during the early winter of 1922. The view is looking west on Plymouth Street (Route 25B) after a major snowstorm. Several townspeople can be seen shoveling their walkways.

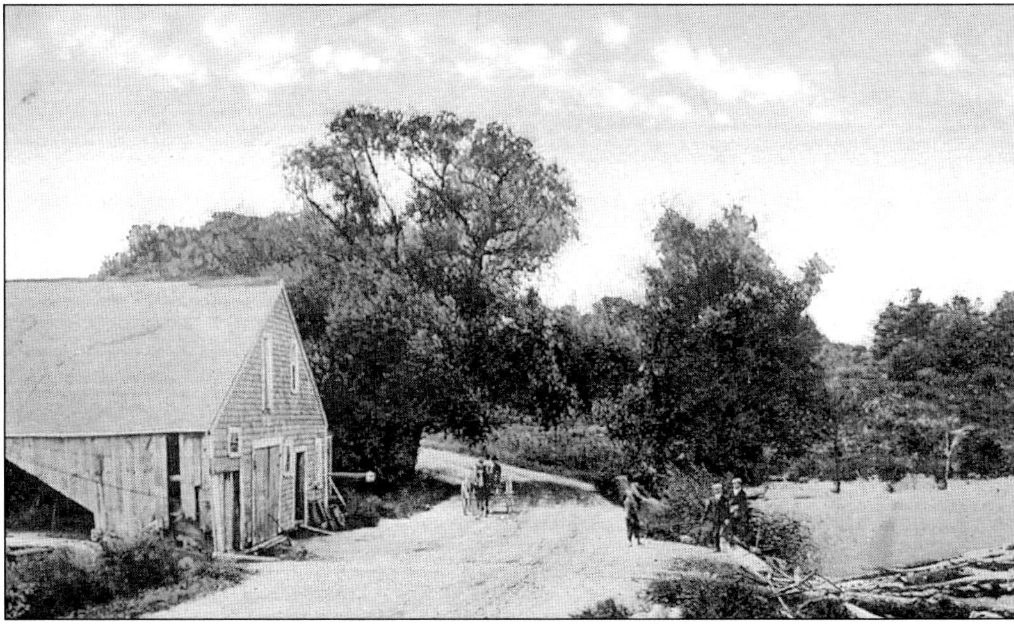

The Old Mill Corner, c. the 1900s. This is a typical country scene of the logging district of Center Harbor.

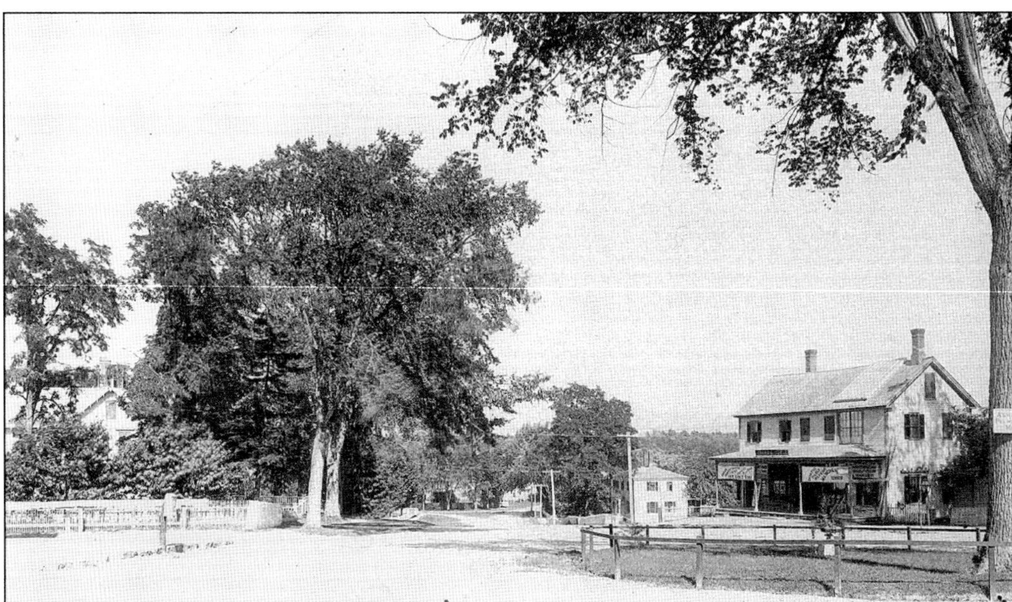

The Village of Center Harbor, Early 1900s. This view, looking northeast, includes the Coe Mansion on the left, and the Bayswater Book Company and Yikes Gallery (once known as Heath's Super Market) on the right.

Four

HOLDERNESS

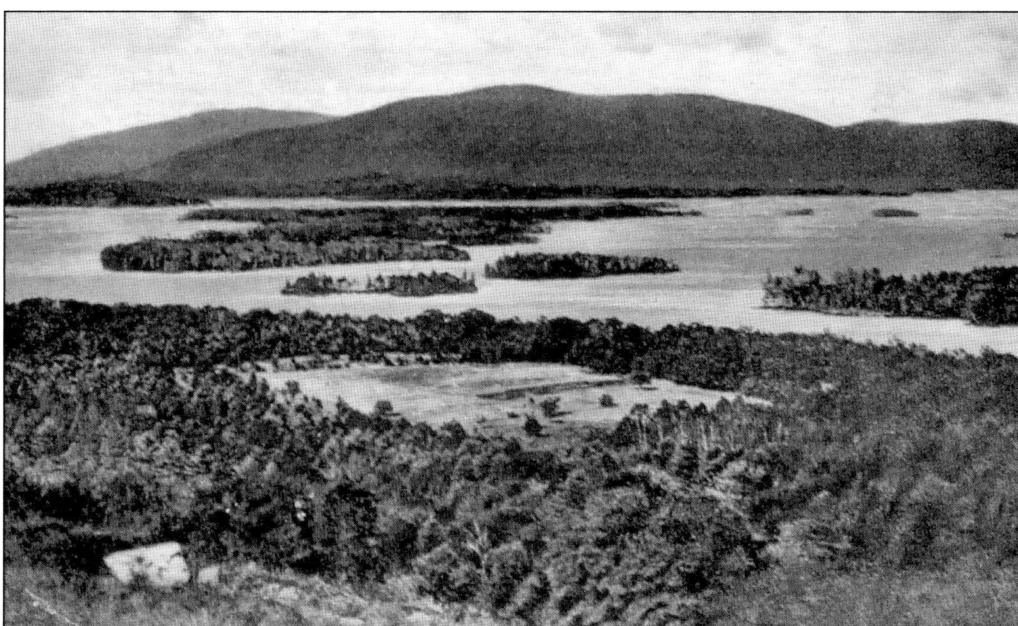

SQUAM LAKE AND RED HILL, FROM MOUNT MORGAN, HOLDERNESS. The limpid purity of Squam Lake, the singular grace of the tree-tufted islands, and the grandeur of the adjacent mountains all combine to make it the most picturesque sheet of water in eastern America. At the head of the lake, Red Hill rises to create a most appropriate background for this view of combined wildness and grace.

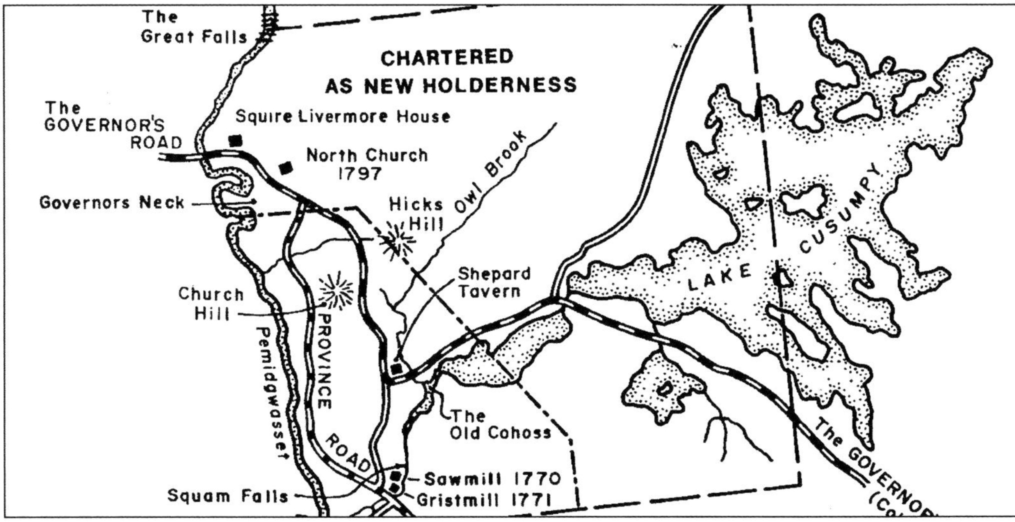

A MAP OF NEW HOLDERNESS IN 1761, FOR ROBERT D'ARCY, EARL OF HOLDERNESS, ENGLAND. The town of Holderness had its beginning when a charter was granted in 1751. However, it was considered unsafe due to the Native American traffic along the Indian trails from St. Francis in Canada to the seacoast at the mouth of the Androscoggin. It is written that Indian raiders had carried many early settlers away through this area and, until the Treaty of Paris, negotiated in Paris in 1753, people were very skeptical of coming to settle here. The decisive defeat of the French at Quebec in 1759 removed the threat of an Indian attack from this region and, in 1761, Governor Wentworth issued a grant for the township, naming it New Holderness, for the Earl of Holderness.

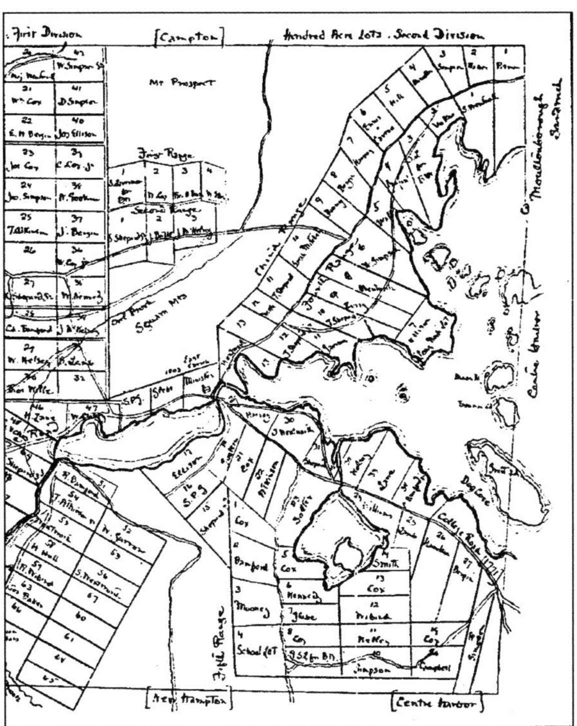

A MAP OF THE HUNDRED-ACRE LOTS OF HOLDERNESS. By 1751, a charter had been granted and a township had been laid out by surveyor Samuel Lane. On October 15, 1751, Benning Wentworth laid before the council "a petition of Thomas Shepard and others, praying for a grant of His Majesty's land of the contents of six miles square on the Pemigewasset River on the east side thereof as surveyed and planned by Samuel Land, surveyor," to which council did advise and consent. The grantees were Maj. John Wentworth and 67 other Episcopalians. An early historian has said that they were, "a company of English emigrant ardently devoted to the creed and worship of the Church of England, and with glowing anticipation of the future for the colony. The founders hoped and believed that they were laying the basis of the great city of New England, the rival of Puritan Boston, and destined to throw it into the shade."

THE LIVERMORE FALLS, HOLDERNESS. In 1761, Governor Wentworth issued grants for 18 townships. It was under these grants that Holderness was finally settled. It incorporated into a township a piece of land six miles square, "beginning at a red oak at the foot of the great Falls of the Pemigewasset River (now Livermore Falls), thence running east six miles, then turning off at right angles and running south six miles, then turning off again and running westerly six miles to a white pine tree marked, standing on the bank of the river aforesaid, then running up said river northerly as that runs to the Bound first mentioned as Bound begun at." Logging was a major industry in the area, but sawmills also dotted the shores of most waterways throughout the Lakes Region.

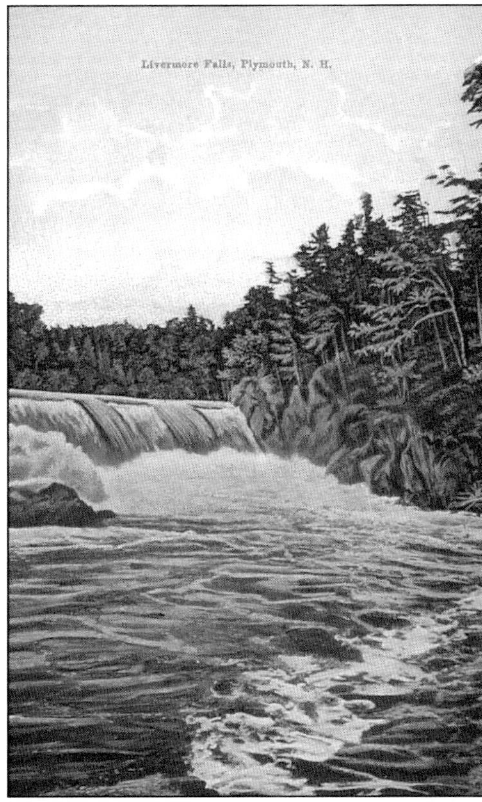

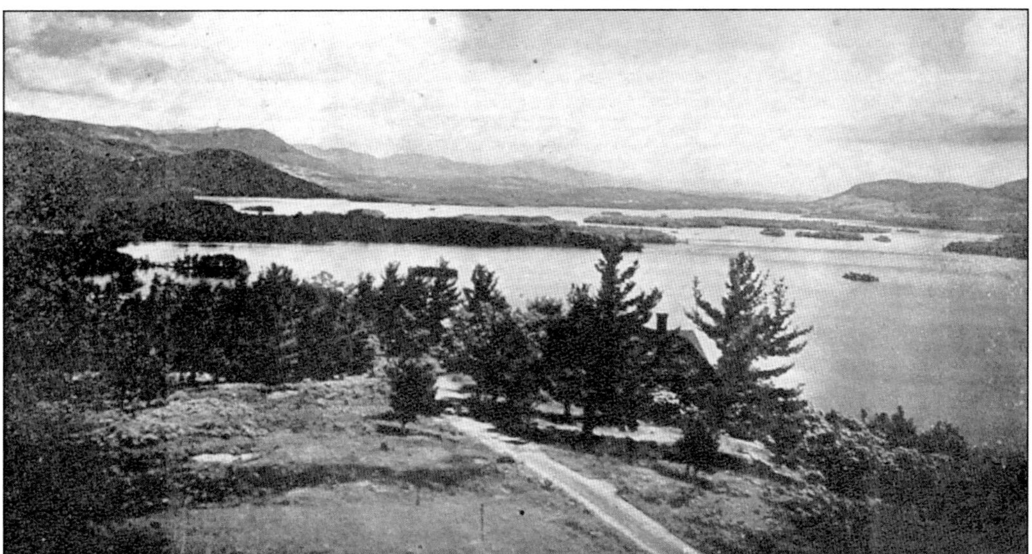

BIG SQUAM LAKE, FROM SHEPARD HILL. From the summit of Shepard Hill, the full breadth of Squam Lake may be enjoyed. The long islands lie across the lake in parallel ranks, with lanes and squares of blue water in between. In the far distance, the whole of the Sandwich Range towers on the horizon, while the Squam Range flanks the northern face of the lake. Starr King writes, "Great Squam, singularly striped with long, narrow, crinkling islands, and, like Wordsworth's river, winding in the landscape 'at its own sweet will.'"

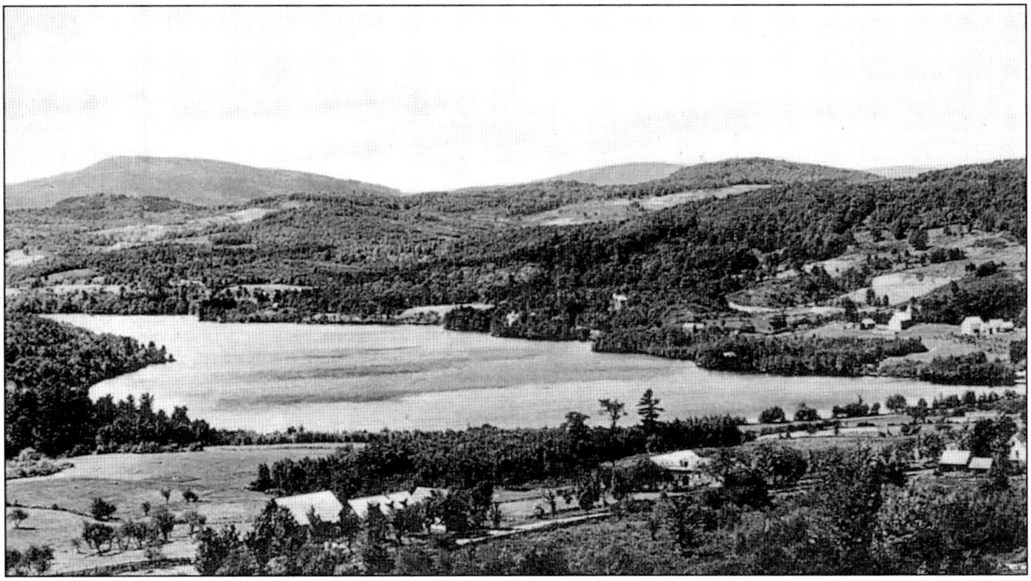

LITTLE SQUAM LAKE, FROM SHEPARD HILL. Unlike Squam Lake, this lake is unbroken by islands. Little Squam is fringed and shadowed by thickets of rich foliage that are arranged around its western shore in a long sweeping curve.

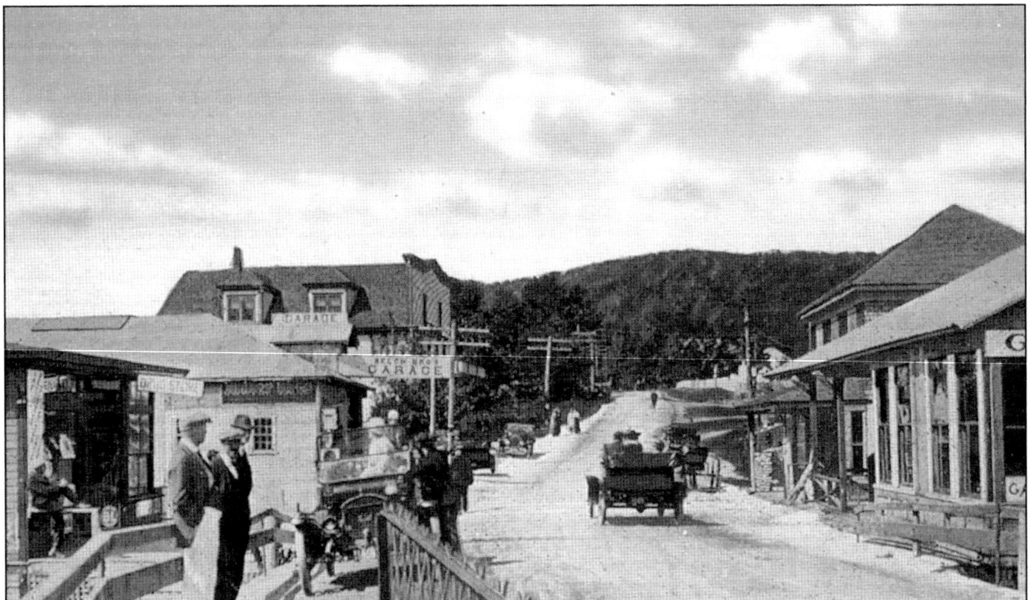

A VIEW OF MAIN STREET, LOOKING NORTH, C. THE 1900S. The village of Holderness is a relaxing resort center in the Lakes Region, with many camps, cottages, hotels, and inns to be found within its confines. Holderness was named for the Earl of Holderness (a friend of Governor Wentworth), and was granted to John Shepard and others in 1751. This area was originally named the "Great Waste," for Native Americans used it to transport captives between St. Francis, Canada, and the seacoast of Maine.

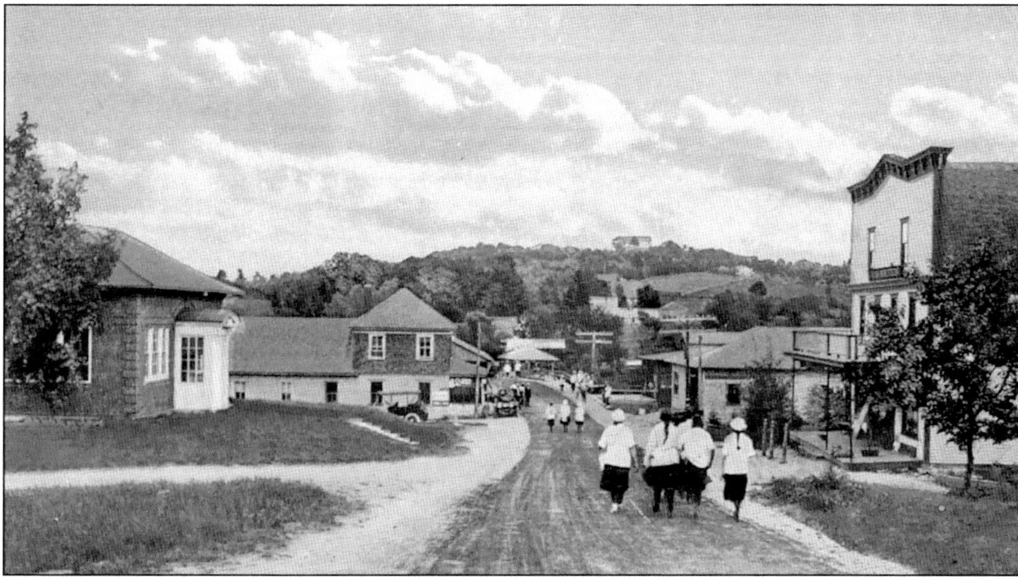

HOLDERNESS VILLAGE, LOOKING SOUTH DOWN MAIN STREET, C. THE 1900S. With the town library on the left and Shepard Hill in the distant center, Holderness begins to blossom as a thriving tourist community and a magnet for the Squam Lake region. The library was founded in 1878. However, it was officially established in 1893, when it was housed in private homes and stores. On September 17, 1906, a major fire destroyed the center of Holderness village, including Whitten's store, which housed the library. Save for 18 books, the entire library collection was lost. The present Colonial Revival library (above) was completed *c.* 1910. The building is home to one of the region's most interesting small libraries, marking the transition from the eclectic architecture of the late 19th century to the more disciplined academic architecture of the early 20th century.

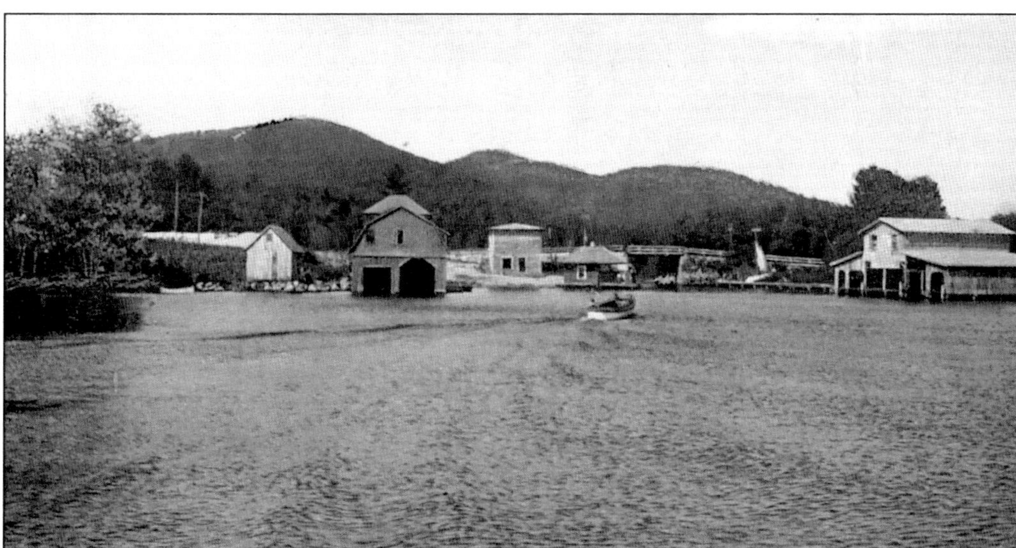

THE SQUAM BRIDGE AT THE UPPER END OF LITTLE SQUAM LAKE. Approaching the bridge via a 19th-century steamer, open boathouses are seen on either side of the channel. The Squam Mountains are seen in the distance.

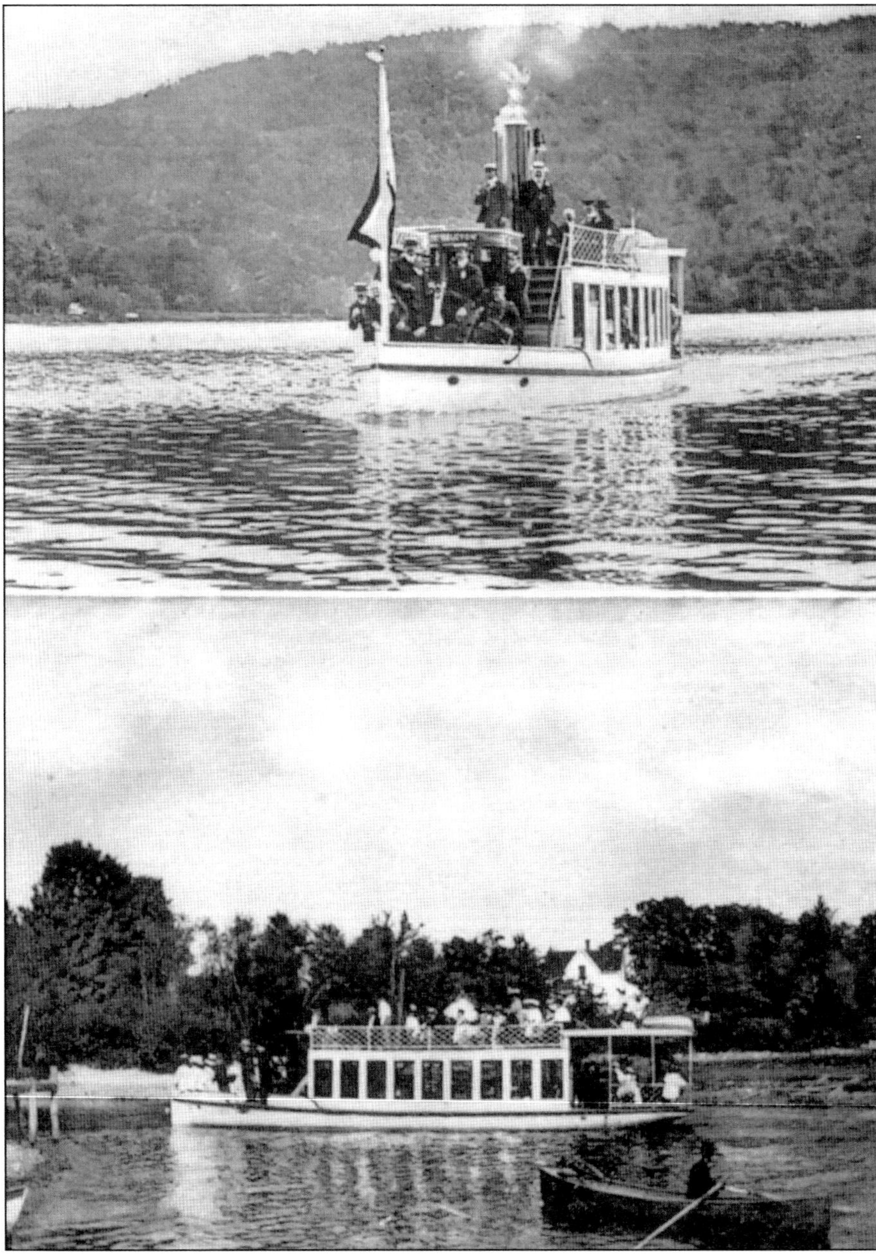

THE STEAMER *HALCYON* ON SQUAM LAKE (UPPER) AND AT SQUAM BRIDGE (LOWER), 1906. This craft was a mail boat that serviced the island residents on Squam Lake. The vessel was built for A.E. Fifield, manager of the Asquam Transportation Company in Ashland. Burt Fifield and his father built it in 1903. The boat measured 50 feet long with a beam of 12 feet. It was fitted out with a 75-horsepower boiler and a 50-horsepower Treat & Paine engine. The vessel could carry more than 100 passengers. The *Halcyon* made its first official trip on Squam Lake and Little Squam Lake in June 1903 with a crew of four men. The pride of the Asquam Transportation Company, the boat became a prime favorite of summer residents. Earlier boat transportation included horse boats and flat barges, which were used to transport logs on the waterways.

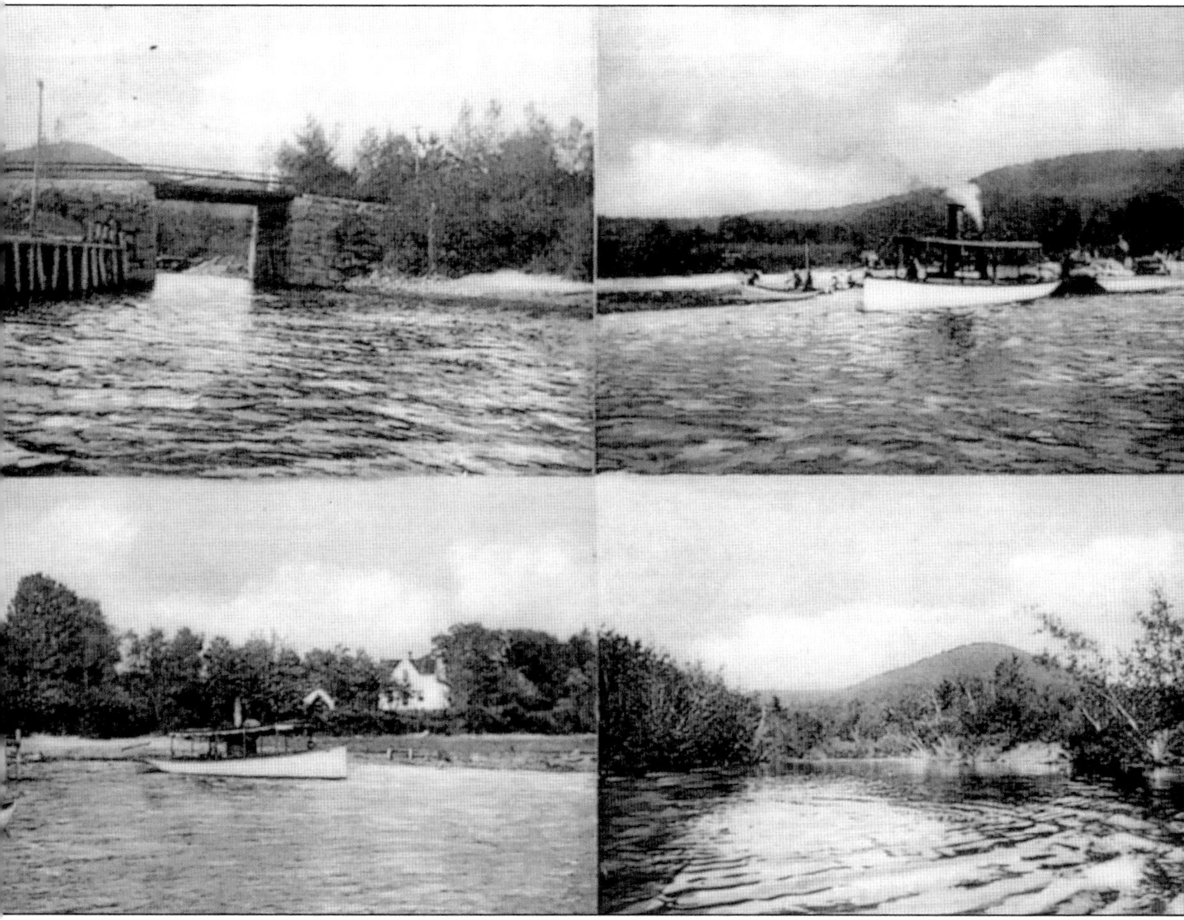

FOUR SCENES AROUND SQUAM BRIDGE, 1906. In the upper left is the water from Little Squam Lake approaching the narrow stream leading to Squam Lake. In upper right are steamboats on Little Squam Lake, west of the bridge. In the lower left is a steamer approaching the bridge. În the lower right, facing east in the channel, is the wake of the steamer as it approaches the bridge and enters Little Squam.

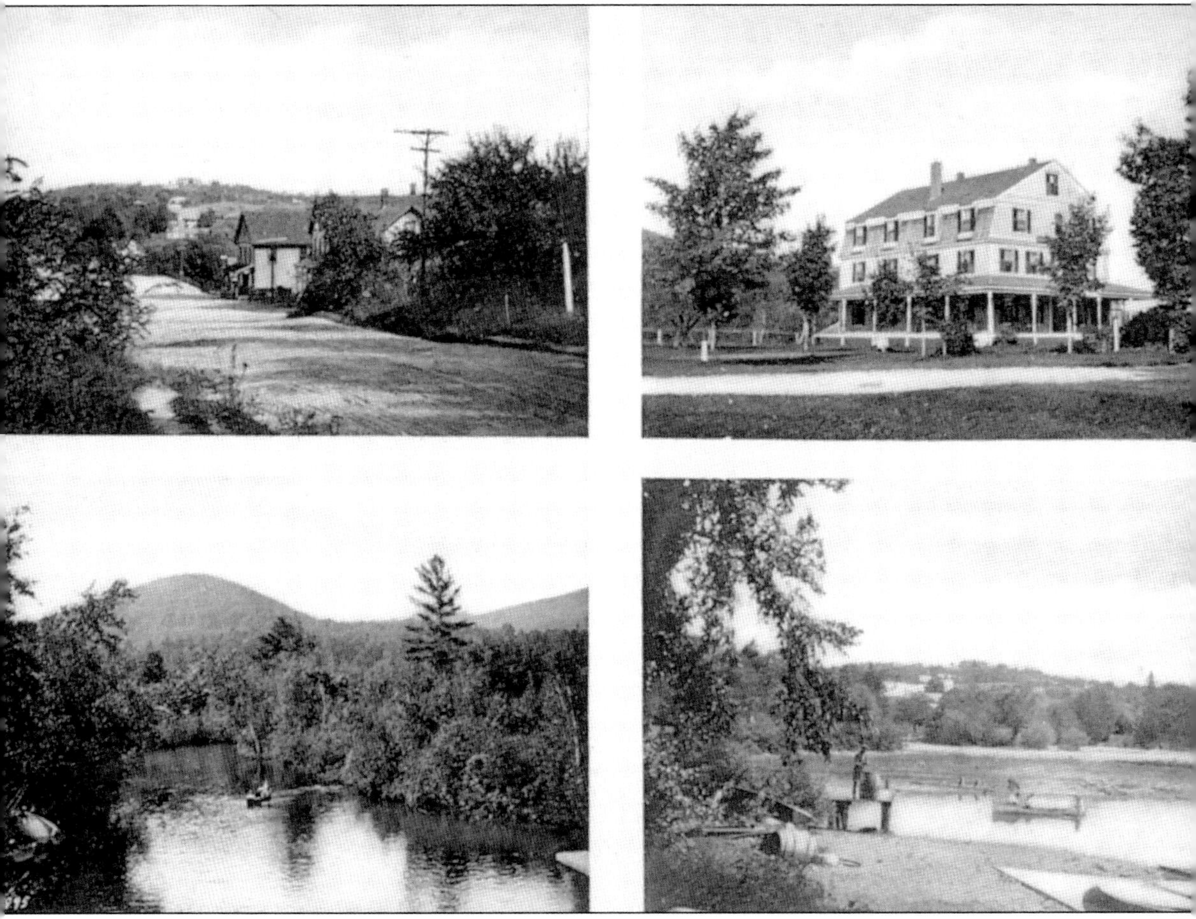

FOUR SCENES NEAR SQUAM BRIDGE, 1906. In the upper left view, facing south to Shepard Hill, is Main Street near the bridge. In the upper right is the Central House. In the lower left view, facing east, is the channel, with the peak of Mount Fayal in the distance. In the lower right is a peaceful view of the beach on Squam Lake.

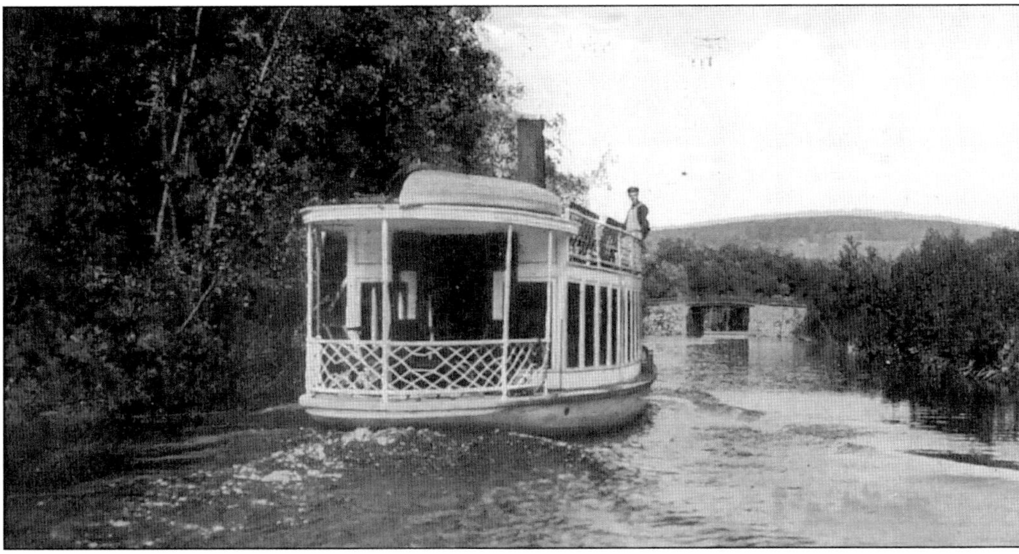

THE LITTLE SQUAM BRIDGE AND THE STEAMER *HALCYON* APPROACHING SQUAM LAKE, C. 1912. Steam-powered vessels were successful, commercially and otherwise. The *Halcyon* became a popular tourist boat that passed under the bridge from Squam Lake to Little Squam Lake daily.

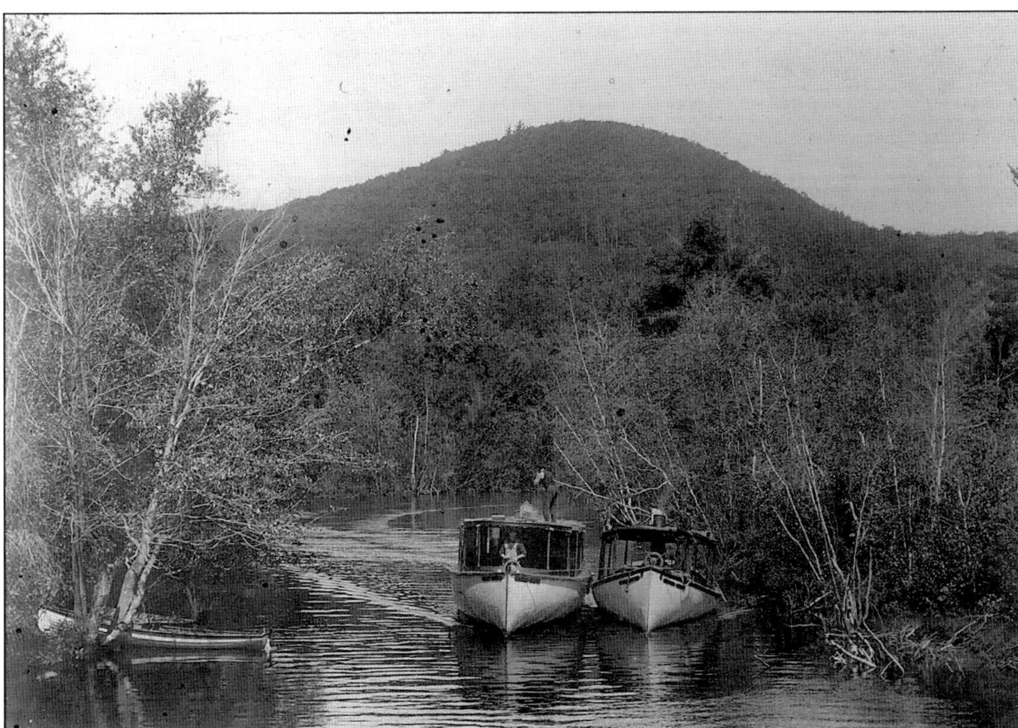

LOOKING UP SQUAM RIVER, C. 1912. Here, two steamers approach the Squam Bridge in Holderness, a junction which connects the lakes.

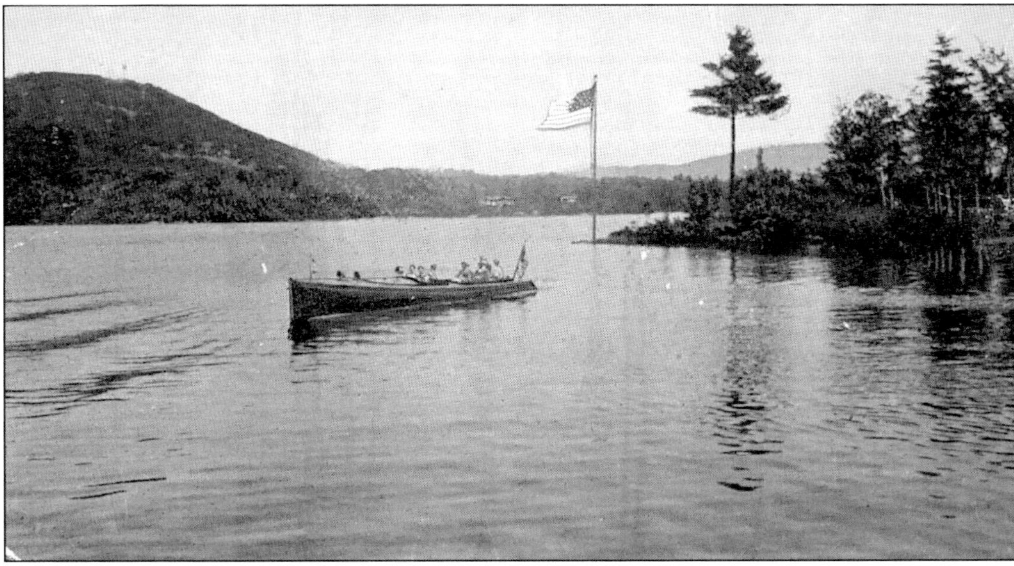

RUHE'S POINT AT BENNETT'S COVE, SQUAM LAKE, 1910. This shows a quiet moment in Bennett's Cove on Squam Lake, as an early inboard speedboat sails from Ruhe's Point.

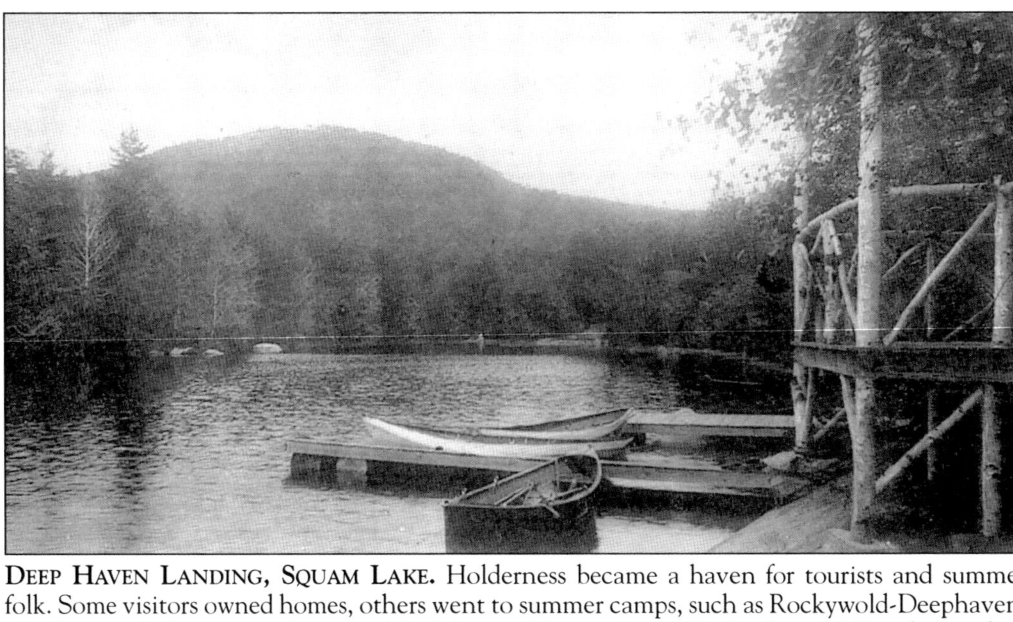

DEEP HAVEN LANDING, SQUAM LAKE. Holderness became a haven for tourists and summer folk. Some visitors owned homes, others went to summer camps, such as Rockywold-Deephaven, which provided guests with a simplified form of living. In 1897, Rockywold-Deephaven had its humble beginning on Squam Lake. According to Megan Thorn's *Roots and Recollections: A Century of Rocky-Deephaven Camps*, "This camp is the legacy of two remarkable women, Mary A. Armstrong and Alice M. Bacon, who, from very different backgrounds shared a vision of what time in fellowship and in nature could. Together they created at this 'deep haven' and this 'rocky wold,' a summer retreat on Squam Lake."

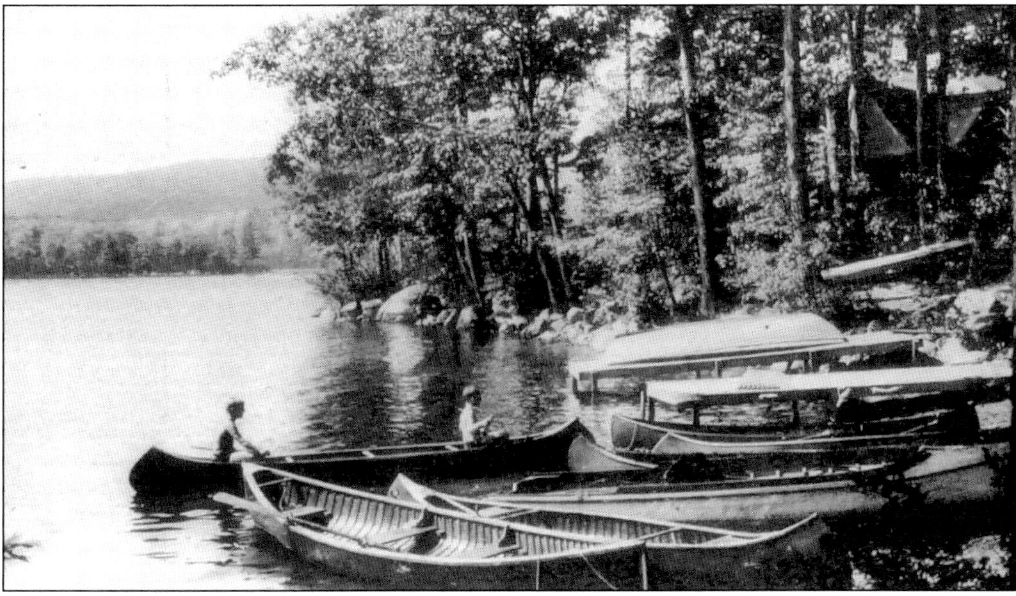

ROCKYWOLD-DEEPHAVEN, SQUAM LAKE. "Champagne in a tin cup" is how this camp is often described. It is considered the very best and the simplest. Camp is a place where families come together to celebrate life with nature. It is where, year after year, families return.

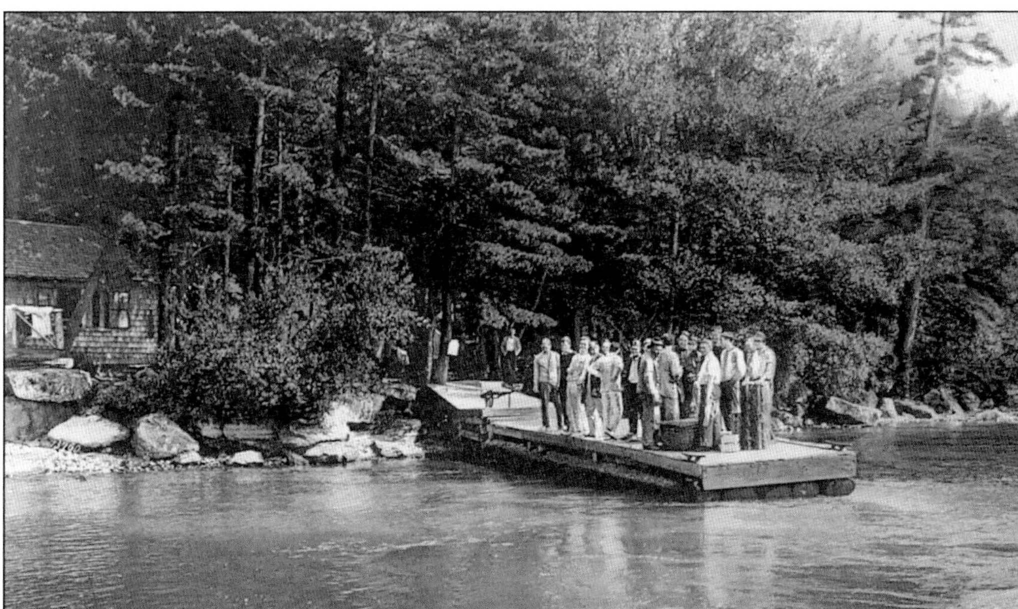

CAMP ALOHA DOCK, SQUAM LAKE, THE 1930S. This summer camp for boys was established in 1904 by Edmund W. Ogden. It was long directed by Emerson A. Kimball and Lambert F. Whetstone, both of St. Paul's School in Concord. The purpose of the camp was to provide boys with summer tutoring that was fit for higher education.

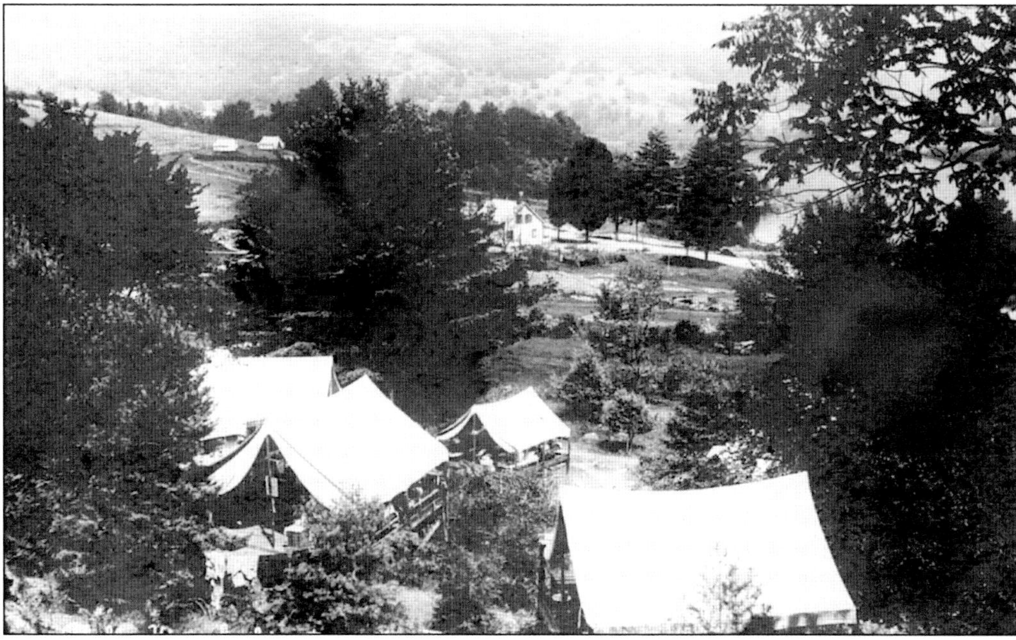

AN EARLY CAMPING VIEW OF CAMP ALOHA, 1920. During the early years of camping, tents on wooden platforms were used. This camp was located off the highway on Mooney's Point. A balance of activities, both physical and mental, was provided for each camper.

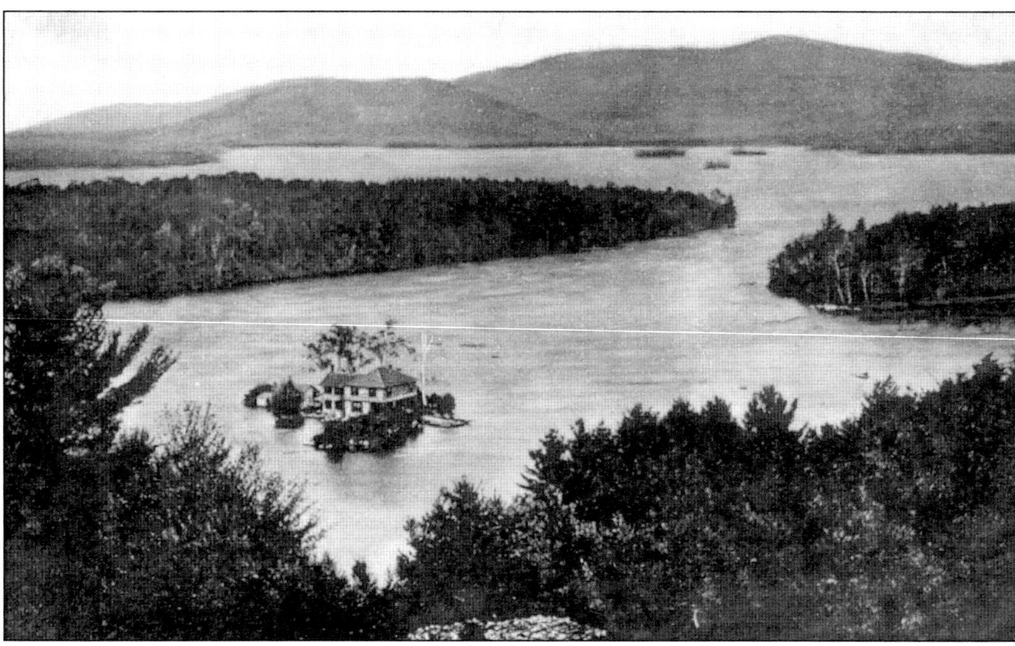

A BIRD'S-EYE VIEW OF CAMP CAIRNS IN WEBSTER COVE ON SQUAM LAKE. This southward view of Squam Lake reveals the intimate coves that are interwoven throughout the lake. This small cove on the north side of the lake quietly frames the solitude of a tiny habitable island.

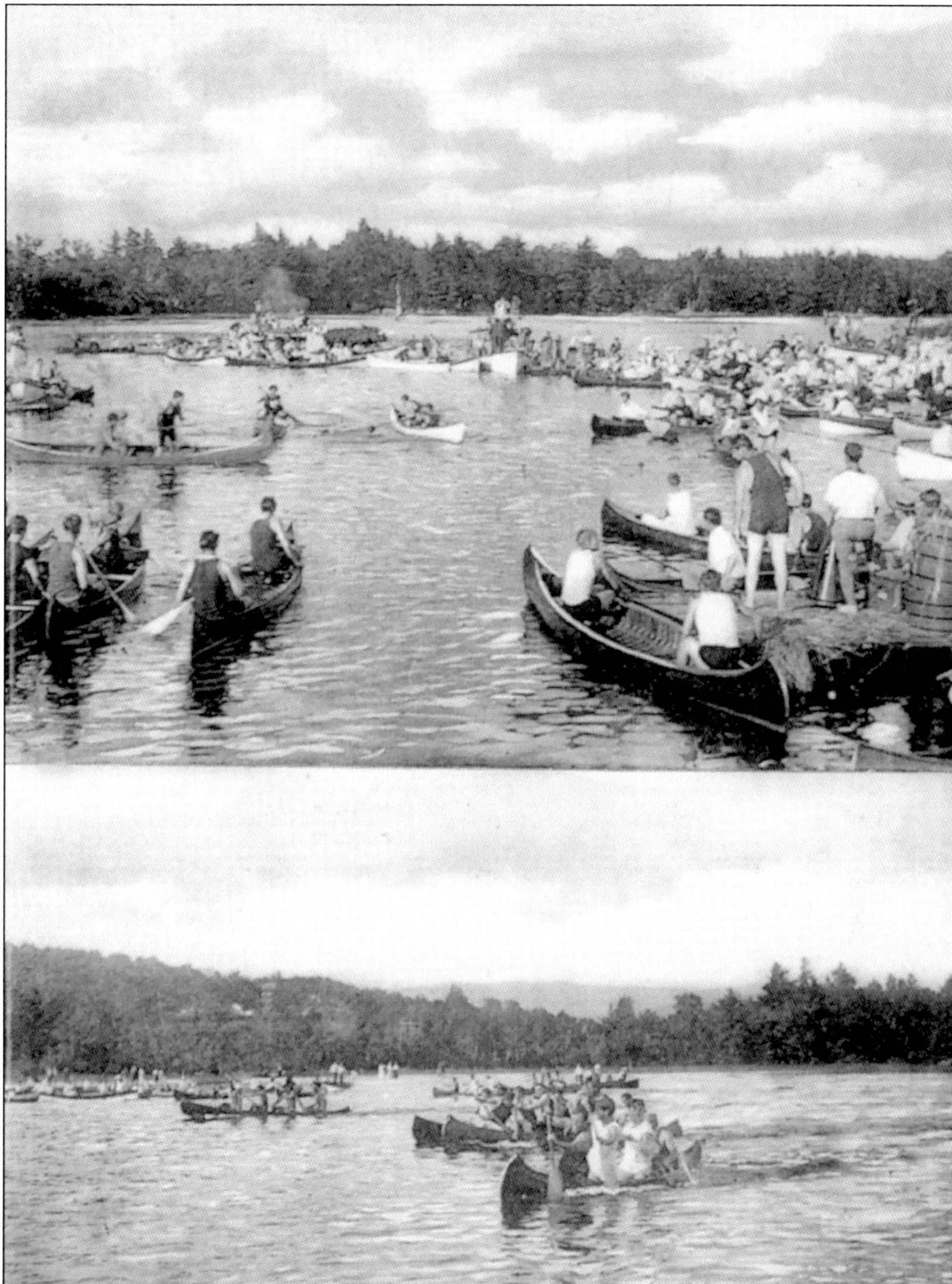

A Carnival Scene, Squam Lake. Water sports were very popular in the Squam Lake region. These two scenes show local campers assembled on the lake for a carnival of healthy competition.

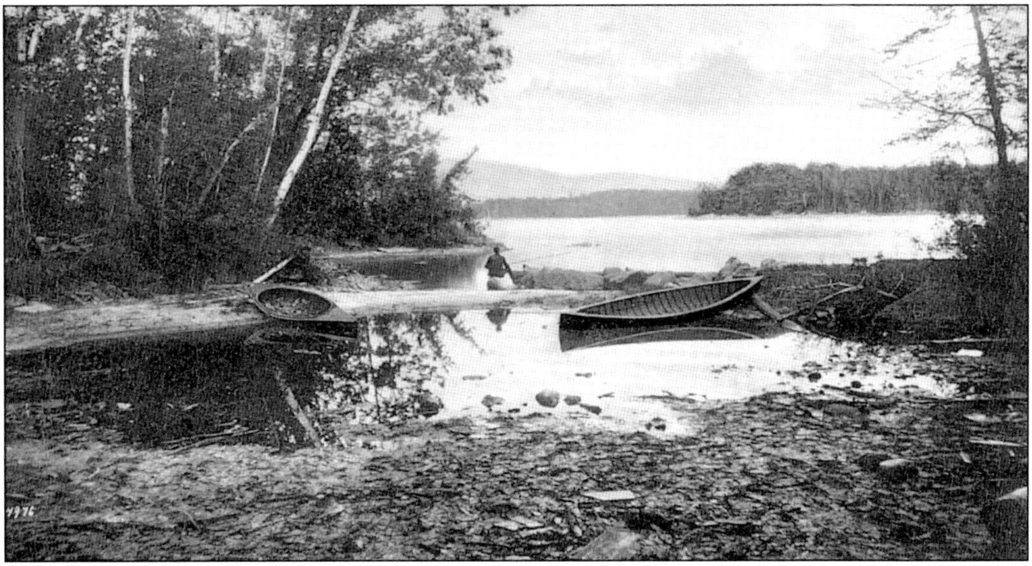

CHOCORUA ISLAND COVE, SQUAM LAKE. On Chocorua Island (Church Island) was located the first organized summer boys' camp in America. With eight boys enrolled, the camp opened in 1881 under the direction of Ernest Balch. It continued until 1889. Each camper was expected to do all of his own work. Originally, the island was called Bunt or Burnt Island. The second oldest camp, Camp Harvard (1882) was taken over by Dr. Winthrop T. Talbot and was moved to this lake, where it was known as Camp Asquam (1884).

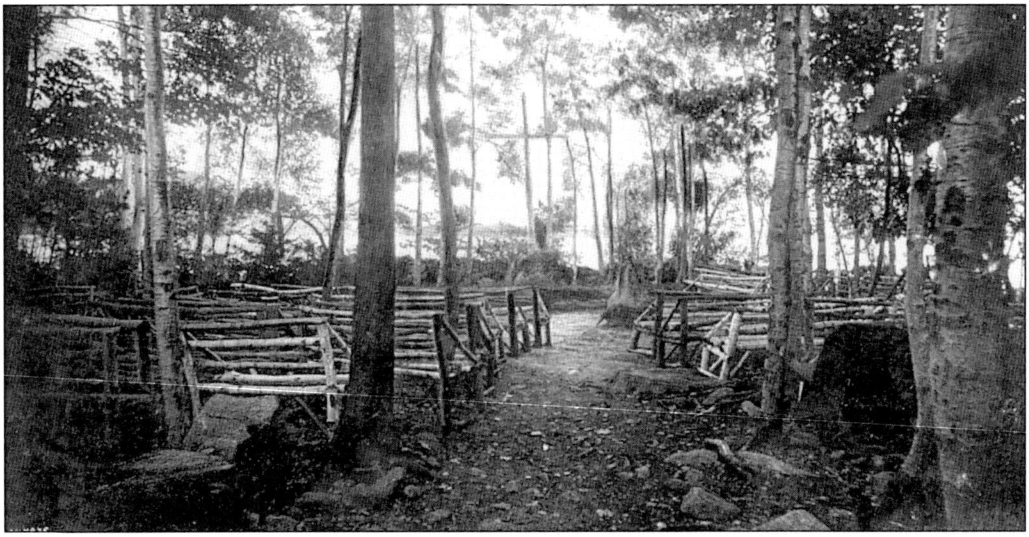

CHOCORUA ISLAND CHAPEL, 1910. After the closing of the camp in 1889, Oliver and Ellen Balch Huntington continued to hold services at the chapel on the island for some of the former campers who returned to vacation at the camp and for others visiting this island on Squam. In 1903, five men met and formally founded a chapel on Chocorua Island. On September 3, 1903, they incorporated the Chocorua Chapel Association. The incorporation articles of agreement declared: "The objects for which this corporation is established is the carrying on of religious services according to the form of the Protestant Episcopal Church, at a suitable place on the shores of Asquam Lake." Today, this chapel is actively used for that purpose. The Chocorua Island Chapel faces the east for a full view of the sunrise.

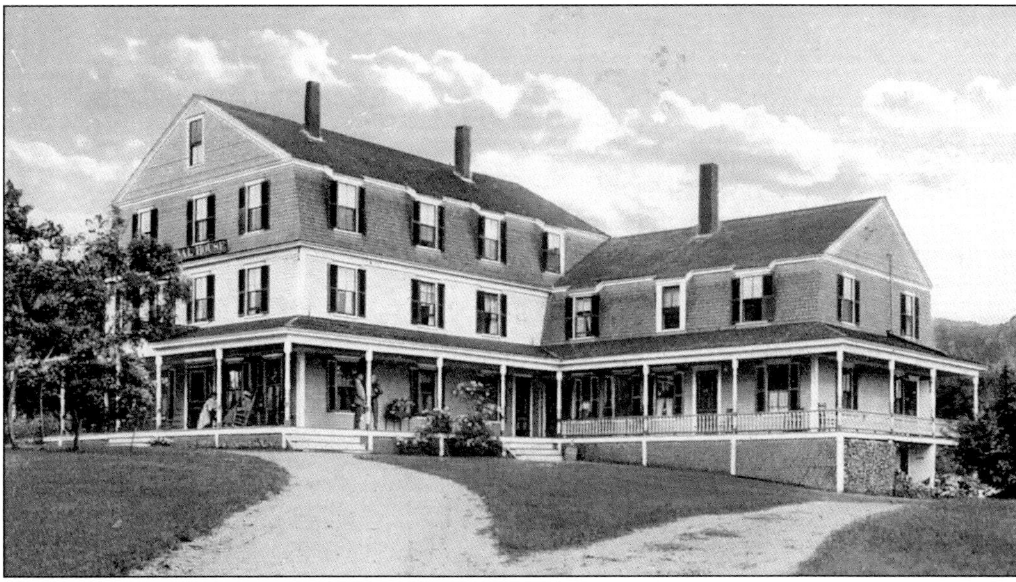

THE HOLDERNESS INN (CENTRAL HOUSE), 1895–1896. The Holderness Inn, distinguished by its surrounding veranda and its quite distinctive gabled mansard roof, is a charming Victorian vernacular building. A late-19th-century hotel, it still retains its three-and-a-half-story main block and one-story veranda that covers the west facade, the south gable end, and most of the east facade of the main block. Prior to the Holderness Inn, John S. Davison converted a Holderness village house into a summer inn named Central House. On June 3, 1895, the Central House was destroyed. Davison rebuilt the house and registered his first guests on July 21, 1896. Although the name was changed to the Holderness Inn, the hotel continued to be owned and operated by the Davison family until 1967, when it was sold to the Squam Lakes Science Center. In 1887, the inn advertised that it had a capacity for 60 guests, and that it cost $2.50 daily and from $9 to $15 weekly.

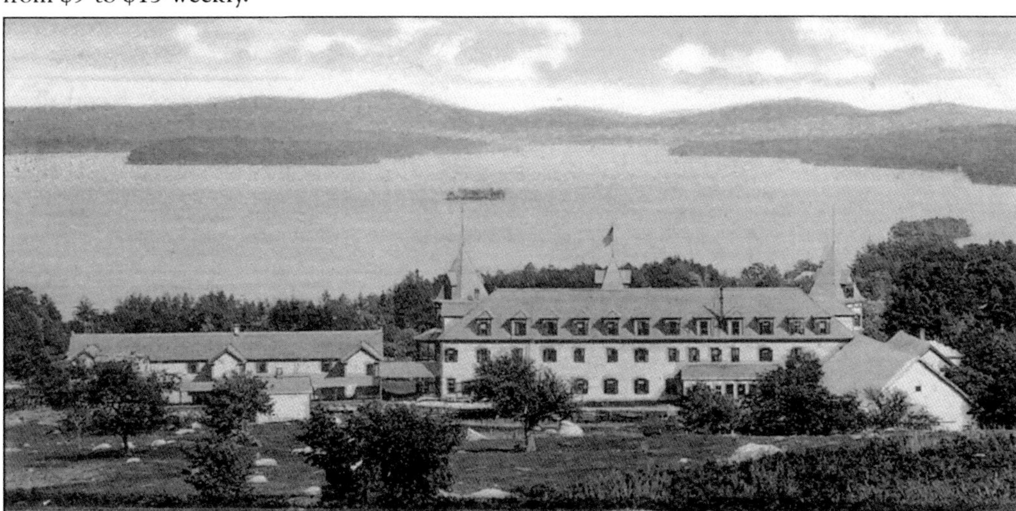

SQUAM LAKE AND THE MOUNT LIVERMORE HOUSE, 1930. This elegant estate reclines on the side of a hill, overlooking Squam Lake. According to *Chisholm's White Mountain Guide*, the daily rate was $2.50 and the weekly rate was from $10.50 to $21 in 1887. Mrs. B.F. Jewell was the proprietor.

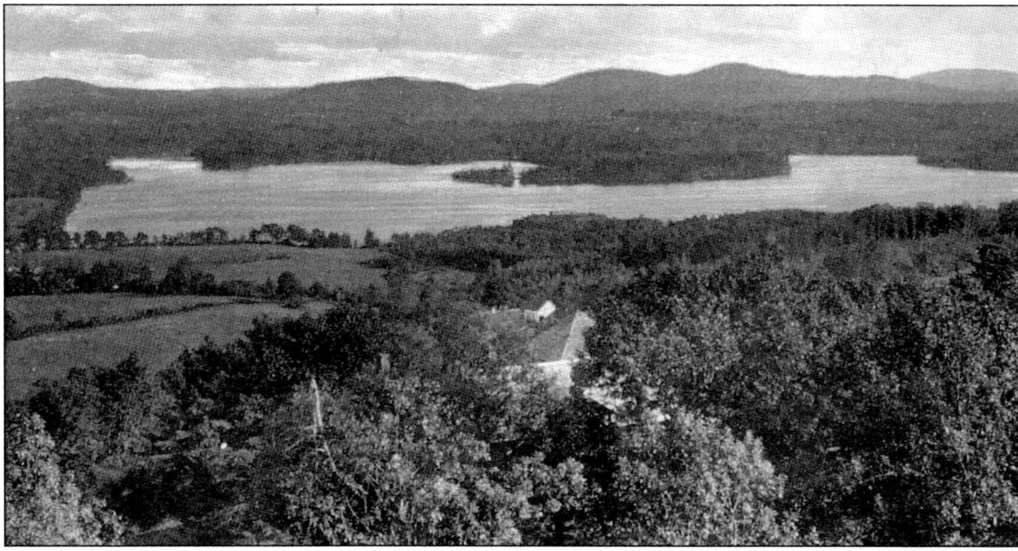

WHITE OAK POND, FROM THE ASQUAM HOTEL, 1954. This is a natural pond raised by a dam. Its altitude is 583 feet above sea level, with an area of 291 acres. The average depth of the pond is 16 feet.

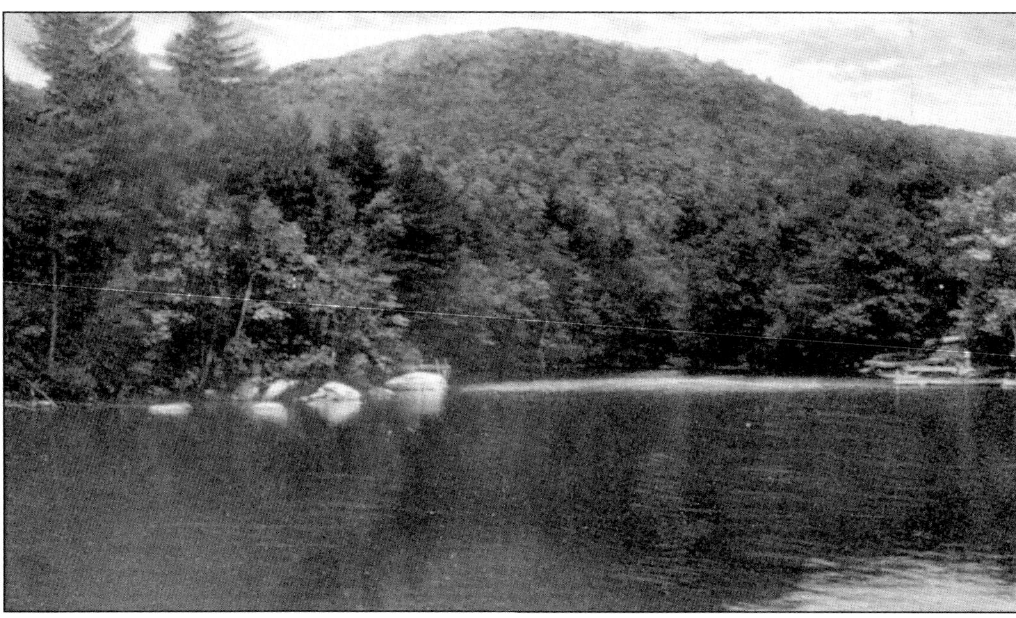

RATTLESNAKE MOUNTAIN, FROM SQUAM LAKE. One of the most spectacular views of Squam Lake is seen from the granite ridge on the summit of Rattlesnake Mountain. The ridge is a 15-minute walk from the road.

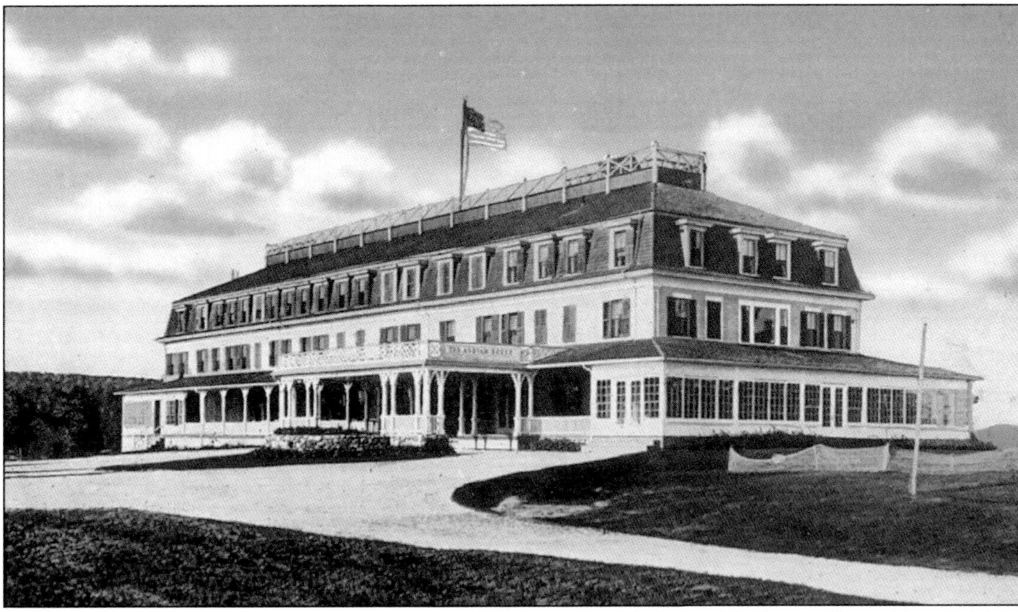

THE ASQUAM HOTEL, 1919. The Asquam House was fashionably located on Shepard Hill on a promontory between Squam Lake and Little Squam Lake. In 1887, this rather large hotel with a capacity of 100 guests commanded a daily rate of $3 to $4 and a weekly rate of $14 to $28.

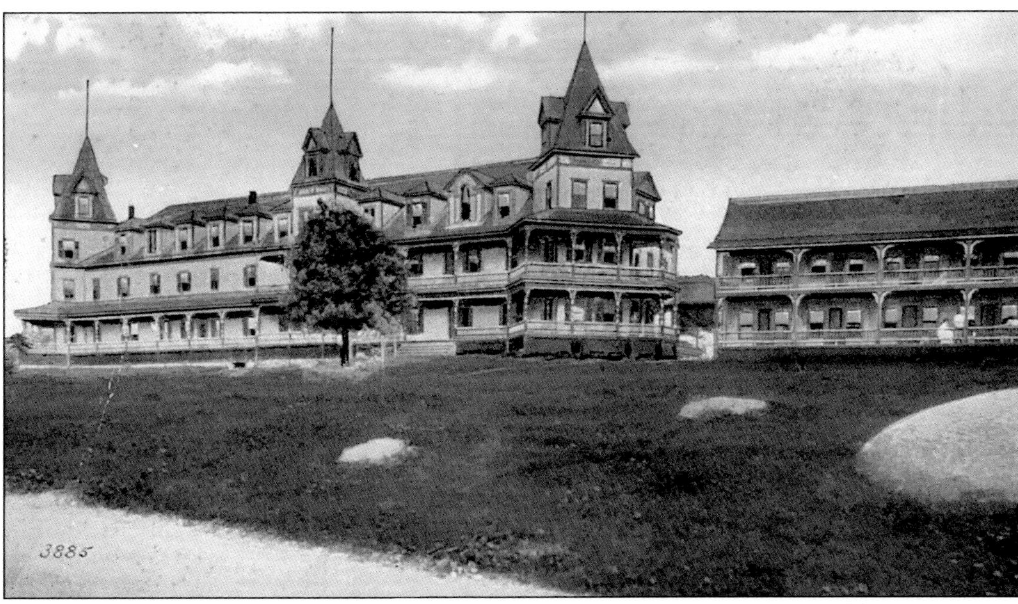

THE TOWERS. During the heyday of tourism at the grand hotels, this establishment—with its formal veranda embracing three-fourths of the building—was considered one of the most popular summer resorts in the Squam Lake region. It was second only to the Asquam House.

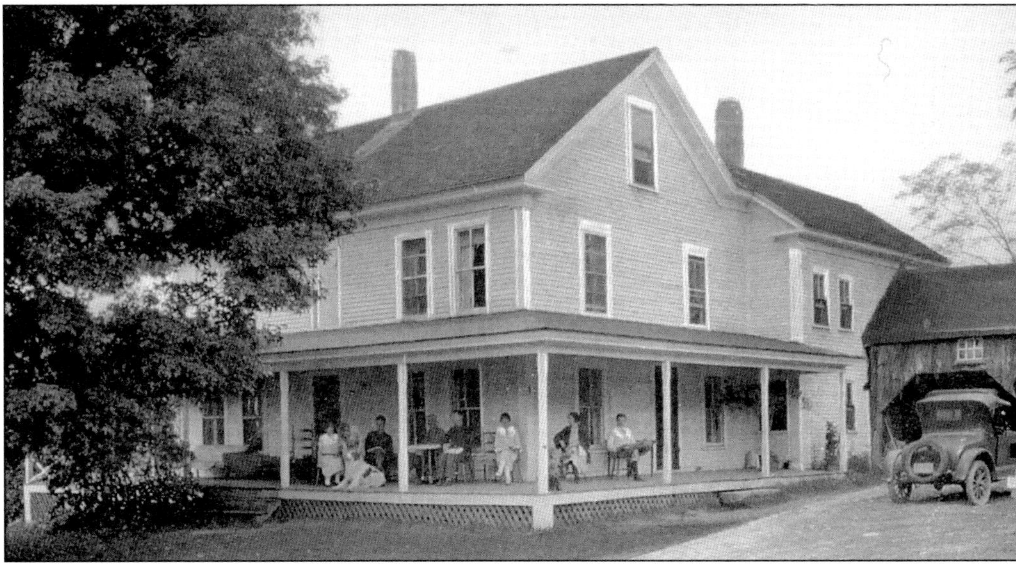

THE LAKE VIEW FARM, ON THE SHORE OF SQUAM LAKE. Pres. Timothy Dwight of Yale College wrote this about Squam (which he afterward named Lake Sullivan): "Many tourists would have tasked his or her imagination for sonorous epithets to describe the lake's scenery, many an artist would have prepared his softest tints to paint its beauty, and many a poet would have strung his lyre to sound its praises in a name that poetry might use. Its pellucid bosom, its undulating shores, its hanging woods, and all its magic beauties are probably destined long to be veiled in obscurity deep as its own seclusion."

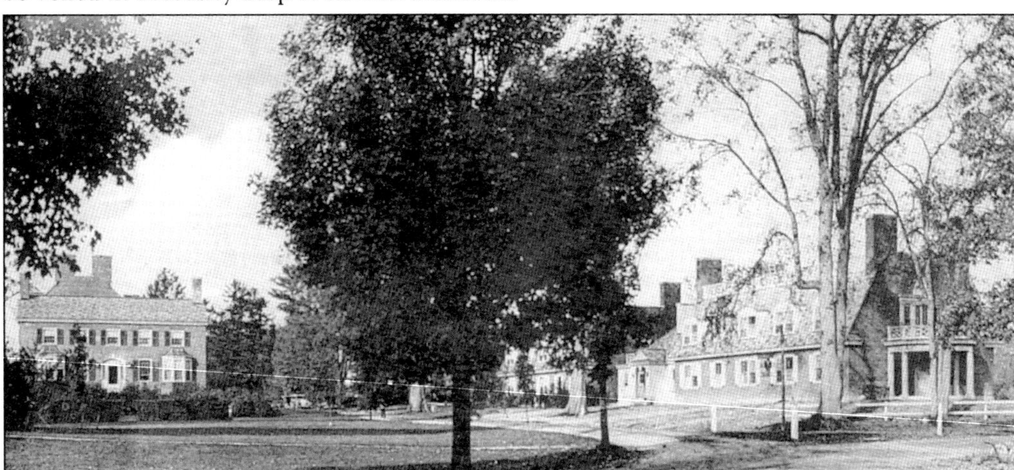

THE HOLDERNESS SCHOOL, WITH SANDERSON MEMORIAL RECTORY, LIVERMORE, WEBSTER, AND NILES HALLS. The Holderness School for Boys is located on a high terrace overlooking the east shore of the Pemigewasset River. The Episcopal diocesan school of New Hampshire, it was founded in 1879. The central building is a fine example of Southern Colonial architecture. The small brick dormitory is notable for its steep sloping roof. Today, Holderness is a coeducational secondary school that is ranked high in the academic community and attracts students from all over the country. The first Holderness School for Boys occupied part of the estate of Judge Samuel Livermore, who was the king's attorney under Governor Wentworth and who was later a U.S. senator and a chief justice. It is said that at one time Livermore owned two thirds of the town of Holderness.

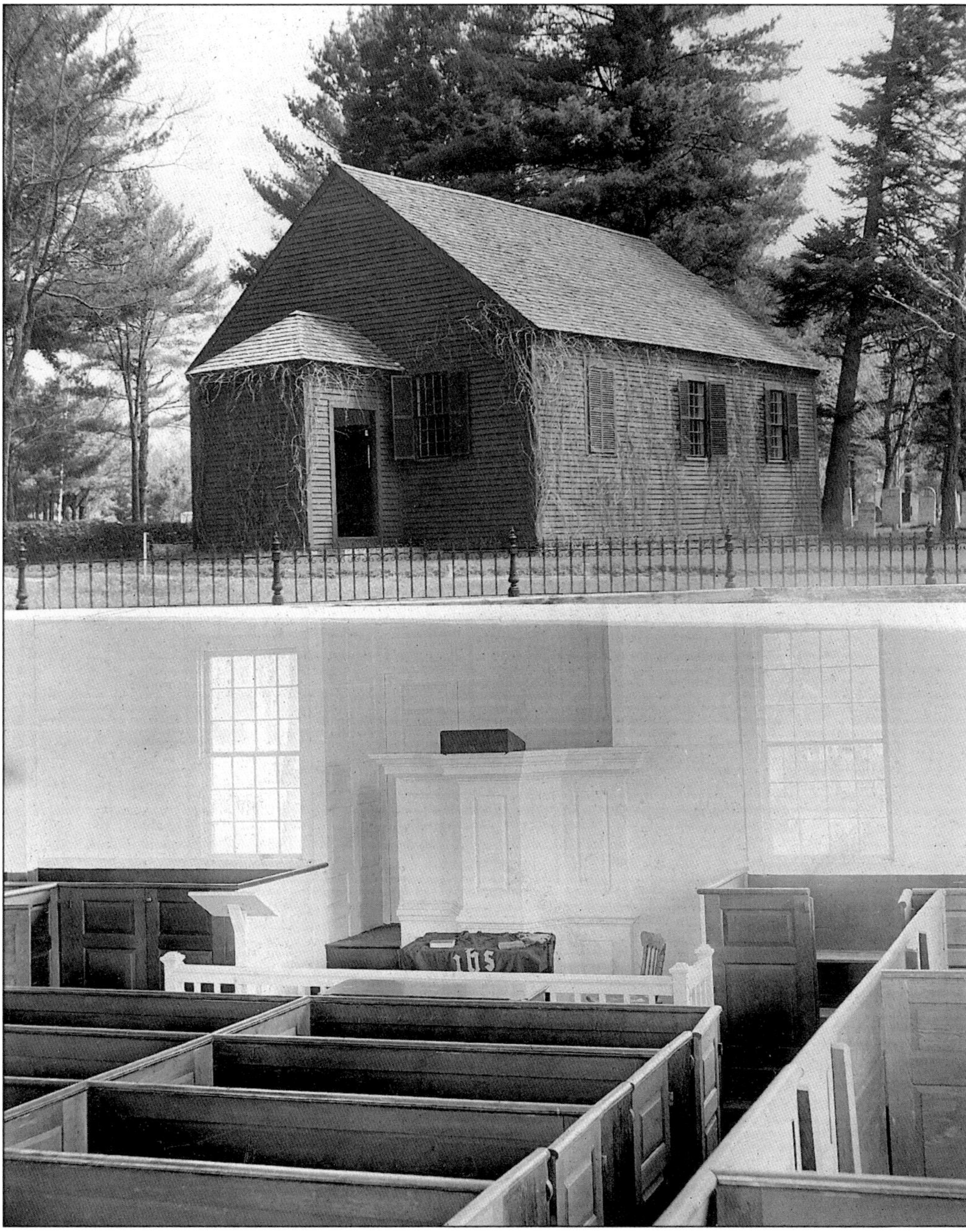

TRINITY CHURCH, NEAR THE HOLDERNESS SCHOOL CAMPUS. This church was dedicated in 1797. This chapel was once called Lady Mary Livermore's Chapel; it is now Old Trinity. Of all the Livermore Holderness buildings, only Trinity Church remains. Samuel Livermore was an Episcopalian who married the daughter of a Portsmouth's Episcopalian pastor. His adopted town of Holderness became one of the state's four communities that supported Episcopalian churches during the 18th century. Trinity Church, the second oldest Episcopal Church in the state, is a modest vernacular building with little architectural embellishment beyond the paneled woodwork on the pews and pulpit. However, it is unique as the state's only 18th-century church that has retained its original appearance.

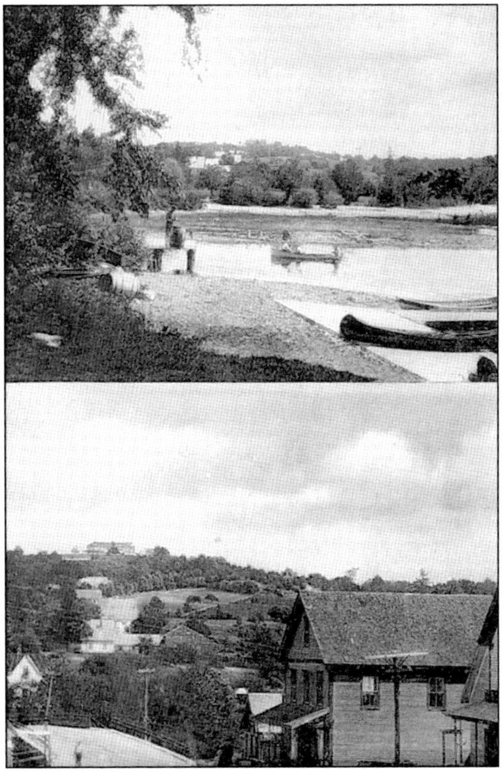

SHEPARD HILL, FROM THE SQUAM BRIDGE IN HOLDERNESS, C. THE 1920S. The upper view of Shepard Hill was taken from the waterfront on Little Squam Lake, and the lower picture from the north end of the village near the town library.

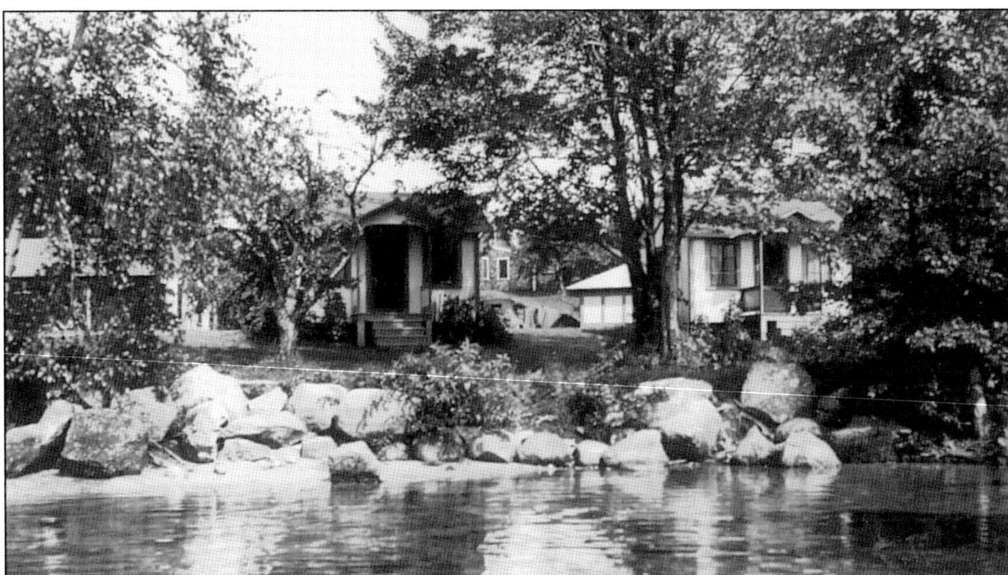

SQUAM LAKE CABINS, HOLDERNESS, 1936. Located on the Daniel Webster Highway, these comfortable period cabins had running water, Simmons beds, and all the conveniences of their day. The were owned and operated by Mrs. Fred L. Perkins, who advertised "Home Cooked Food & the Finest of boating and bathing." During the first half of the 20th century, Holderness had many cabin colonies to serve travelers to the Squam Lakes region. Most of them are no longer in existence, but they have been replaced by country inns, motels, and private cottages.

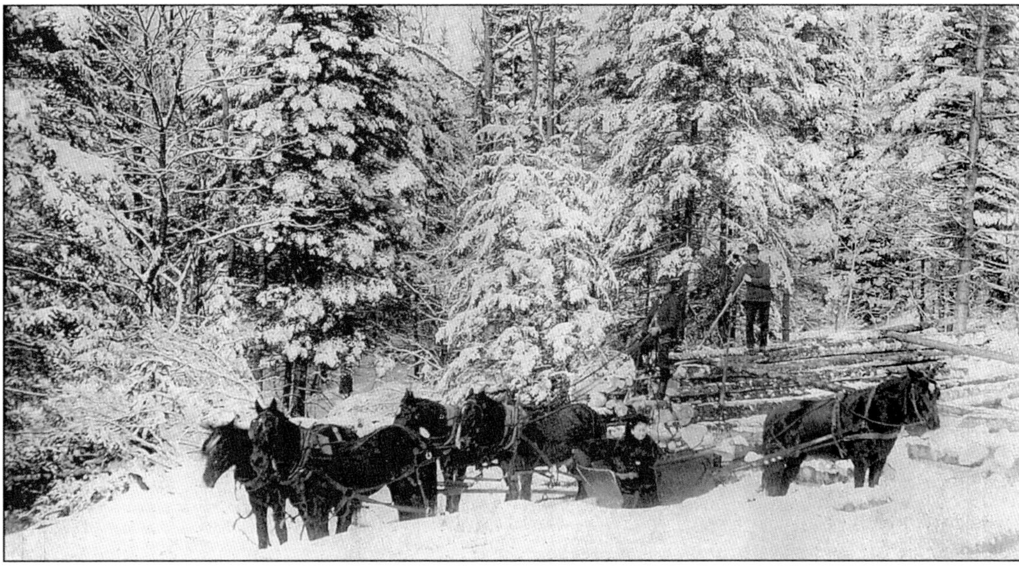

A LOGGING SCENE. According to the original charter of Holderness in 1761, "five conditions accompanied the privileges of settlement, namely: that every grantee shall cultivate five acres out of every fifty, within two years; second, that all white and other pine trees, suitable for making masts for the Royal Navy, be reserved for that purpose; third, that a tract of the township be marked out for town lots; fourth, that for four years, the tax on the township shall be one ear of Indian corn, to be paid on Christmas Day; and fifth, that after that time, every proprietor, settler, or inhabitant shall pay annually on every hundred acres which he owns, settles or possesses. This area of Central New Hampshire was rightly called the 'Kingswoods' for His Royal Navy."

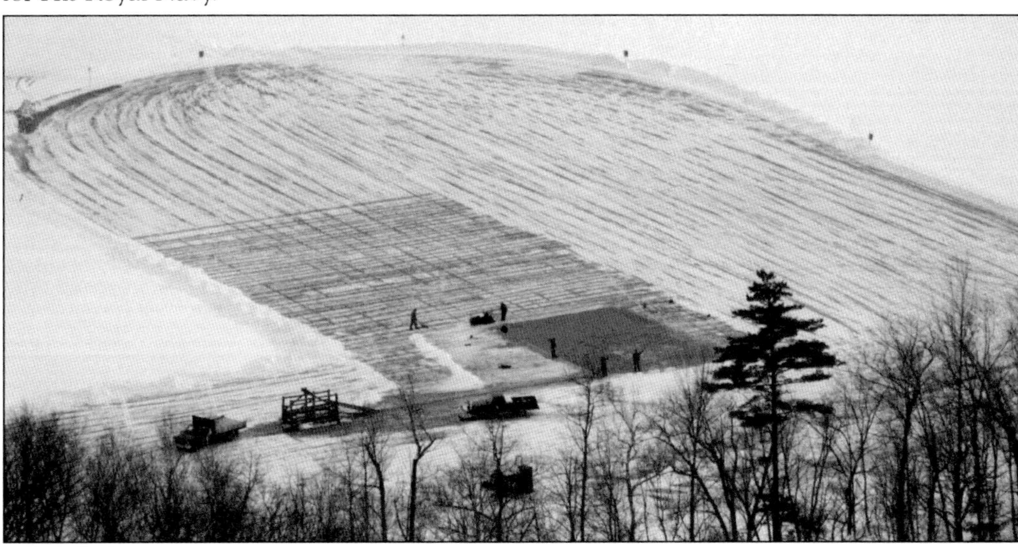

HARVESTING ICE ON SQUAM LAKE, C. THE 1900S. During the early 1900s, ice harvesting on Squam Lake, after the January thaw, was big business. Although no longer big business, ice harvesting on Squam Lake continues to this day. Once, many icehouses were clustered around lakes throughout the region. During the spring and summer months, ice trucks were loaded and bound for the cities to fill iceboxes. Today, some of the remains of the old icehouses stand abandoned on lakeshores.

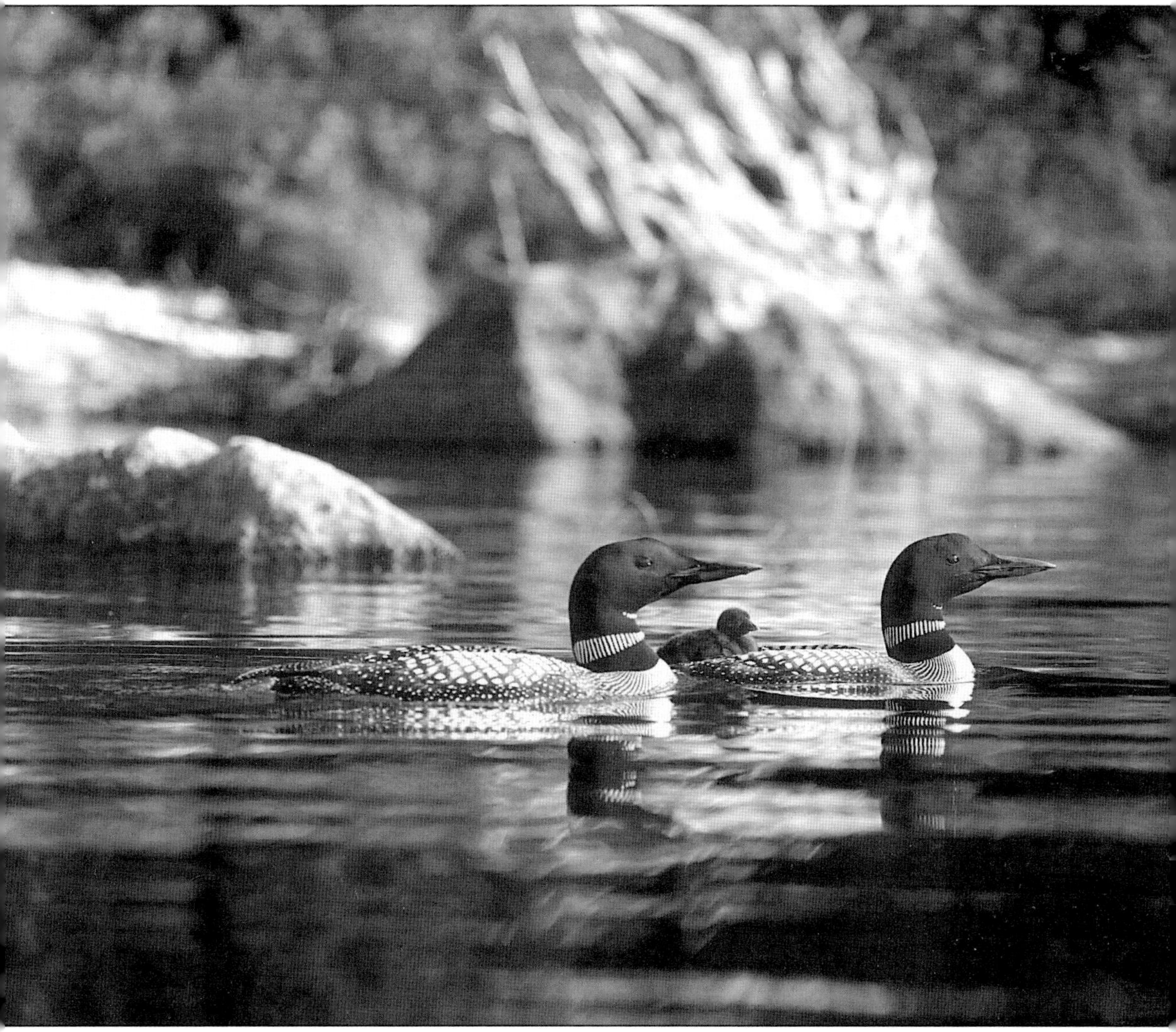

A Family of Loons, Squam Lake. Loons, such as this elegant family, are found on both Squam Lake and Little Squam Lake.

Five

MOULTONBOROUGH

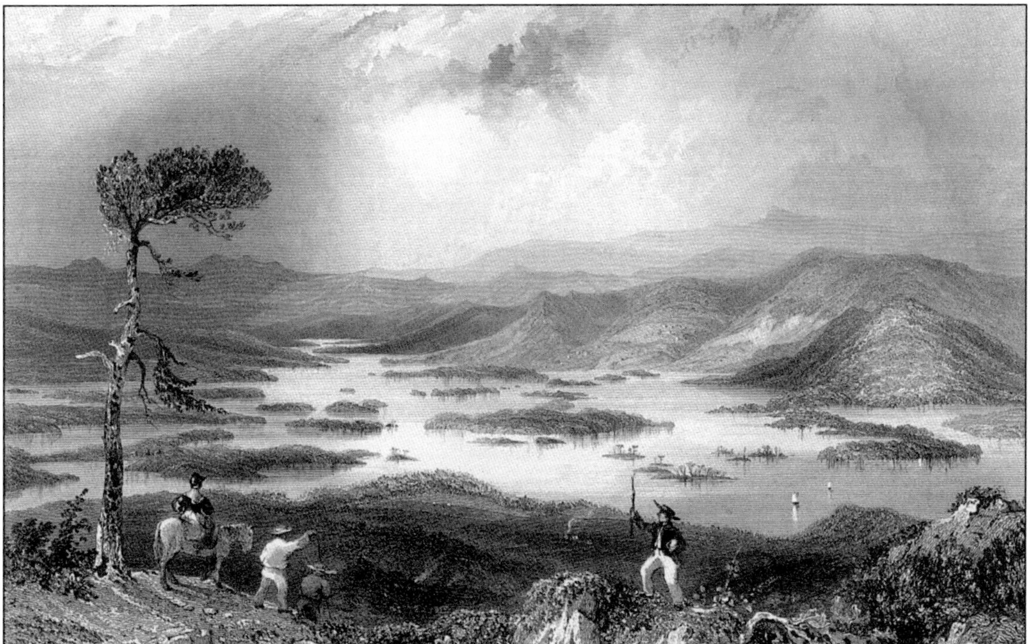

SQUAM LAKE, FROM THE SUMMIT OF RED HILL, 1834. Thousands of visitors have ascended Red Hill. The summit of the northern peak is 2,029 feet above sea level. Looking northwestward, the full grandeur and majesty of Squam Lake and its surrounding mountain ranges is apparent. Seen here are early tourists enjoying the full panorama. (Bartlett print.)

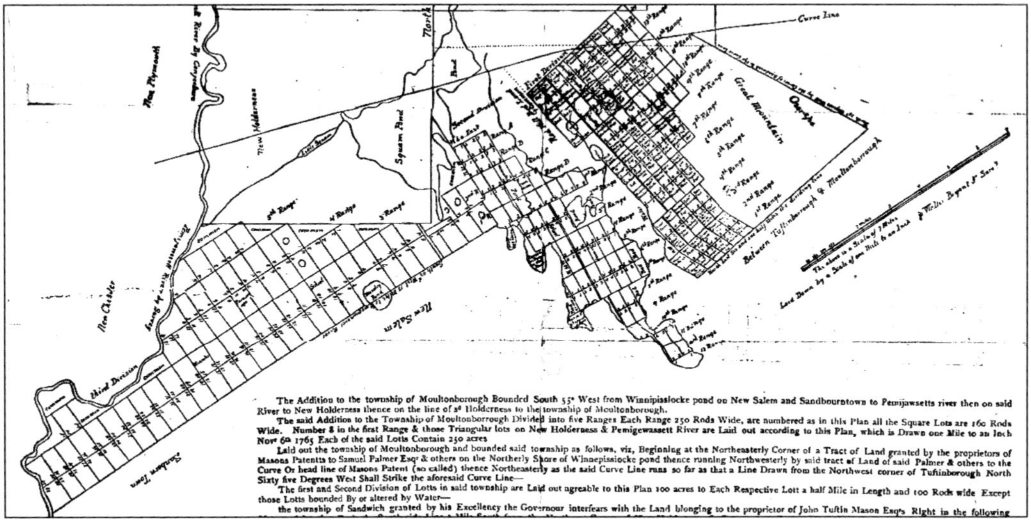

A MAP OF MOULTONBOROUGH, NOVEMBER 6, 1765. Moultonborough was granted to Revolutionary War hero Col. Jonathan Moulton and others by the Masonian proprietors in 1763. Moultonborough Gore (Addition) was later annexed in 1765, and the town was incorporated in 1777. Moultonborough sits astride the northern end of Lake Winnipesaukee and Moultonborough Neck reaches down into the lake, for a total of 50 miles of shoreline beauty. With the addition of 15 miles on Squam Lake, and frontage on Lake Kanasatka, Berry Pond, and 10 smaller ponds, Moultonborough has more shoreline than any other town in New Hampshire.

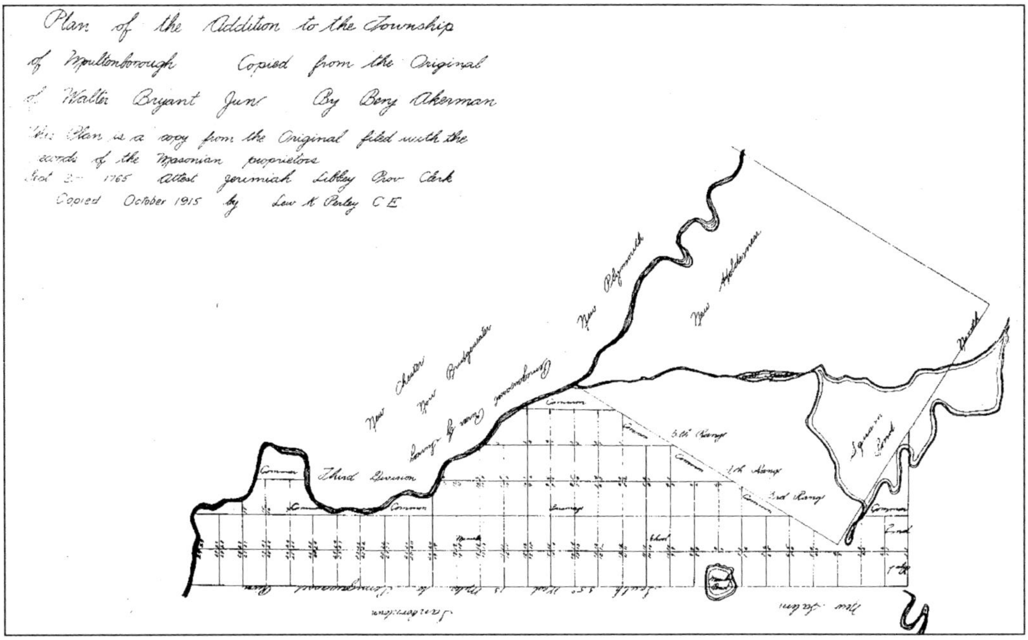

A MAP OF MOULTONBOROUGH ADDITION, 1765. In 1765, the territory of New Hampton was granted to Moulton and became known as Moultonborough Addition. The original plan was filed with the records of the Masonian Proprietors on September 2, 1765. The above plan was copied in October 1915 by Lew K. Perley, a civil engineer, from an earlier copy by Benjamin Akerman of the the original plan of Walter Bryant Jun.

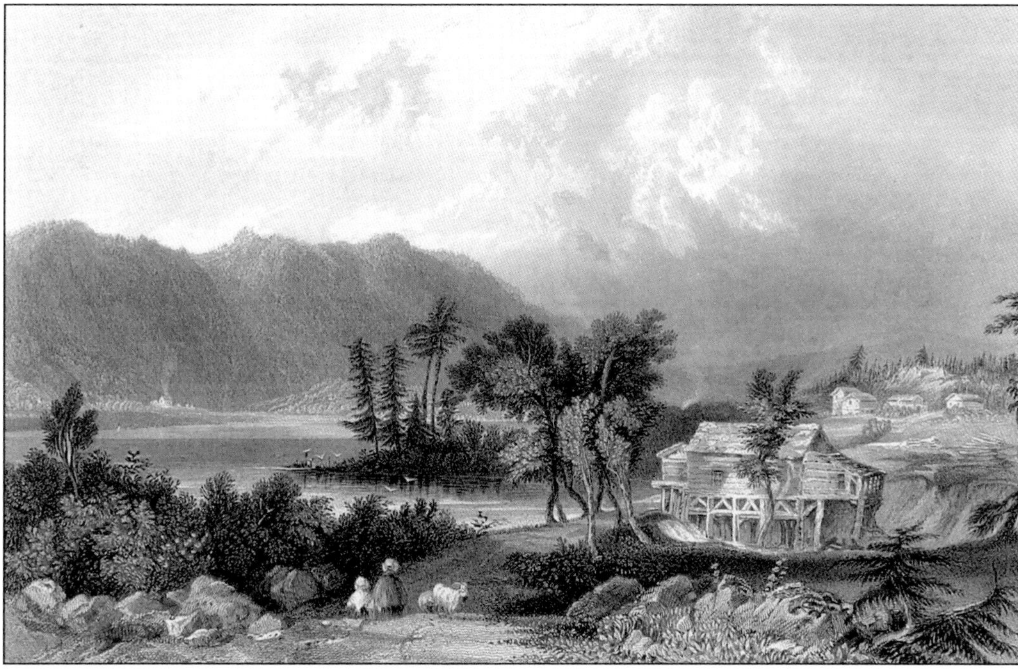

A SAWMILL AND A LOG CABIN. Nestled at the foot of Red Hill, an old sawmill sits on the shore of Long Pond (left). Today, Long Pond is known as Lake Kanasatka. According to town historians, the mill had several owners. Originally, this property was granted to Benning Moulton, a son of General Moulton. It was purchased by the Senters of Center Harbor in 1793 and by John Coe during the first half of the 19th century. It was later replaced with the present Red Hill House. Early town papers indicate that "20 acres of common land on each side of the mill were held by the town. The road was much lower, and the hills steeper at that time. It is recorded that in 1867, Curtis Coe was ordered to remove buildings and logs from the town property Between 1880 and 1890, the mill was owned and operated by Frank Brown and his son Fred. At that time the supply of logs were floated in Long Pond, each log being 'snaked' across the road to the mill as needed." To this day, there appears to be a large deposit of sawdust at the mouth of the brook into Lake Winnipesaukee. (Bartlett print.)

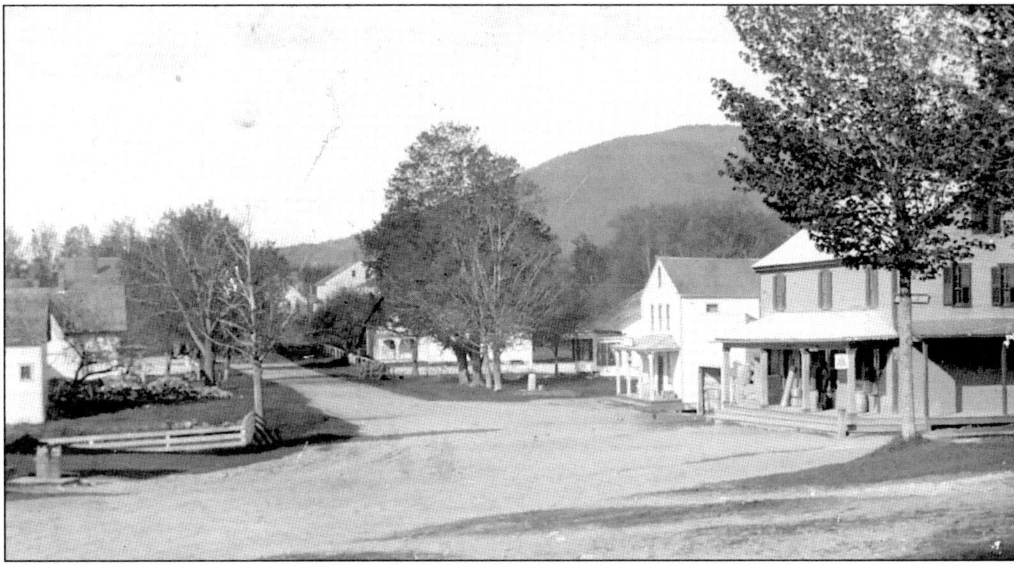

MOULTONBOROUGH CORNER, LOOKING WEST, THE 1880S. As the town grew, this intersection of three roads became a natural focus for town activities. According to Helen S. Matthews and the Moultonborough Historical Society, "The northern boundary of Moultonborough, when granted in 1763, followed the curve of John Mason's Claim as run by the earliest state surveyors. On maps printed about 1800, it is shown that this curve was resurveyed by a Robert Fletcher, Esq., in 1788. In that year the state fixed the boundary between Moultonborough and Sandwich. By 1840 there was a significant settlement at Moultonborough Corners." Being a center for commercial activities, the corner soon became the site of stores, a church, a town house, a school, and private homes.

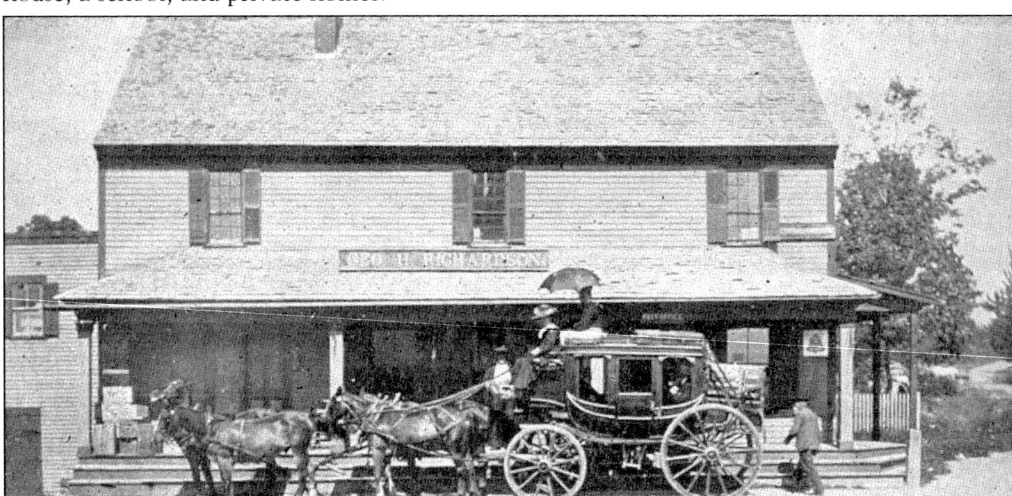

THE POST OFFICE AND THE OLDE COUNTRY STORE, MOULTONBOROUGH CORNER, THE 1880S. This view of George H. Richardson's store shows the Concord Coach with two pairs of horses en route from the Conways to Concord. The Olde Country Store, currently listed on the National Register of Historic Places, houses an original Concord Coach. The boardinghouse and stagecoach era of the 1880s contributed to the growth and development of Moultonborough Corner. This was a major thoroughfare for the Concord Coach from Center Harbor to the Conways in the White Mountains.

THE WOODEN INDIAN ON THE PORCH OF THE OLDE COUNTRY STORE. In front of the store is the full-size statue ready to welcome all travelers to the Olde Country Store. The Wooden Indian was carved prior to 1800.

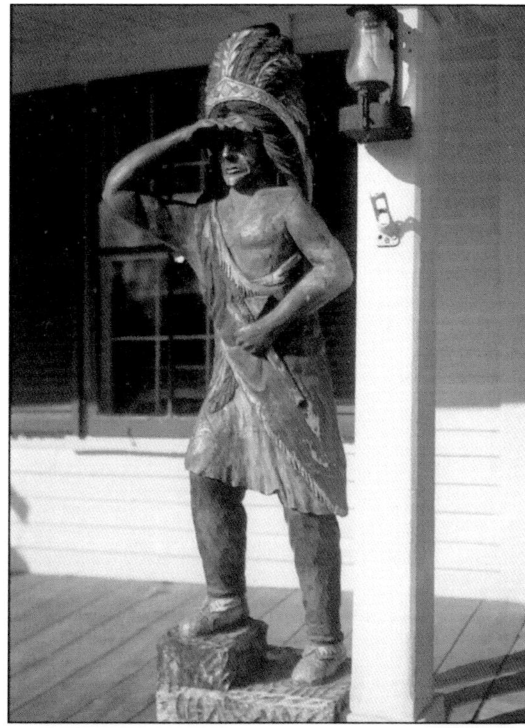

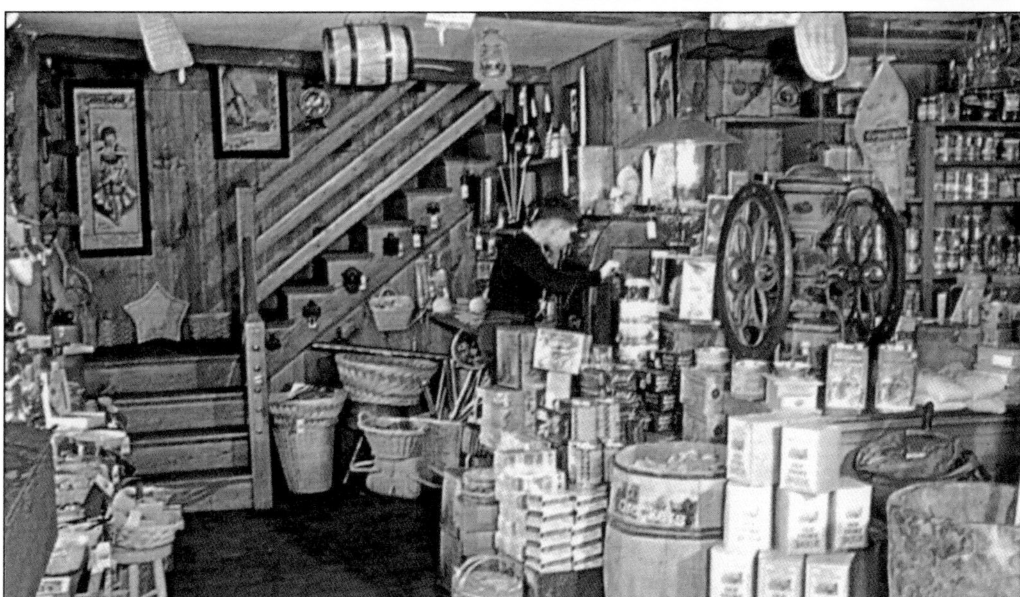

THE INTERIOR OF THE OLDE COUNTRY STORE, 1977. This store dates back to 1781, when it was known as Freeze's Tavern and served as the social and political center of the community. Eventually, this building came to be used as a town meeting hall, post office, library, and trading center of goods. Today, the store holds the old-time tradition as a true country store with all the elements of colonial mercantilism. The store offers all sorts of wares, including cheddar cheese that has been aged on the premises, pickles, and penny candy. An added attraction is the museum on the second floor, which is well stocked with artifacts of the town's history.

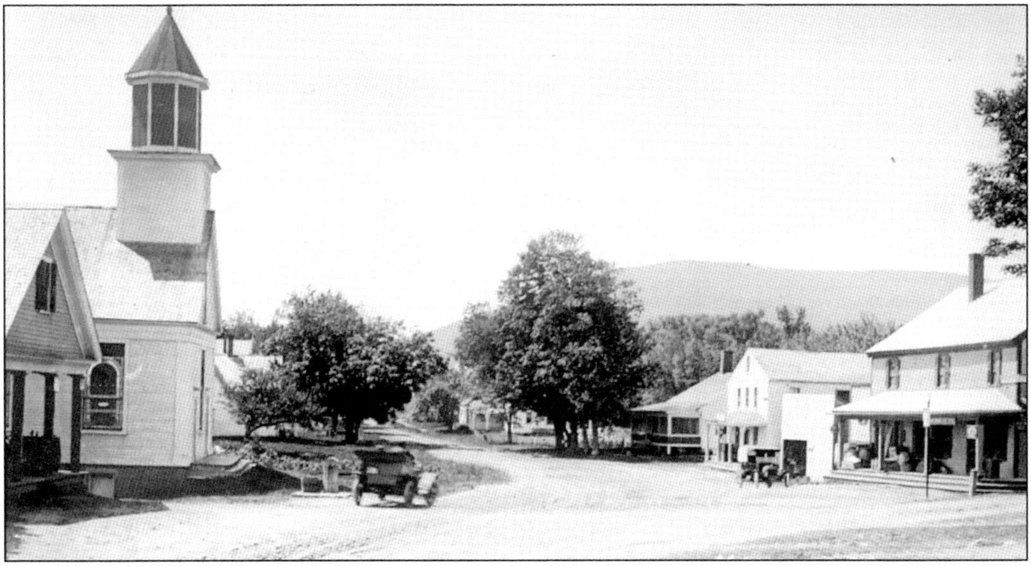

MOULTONBOROUGH VILLAGE, LOOKING WEST, THE 1920S. This view shows the Methodist church (left), Moulton's Store, Maplehurst, Tilton's General Store, and the Olde Country Store (far right).

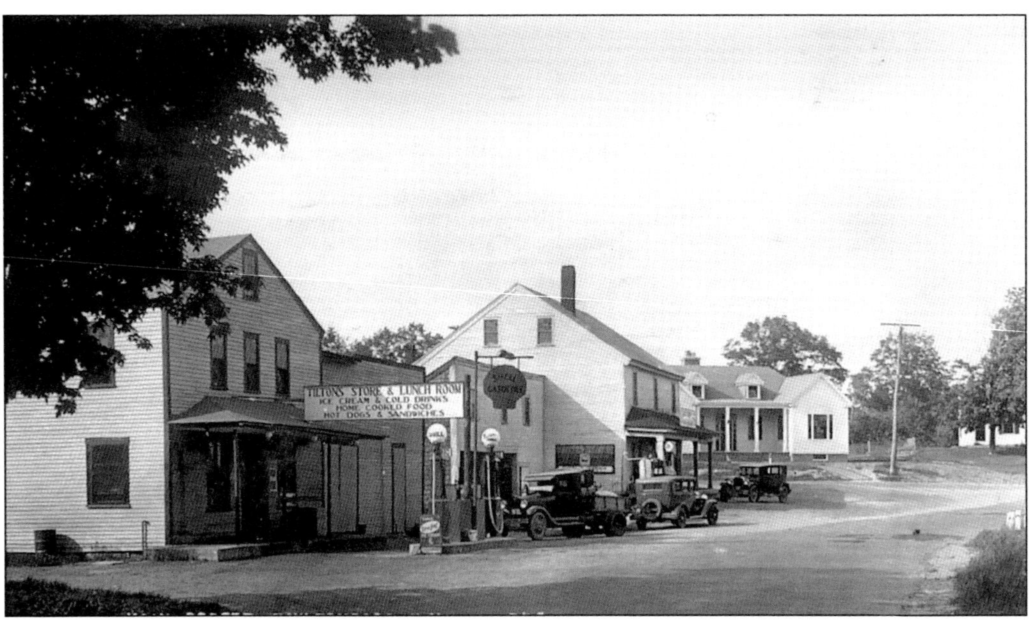

MOULTONBOROUGH VILLAGE, THE 1930S. This view, looking east on Main Street, shows Tilton's General Store (left), the Olde Country Store (center), and the town library.

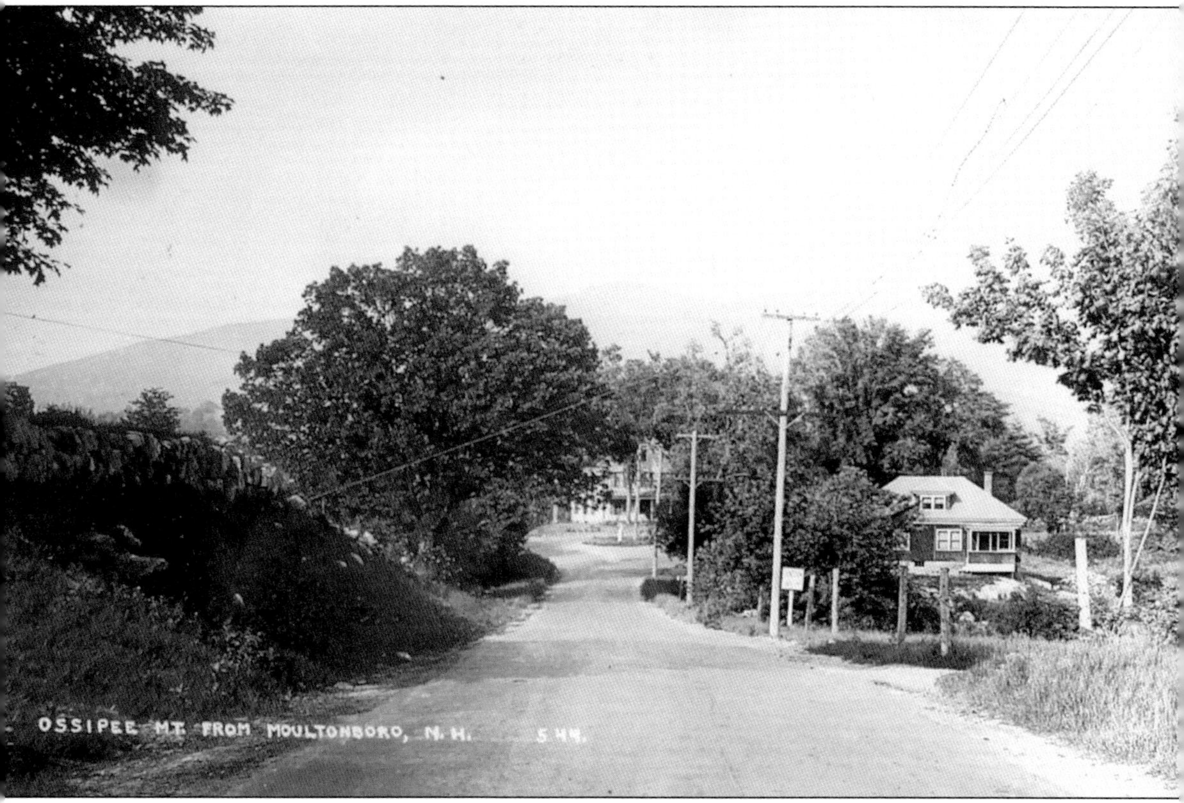

THE OSSIPEE MOUNTAINS, LOOKING EAST FROM MOULTONBOROUGH CORNER, THE 1930S. This view is of the present Route 25, with Marion Goodwin's house on the right.

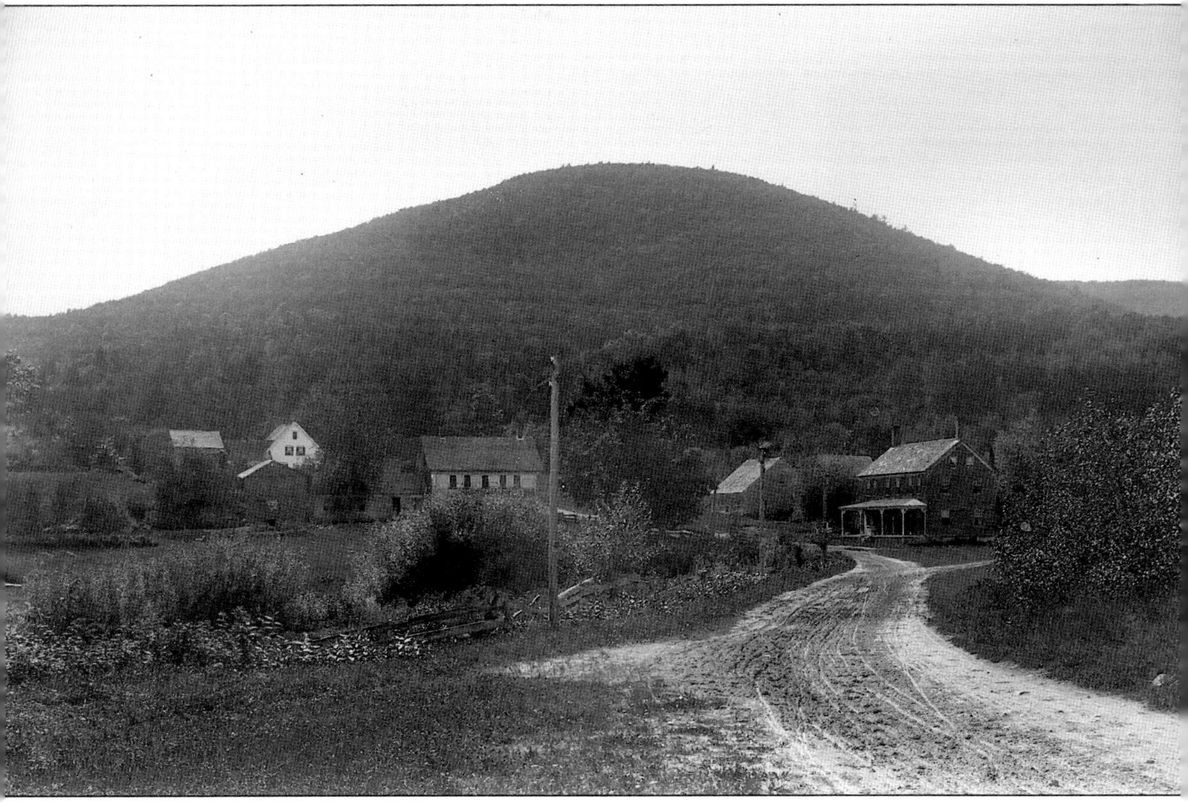

MOULTONBOROUGH FALLS, FROM THE BRIDGE, 1899. Due to the increase of population, the Falls became the second center of Moultonborough, and was named Moultonborough Center on 19th-century maps. According to town records, there were at one time three stores, two hotels, a tannery, a currier's shop, a blacksmith shop, a sleigh and carriage maker, a saddle and harness maker, a printing office, shoe shops, mills, and a cluster of homes.

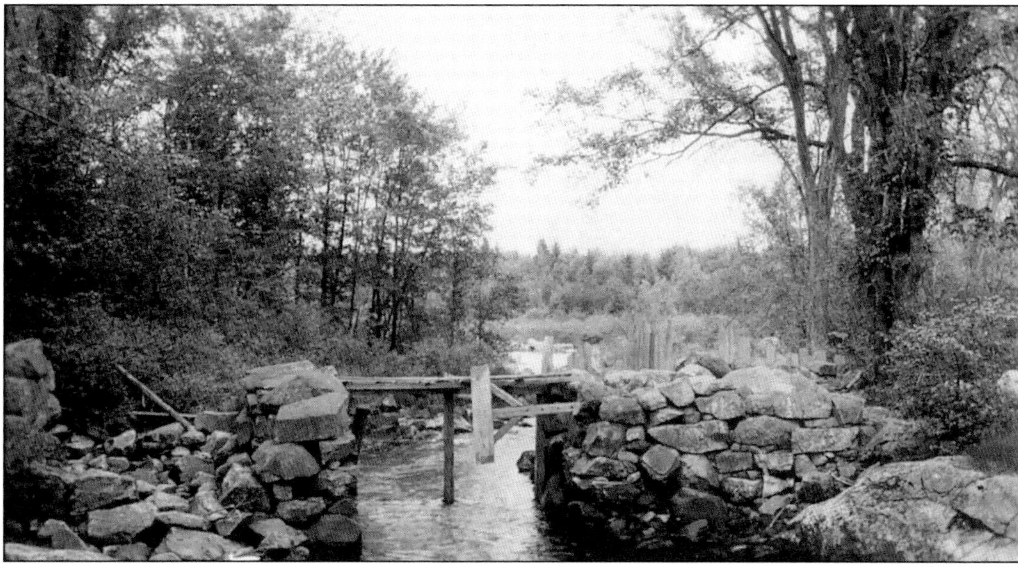

THE OLD DAM AT MOULTONBOROUGH FALLS, 1916. It was here in 1765 that Jonathan Moulton built a gristmill and sawmill, which later expanded to include a carding and fulling mill.

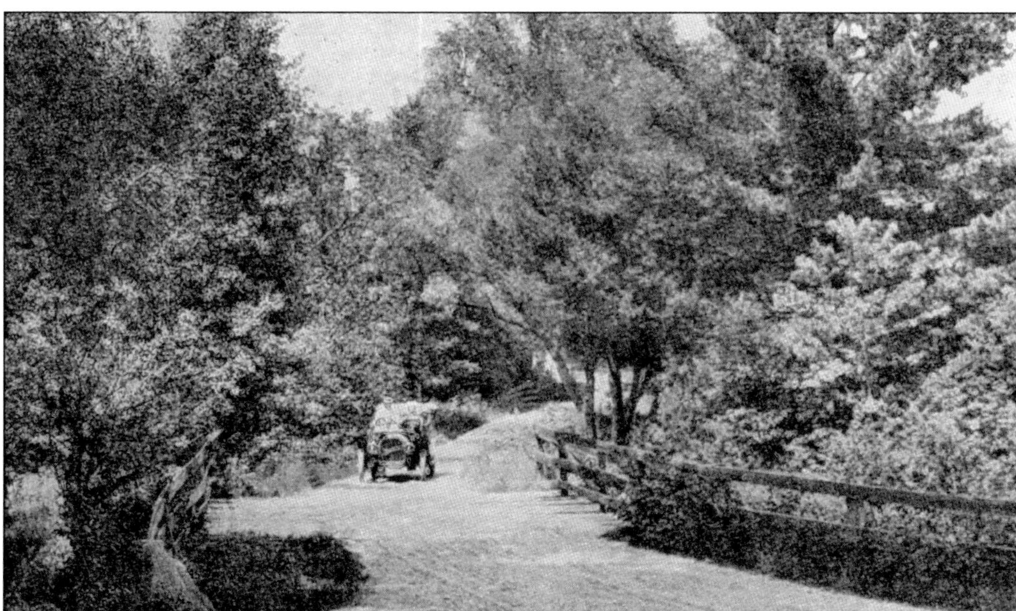

THREE BRIDGES, MOULTONBOROUGH, 1921. This vintage photograph was taken at the Shannon Brook Junction, near the States Landing Road at the present junction of Routes 171 and 109. According to early town records, this area was considered the first center of Moultonborough. Note the Ford convertible traveling the early dirt road to Wolfeboro. During the 1800s, this area had several mills along the stream.

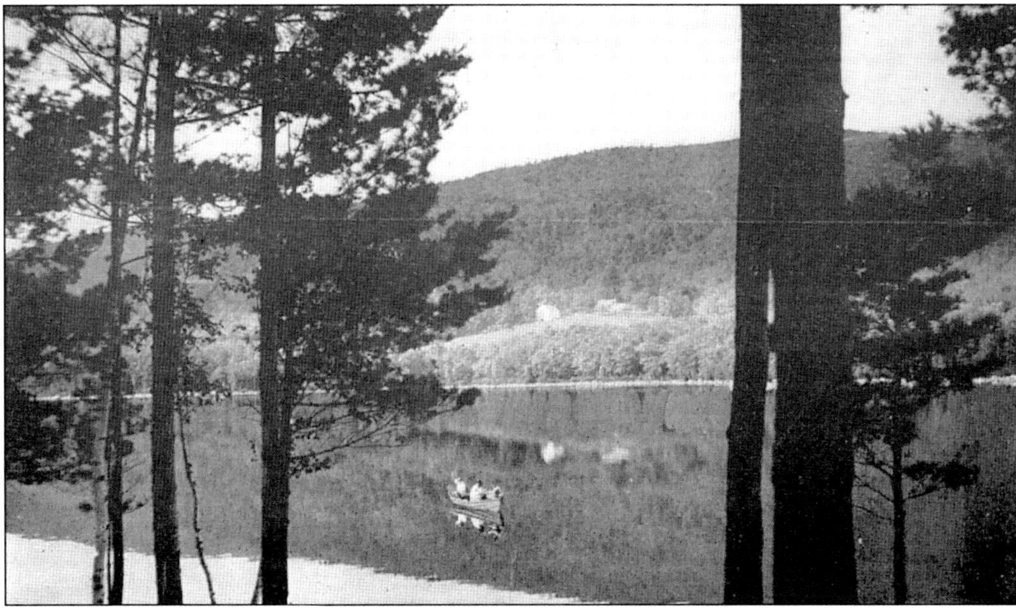

CAMP VONHURST, FROM THE PORCH OF THE PINES ON LAKE KANASATKA. Camp Vonhurst was a camp for adults and their families. There was a central lodge, cottages, a 60-acre forest, and a beach. Fishing, swimming, and hiking were popular activities.

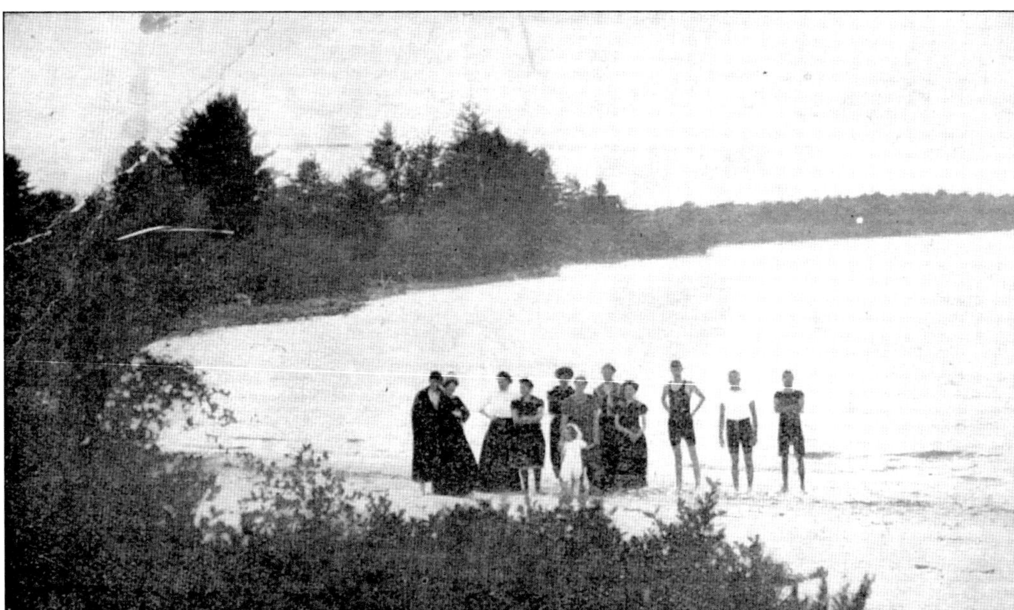

A BATHING SCENE ON LONG POND (KANASATKA) IN MOULTONBOROUGH. This charming lake is located one mile east of the Center Harbor village. This body of water empties into Lake Winnipesaukee by a stream located between the Second and Third Moultonborough Necks. From this lake, the old Indian Carry connects Kanasatka with Squam Lake to the west. This beach is better known as Sandy Cove.

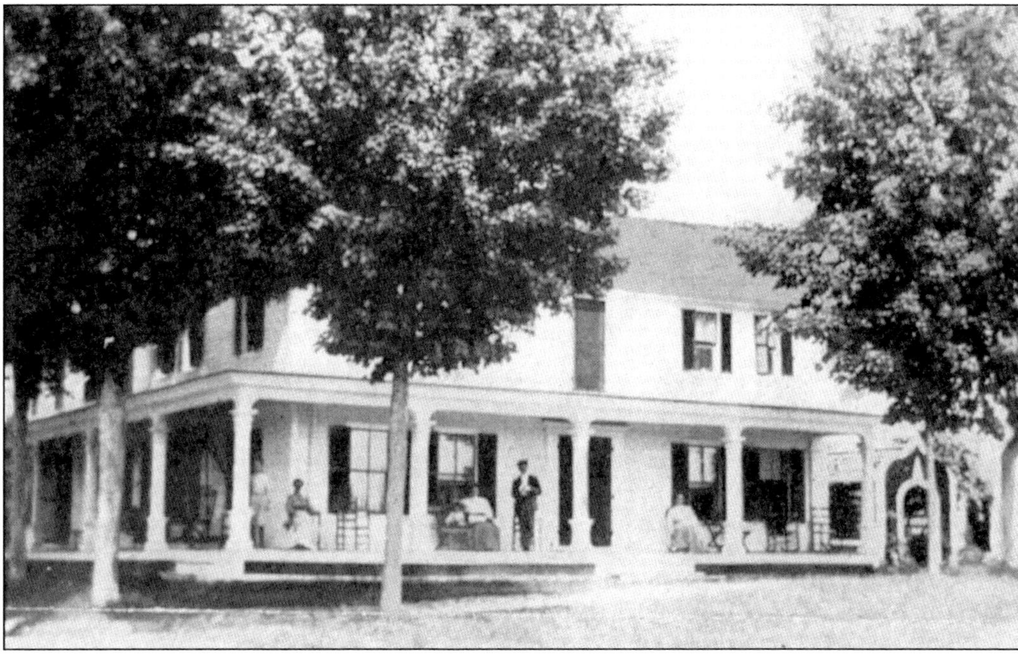

The Homestead, Owned by George A. Blanchard, 1910. George A. Blanchard was the proprietor of the Homestead. In 1910, the daily cost was $2 and the weekly cost was $7 or $8. During the late 1800s, travel to the Lakes Region and White Mountains was easy and fashionable. Boardinghouses met the demand for accommodation of visitors from the cities. Typically, the visitors came by train, steamboat, and stagecoach.

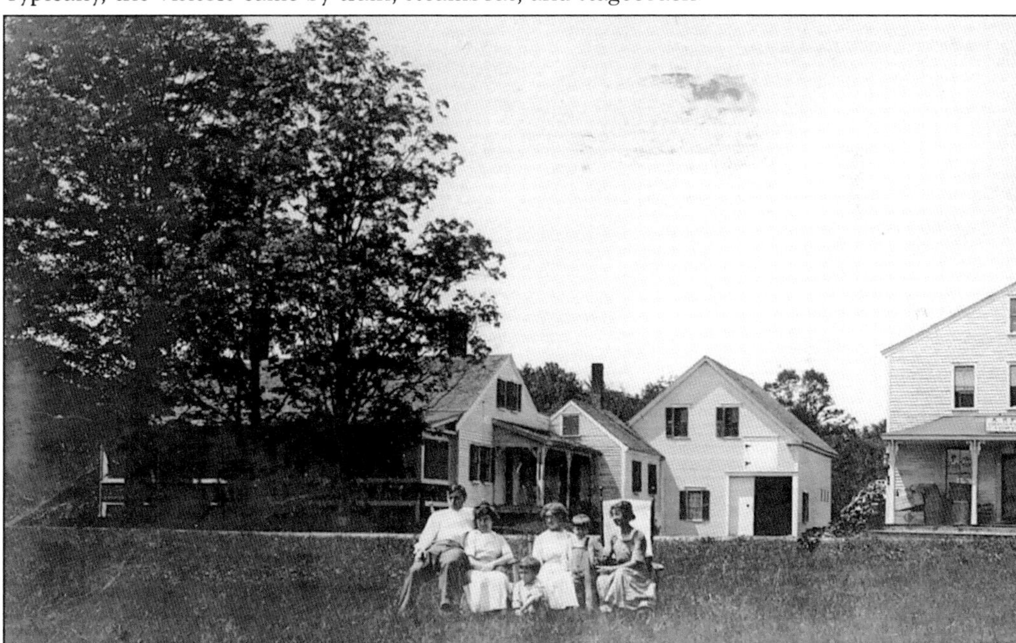

The Maplehurst, Owned by R.S. Freese, 1914. Once the tourists found their favorite summer inn or boardinghouse, they often stayed for the entire summer. These boardinghouses took on a popular appeal, and soon the grand hotels met the needs of the booming tourist trade.

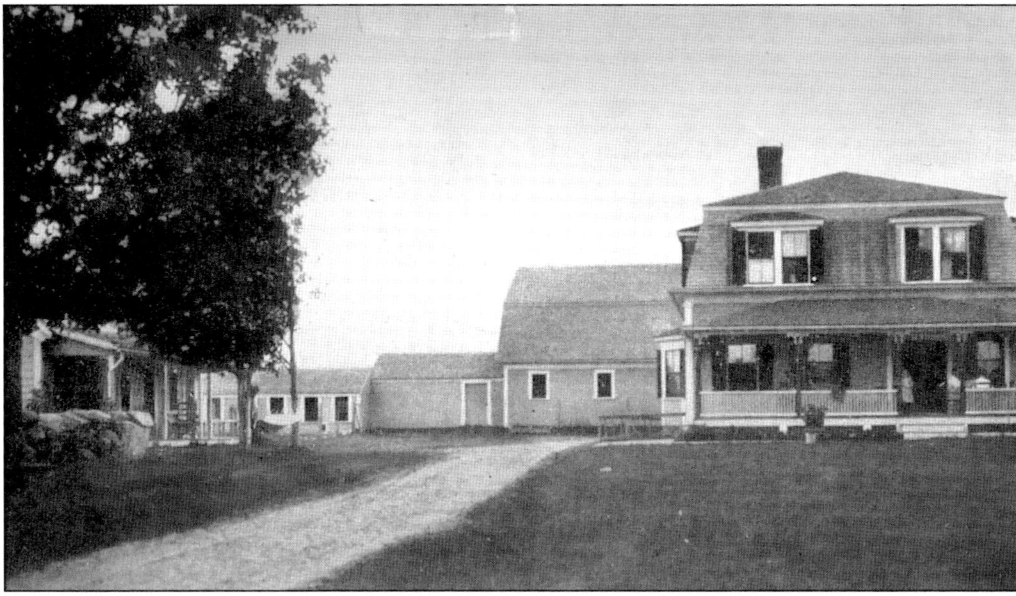

THE NEW CAMBRIDGE HOUSE, 1905. Located near Greene's Corner, the Cambridge House is thought to have been one of the earliest boardinghouses in town. After some years of operation, the original house was destroyed by fire. It was replaced by the yellow house that stands to the north of Route 25 today. Many other boardinghouses and private homes—like the Cambridge House—were built in the neighborhood, making Greene's Corner a popular stop for summer visitors.

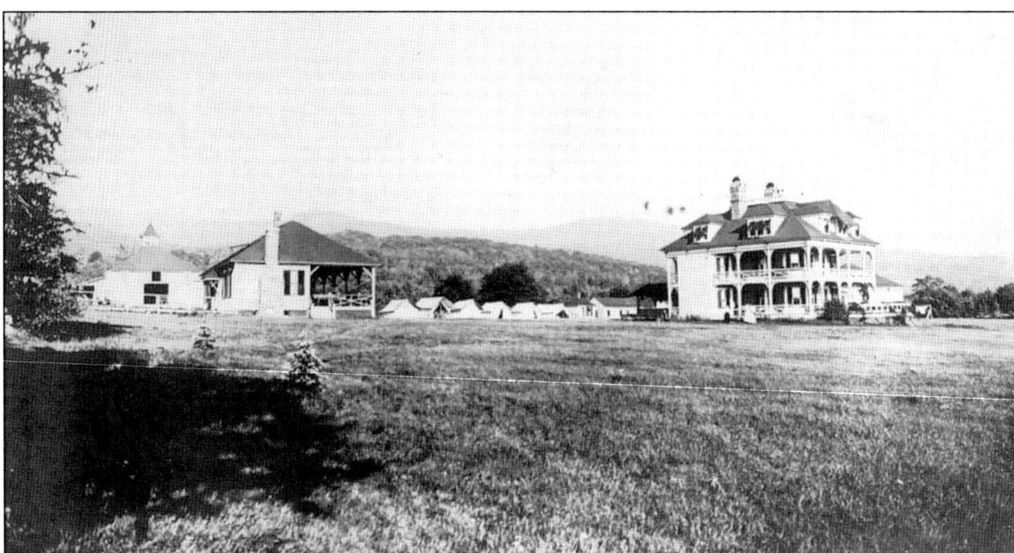

THE PARK HOUSE, OSSIPEE MOUNTAIN PARK, THE EARLY 1900S. In 1879, B.F. Shaw of Lowell, Massachusetts, purchased land at the Lee Settlement and developed it into the Ossipee Mountain Park. Here, he built a beautiful Queen Anne–style home on the mountain. Shaw and his family and friends spent the summer months here. The Park House, or Weelahka Hall as it was called, became a popular vacation resort and was visited by several famous people, including poets John Greenleaf Whittier, Lucy Larcom, and Robert Frost. After Shaw's death in 1890, his residence was operated as a boardinghouse by Mrs. E.F. Pettengill.

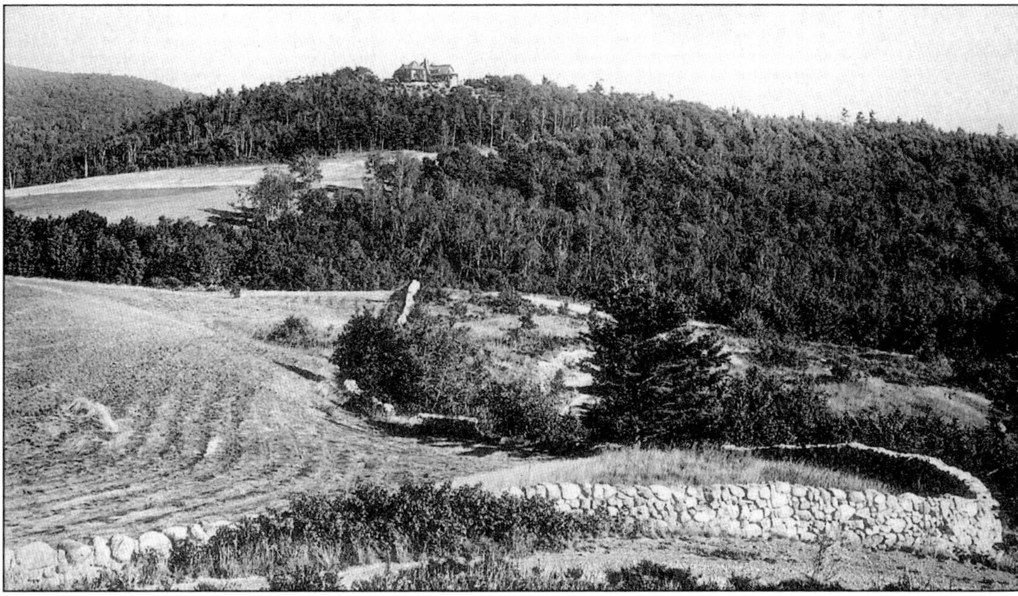

LUCKNOW, THE THOMAS PLANT ESTATE, OSSIPEE MOUNTAINS. This early-20th-century view shows the estate in the distance with fields, stone walls, and woods in the foreground. When Thomas Plant purchased the property, he leveled some of the farms but kept Weelahka Hall, operating it as the living quarters for many of the workers on his new estate. The final plans for his home were completed between 1912 and 1913, and work began in the spring of 1913.

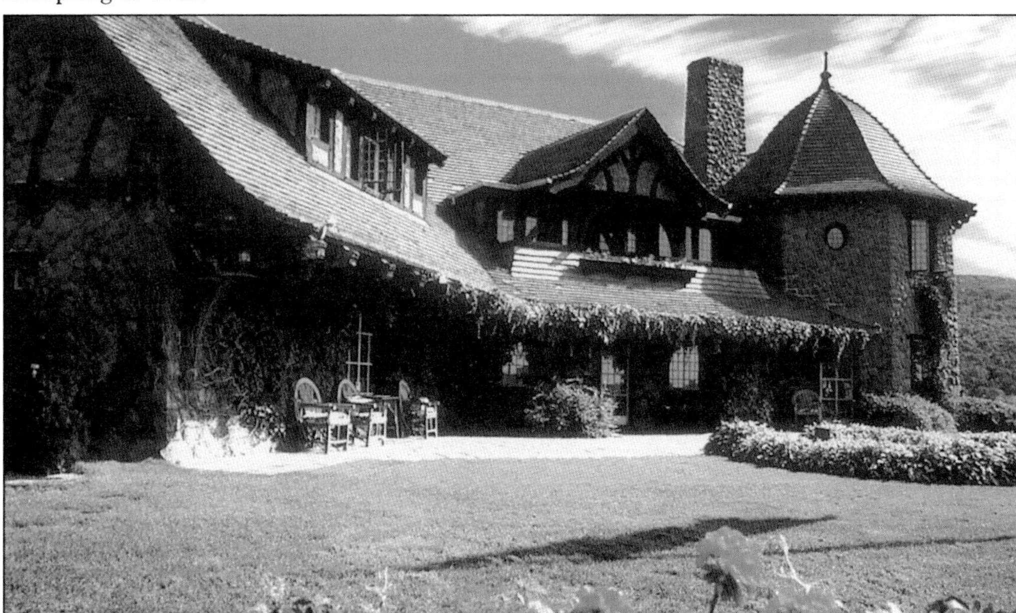

THE CASTLE IN THE CLOUDS. This recent view of Lucknow shows shows the terrace side of the building with a round tower on the far corner and geraniums in the foreground. Thomas Plant lived in this house from 1913 until his death in 1941. Later in the 20th century, the estate was called the Castle in the Clouds and was opened to the public. It is located on the brow of the Ossipee Mountain Range overlooking Lake Winnipesaukee.

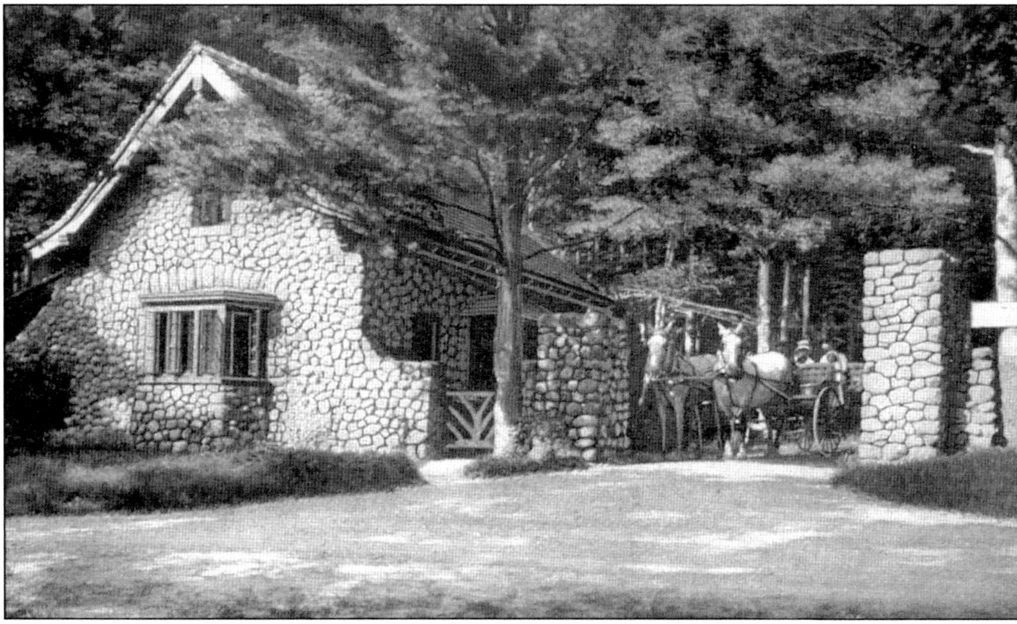

THE ENTRANCE GATE AND LODGE, THE OSSIPEE MOUNTAIN PARK, 1920. Seen here is a wagon with a pair of white horses coming through the gate.

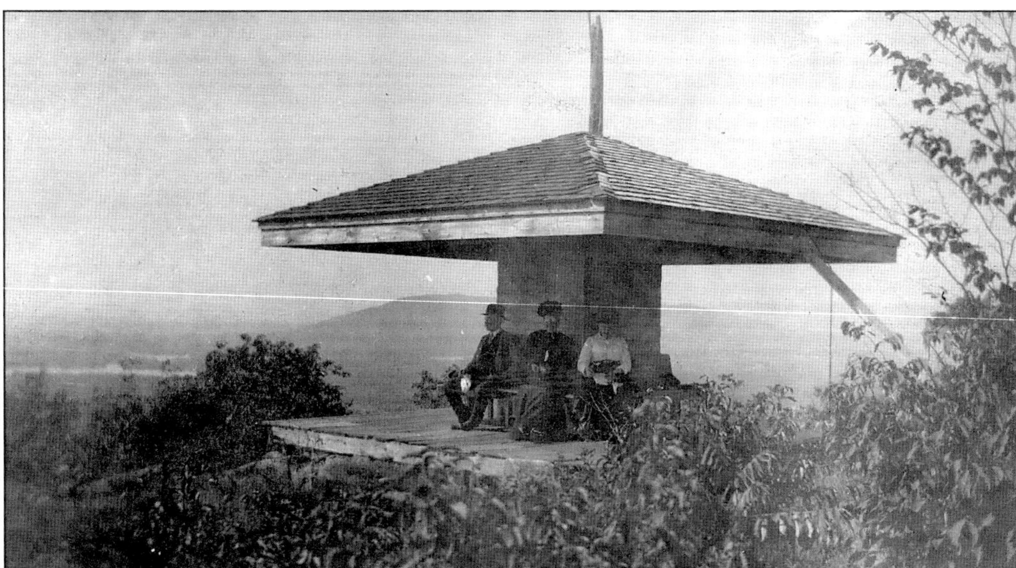

THE CROW'S NEST. B.F. Shaw built this lookout seat with an overhanging roof on a spot where the Castle in the Clouds now stands. The Ossipee Mountain Park was a widely known resort in the late 1800s and early 1900s. Each year thousands of visitors sat in the Crow's Nest and viewed the scenic beauties of the park.

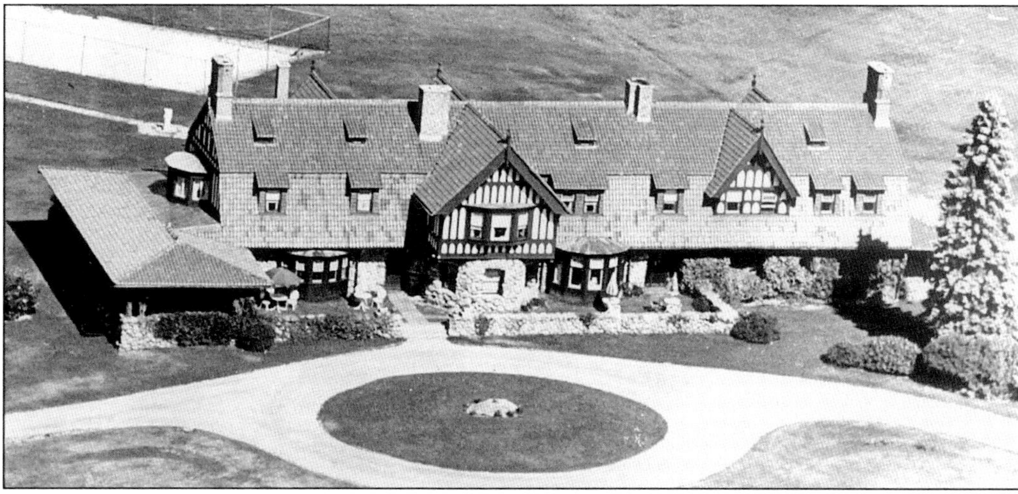

THE KONA FARM, 1948. In 1899, Herbert Dumaresq, part owner of Jordan Marsh department stores in Boston, retired and started plans for a country home on the shore of Lake Winnipesaukee. The Kona Farm is one of the finest estates in the Lakes Region. This 1,186-acre estate sits atop a hill by the shore of Lake Winnipesaukee.

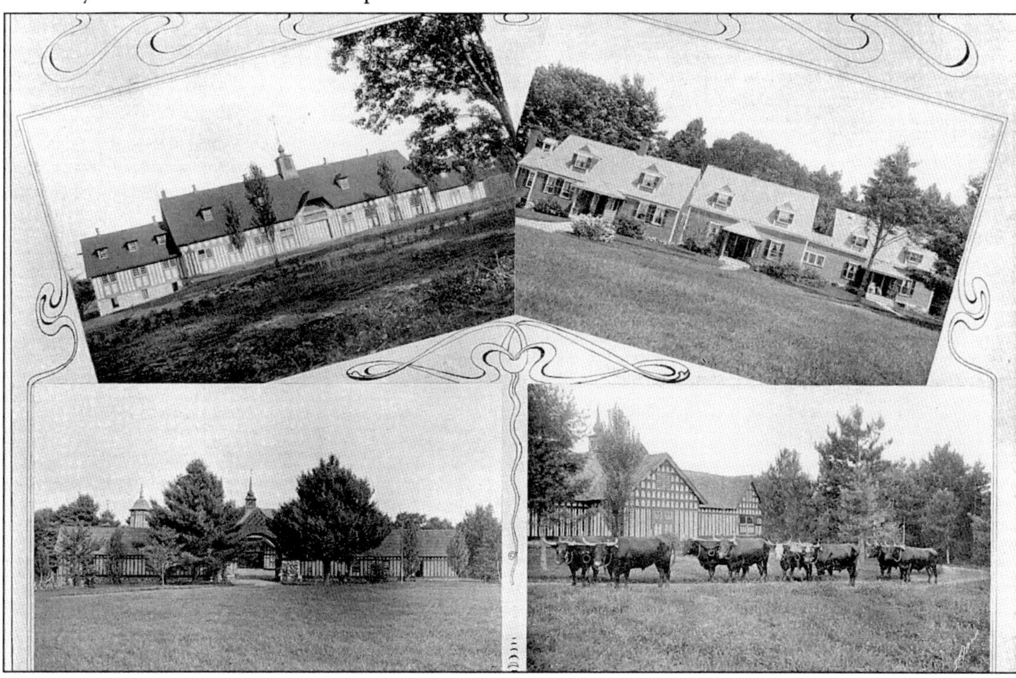

THE KONA FARM. This gentleman's farm included several outbuildings. All of the buildings had white siding with green overlays, except the three Capes, which were painted red. The stock barn was a large structure built on all four sides of a 120-by-65-foot barnyard. It was transformed into a motel, but the original interior was preserved. In the upper left is a sheep barn, which has dormer windows and a cupola with a ball decoration. In the upper right are three attached Capes. One was the home of the farm overseer; another was the home of the caretaker of the mansion; the third was used by the Dumaresqs when they came to Moultonborough in the winter. Generally, the family spent winters on Commonwealth Avenue in Boston, Massachusetts.

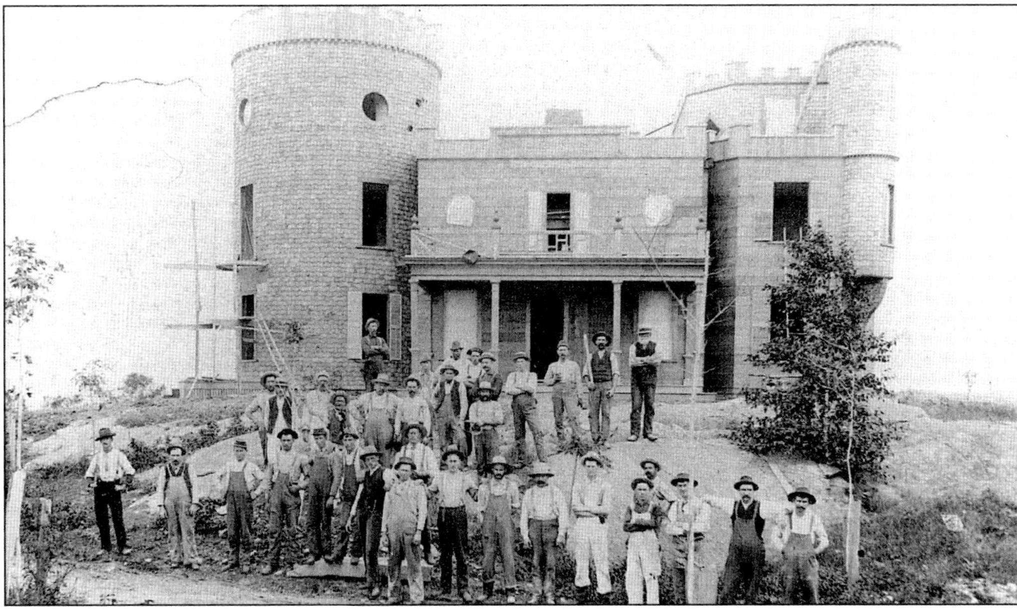

The Roxmont Estate and Workmen. In 1885, Dr. J. Alonzo Greene fixed his heart upon New Hampshire as a home. He chose Winnipesaukee's Long Island and built the Roxmont there in 1895. His estate, located on the second lot from the bridge, consisted of 40 acres and commanded an unobstructed view in every direction. His castle had an air of oriental romance, as its interior was intricately decorated with treasures from the Far East. The structure burned 35 years after it was built and, today, all that remains of the Roxmont is its stone gateway.

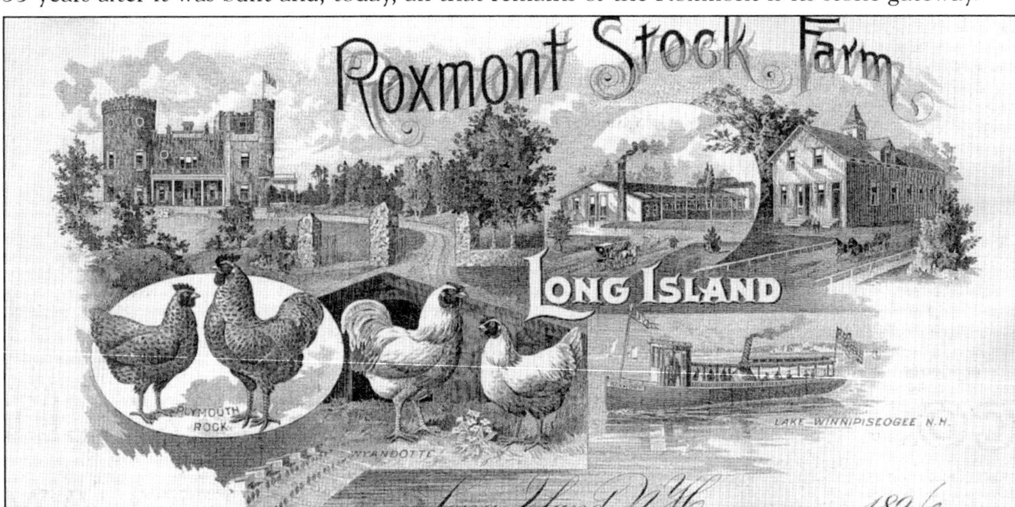

The Roxmont Stock Farm. This is a November 1, 1896 advertisement for Roxmont Stock Farm on Long Island. This farm was highly stocked with fancy breeds of fowl and cattle and was a source of much pleasure to its owner, who spent the greater part of his time overseeing it and hunting and fishing in the neighboring country. Local author and historian William H. Genne stated the following in his book *Geneva Point Center 1919–1989*: "In 1896, the Roxmont Poultry operations ceased and the barn was converted into an Inn for the growing tourist business. Broad verandahs were built on three sides of the building and a broad stairway was built from the western verandah." The inn was properly named the Winnipesaukee Inn.

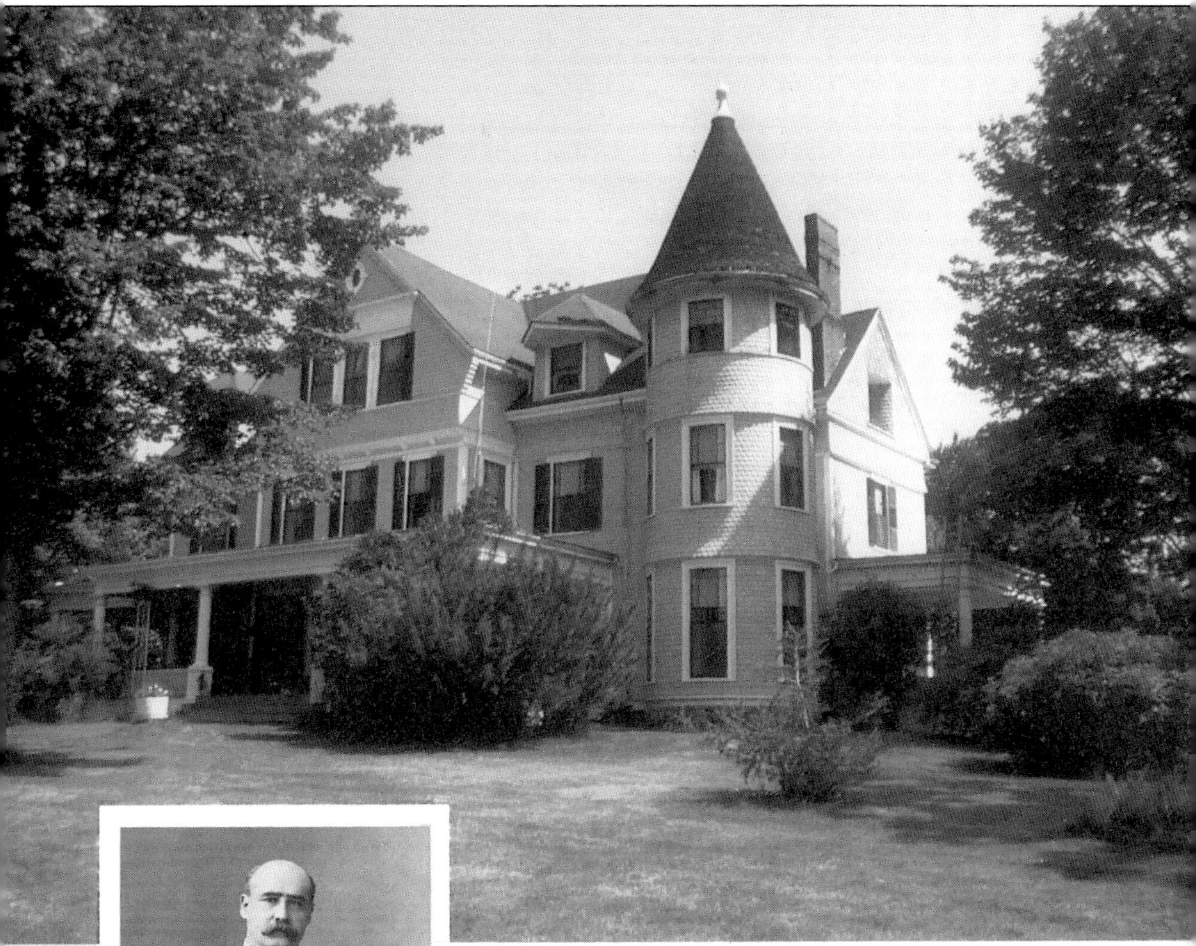

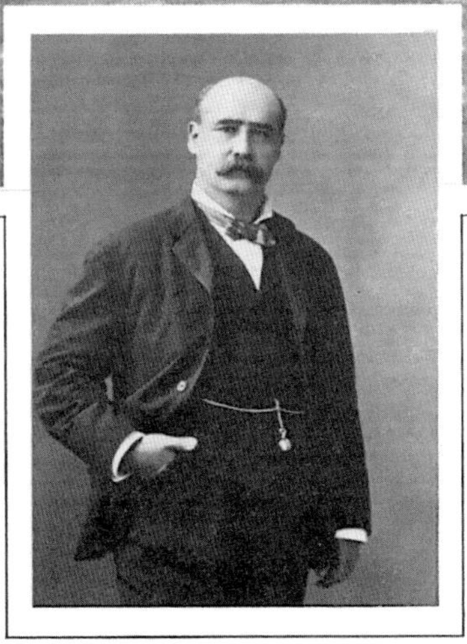

Dr. Frank Eugene Greene

THE WINDERMERE ESTATE, 1891. This estate dates back to 1891, when Dr. Frank Eugene Greene purchased the Lamprey acreage on Long Island. The construction of Windermere and its related buildings was spread over a two-year period. All the materials used came by boat from Lakeport. Approximately 100 workmen camped in tents on the property while the mansion was under construction. The name that Greene and his wife chose came from their visits to Lake Windermere, England, which they often described poetically for its beauty and peaceful charm. Today, this beautiful estate graces the landscape at the southern end of Long Island on the shore of Lake Winnipesaukee.

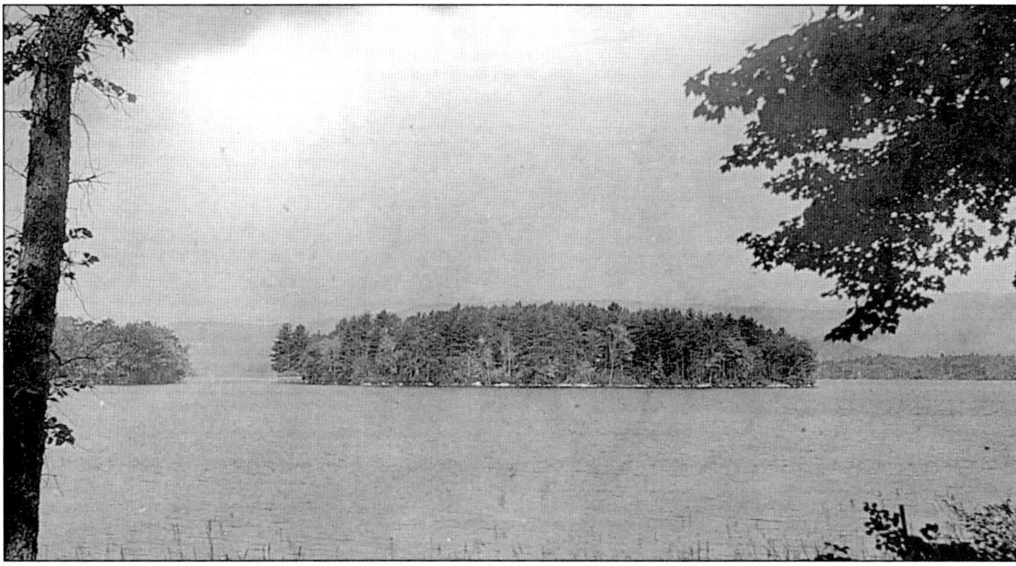

KENT ISLAND, SQUAM LAKE. This secluded island, visible from the Bean Road between Center Harbor and Center Sandwich, is located off the eastern shore of Brown Point and Nichols Cove at the eastern end of Squam Lake.

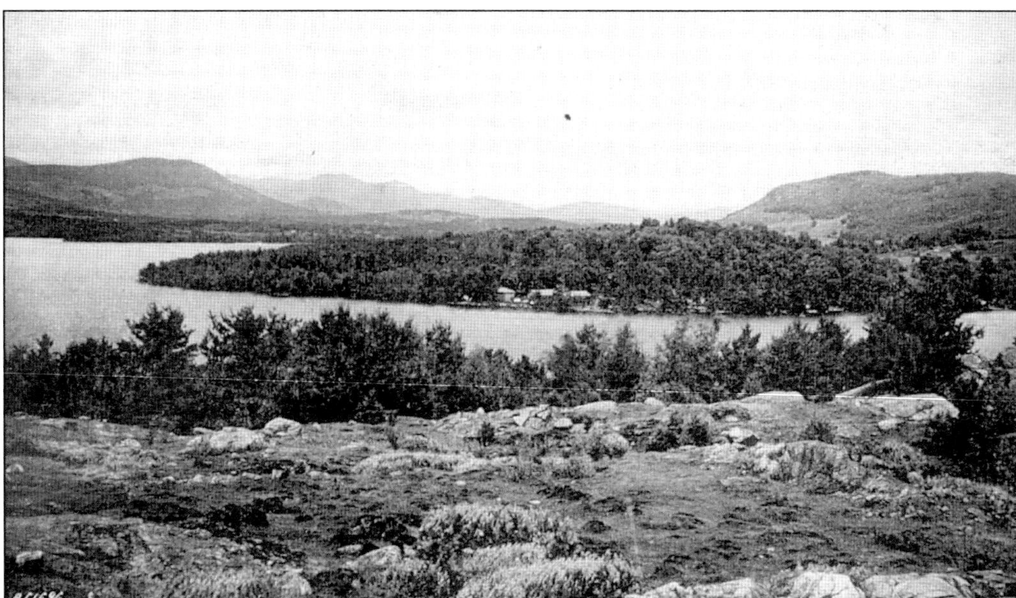

SQUAM LAKE AND HARVARD ENGINEER CAMP, FROM HIGH HAITH, C. 1910. At an engineer camp in Moultonborough Bay, young men from Harvard University lived in tents and worked in drafting rooms of the main lodge, building imaginary railroads. The first official Harvard prospectus dates to 1902, and about 168 students were enrolled and housed in 41 tents along the shore of Squam Lake. The camp remained in operation until the outbreak of World War II and, by the end of the 1941 season, the camp had closed it doors.

Six

SANDWICH

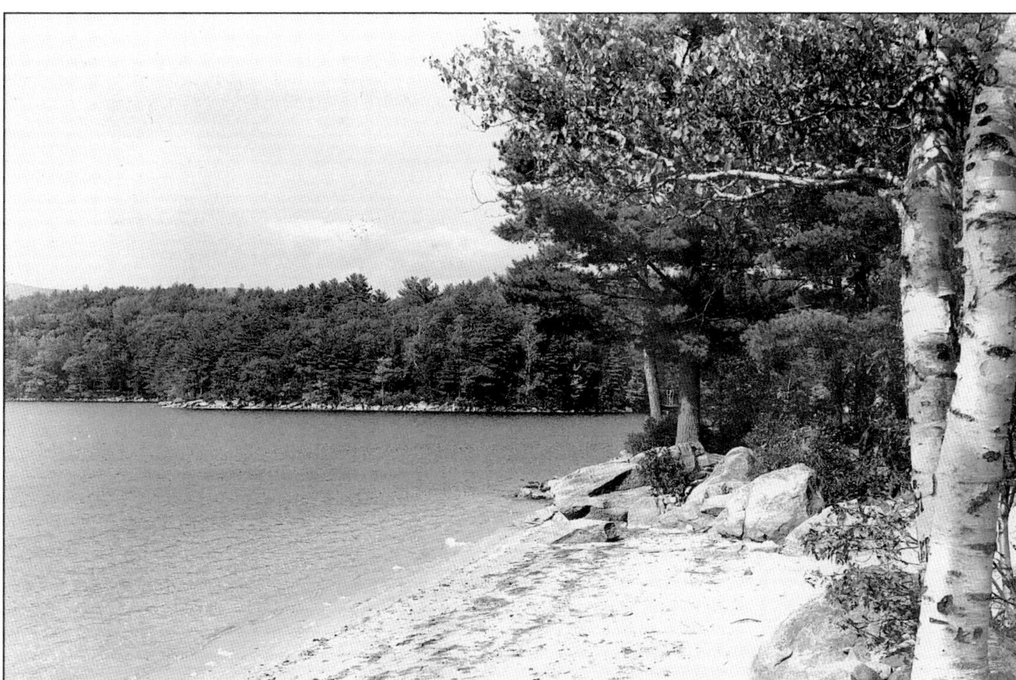

SQUAM BEACH, C. 1950. One of the finest beaches in the Squam Lake region may be found in Sandwich; it is sandy, clean, and very well maintained by the town.

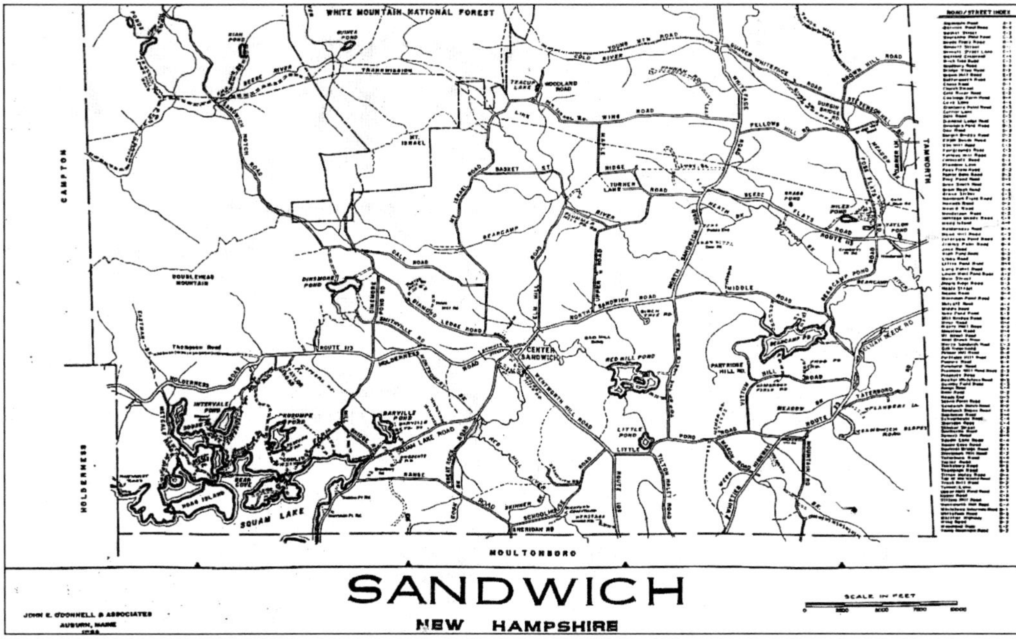

A Map of Sandwich, 1892. Sandwich, located at the eastern end of Squam Lake, covers 64,000 acres of land—six miles square. In 1763, a grant was drawn up for the town; however, the grantees noted that the north and west sides were "so loaded with inaccessible mountains and shelves of rocks as to be uninhabitable," whereupon Governor Wentworth made it 10 miles square. Sandwich was first settled in 1768, and in 1775 it had 245 inhabitants.

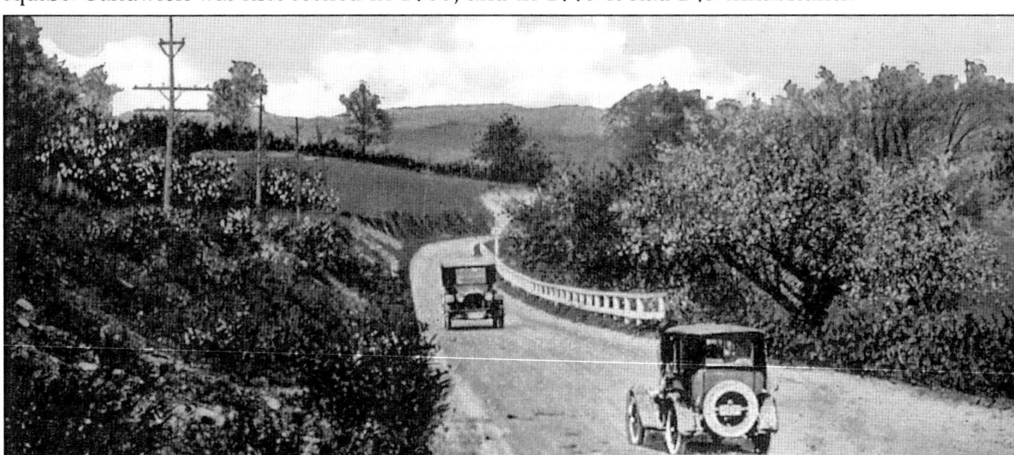

Greetings from Center Sandwich. A party headed by Col. Jacob Smith visited Sandwich to hunt and trap *c.* 1760. The group discovered a little river, which they called Bearcamp—a name that has been closely associated with this region ever since. Three years later, a charter was granted by Gov. Benning Wentworth to grantees who were largely his relatives and friends. The most prominent grantees were Nicholas Gilman, who served on the Committee of Safety during the Revolutionary War, and John Taylor Gilman, who later became the state's governor. In 1770, some of the proprietors sold their rights to John Phillips, now honored as the founder of Phillips Academy at Exeter and at Andover, Massachusetts. The Phillips fortune was founded largely on the marriage of John Phillips to the widow of Nathaniel Gilman, an original proprietor of Sandwich.

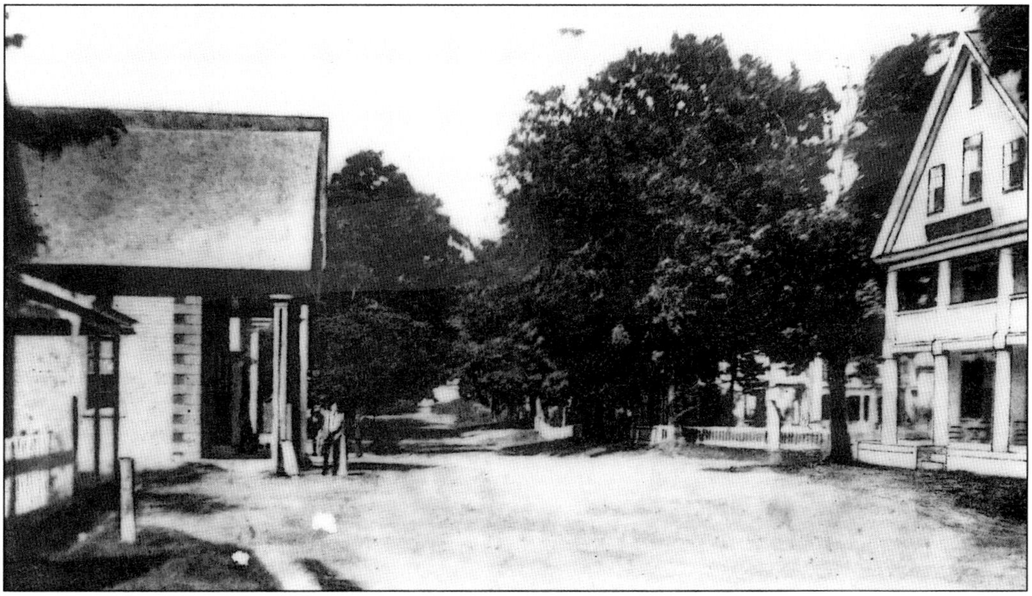

MAIN STREET, CENTER SANDWICH. This view shows the general store on the left and the Sandwich House on the right. By the 1870s, this area was already a thriving business and social center of the town. The Holderness Road skirts the entire north shore of Squam Lake, with Holderness village at its end.

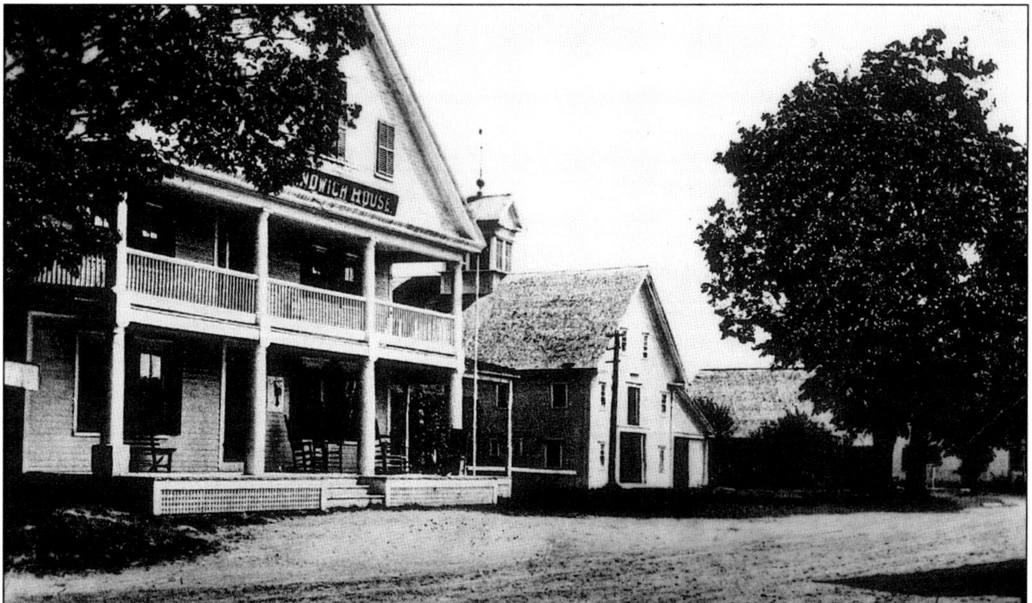

THE SANDWICH HOUSE. During the 1880s, there were three hotels in Center Sandwich: the Pleasant House, the Maple House, and the Sandwich House. Henry F. Dorr opened the Sandwich House in 1888. Previously, it had been the residence of C.C. Fellows, and before that the Red Hill House Hotel. This house could accommodate 30 guests and seat 50 people in its dining room. Situated on the southeast corner of Main and Maple Streets, it was considered the main hotel in town until it burned in 1916.

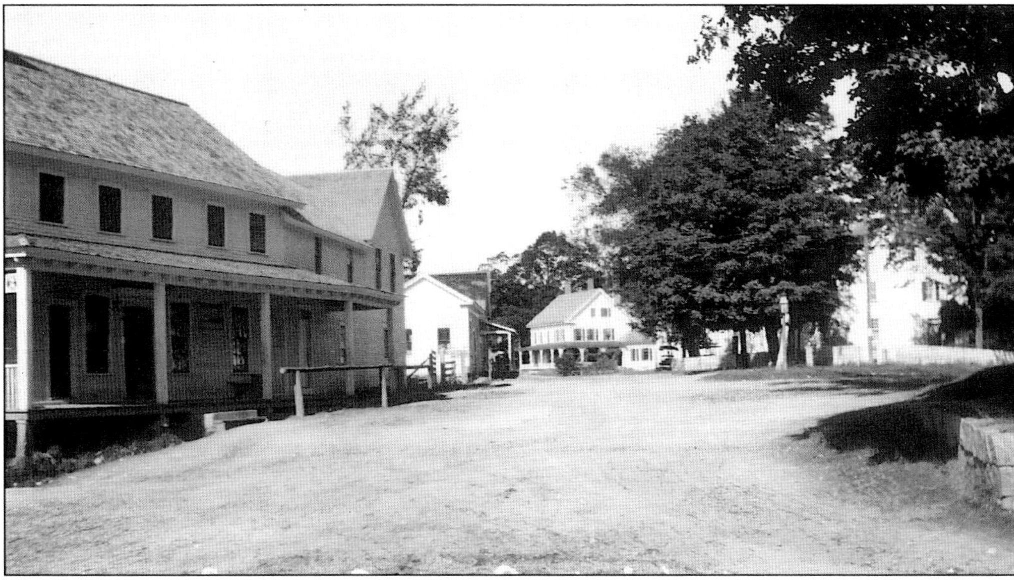

MAIN STREET, UPPER SQUARE. The village is located in a picturesque glen, surrounded by an amphitheater of mountains. This view looks north from the junction of Squam Lake Road, Main and Holderness Roads. The general store is in the distance on the left, and the Sandwich Inn is on the right. This village has been a favorite resort of many tourists. It is one of the best points from which to view Squam and Little Squam Lakes and Mounts Israel and Whiteface in the Sandwich Range.

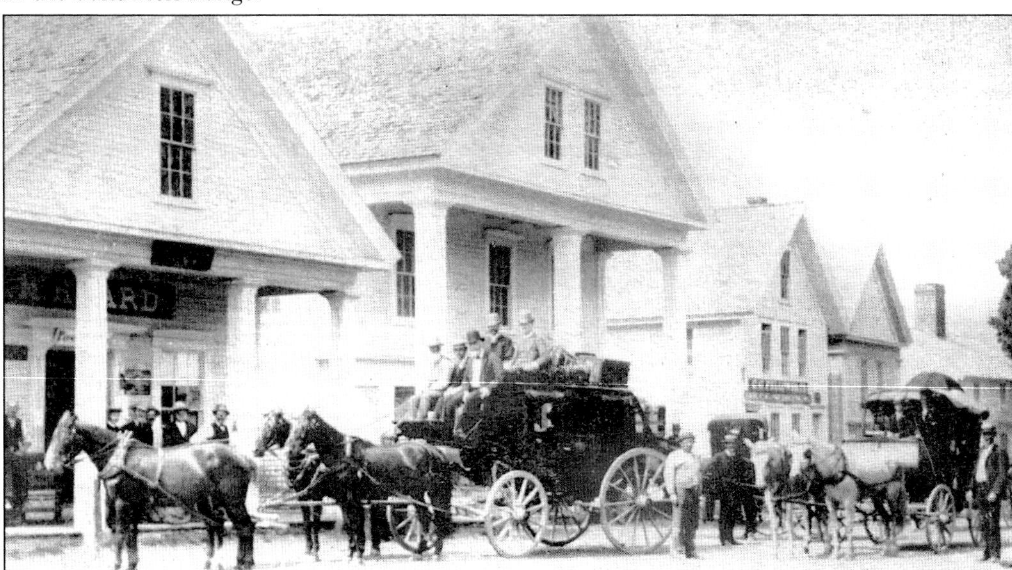

THE STAGECOACH LEAVING CENTER SANDWICH, LATE 1800S. The rail system never entered the bounds of Sandwich. However, the stagecoaches certainly made the town accessible to the outside world. In 1875, three stage routes passed through Sandwich: one from the Conways to Meredith, one from Sandwich to Wolfeboro, and one from Sandwich to West Ossipee. A mail route was added in 1896; the coach left Sandwich at 5:00 a.m., picked up passengers in North Sandwich, and arrived in West Ossipee at 7:30 a.m. From West Ossipee, passengers could take the Boston & Maine Railroad to Boston.

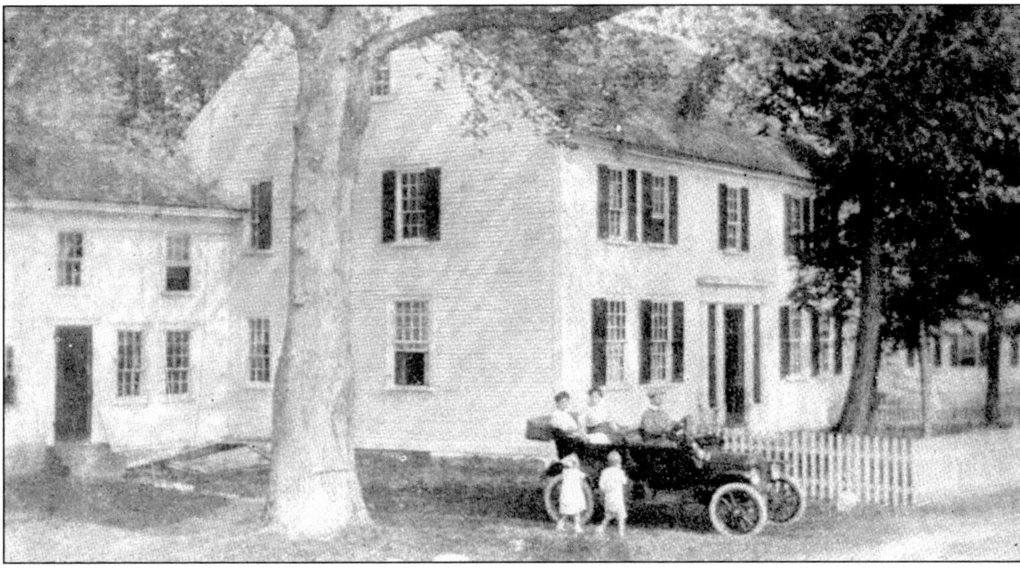

THE SANDWICH INN, MAIN STREET, THE 1920S. This popular inn was located in the center of Sandwich on Holderness Road. Today, the Colonial-style house serves as the Denley Emerson Real Estate office. A five-minute drive north from Sandwich Center is Diamond Ledge, from which a 50-mile view of the White Mountain ranges and lakes is seen. The view includes Lake Winnipesaukee, Squam Lake, Mount Chocorua, Rattlesnake Mountain, Whiteface Mountain, and Red Hill Mountain.

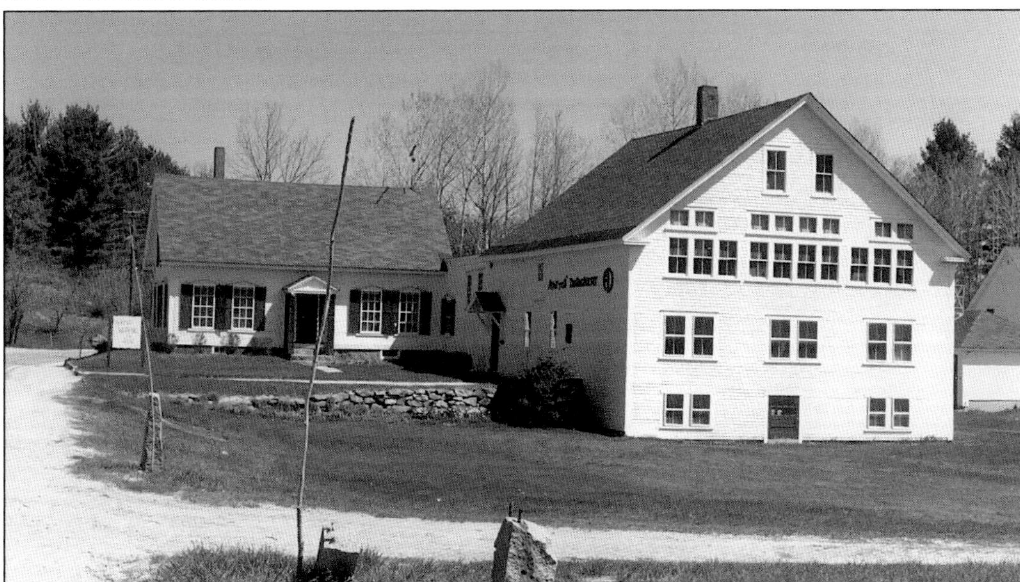

THE QUIMBY SCHOOL, CENTER SANDWICH. The Quimby School was originally founded in 1923. It was endowed by Alfred E. Quimby of Manchester to teach agriculture to young men and home economics to young women. In 1963, the school ceased operation and closed its doors. As part of the Inter-Lakes School System, students who had attended the Quimby School were transported to Inter-Lakes High School in Meredith. In 1966, Robert and Roberta Ayotte bought the old Quimby School and marketed their talents in weaving and design. They taught their craft to others, both in an innovative series of mail-order lessons and in classes at3 their shop.

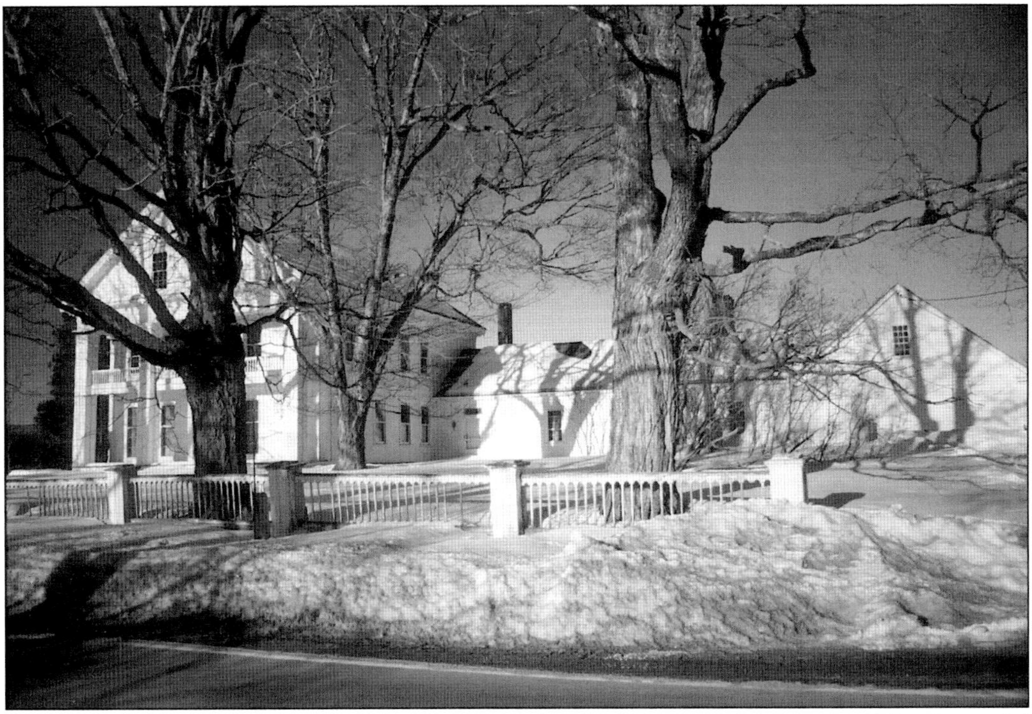

THE PAUL WENTWORTH HOUSE, WENTWORTH HILL, CENTER SANDWICH. This beautiful Greek Revival house, built in 1850 by Col. Joseph Wentworth (1818–1901), commands a magnificent panorama of the Sandwich Mountains and the quiet village of Center Sandwich. Wentworth was a dedicated farmer, postmaster, and storekeeper in Lower Corner. In 1870, he moved to Concord and deeded his estate and store to his son, Paul Wentworth (1846–1915).

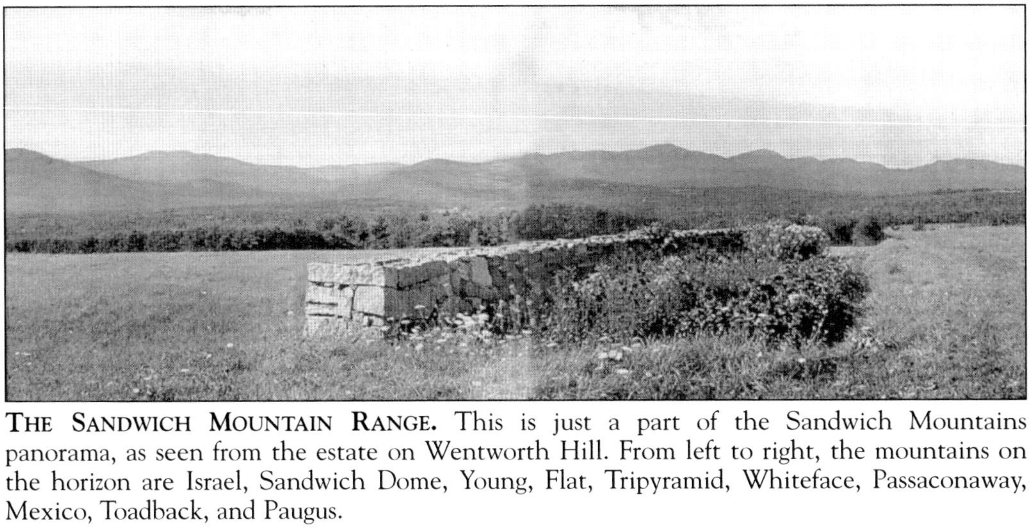

THE SANDWICH MOUNTAIN RANGE. This is just a part of the Sandwich Mountains panorama, as seen from the estate on Wentworth Hill. From left to right, the mountains on the horizon are Israel, Sandwich Dome, Young, Flat, Tripyramid, Whiteface, Passaconaway, Mexico, Toadback, and Paugus.

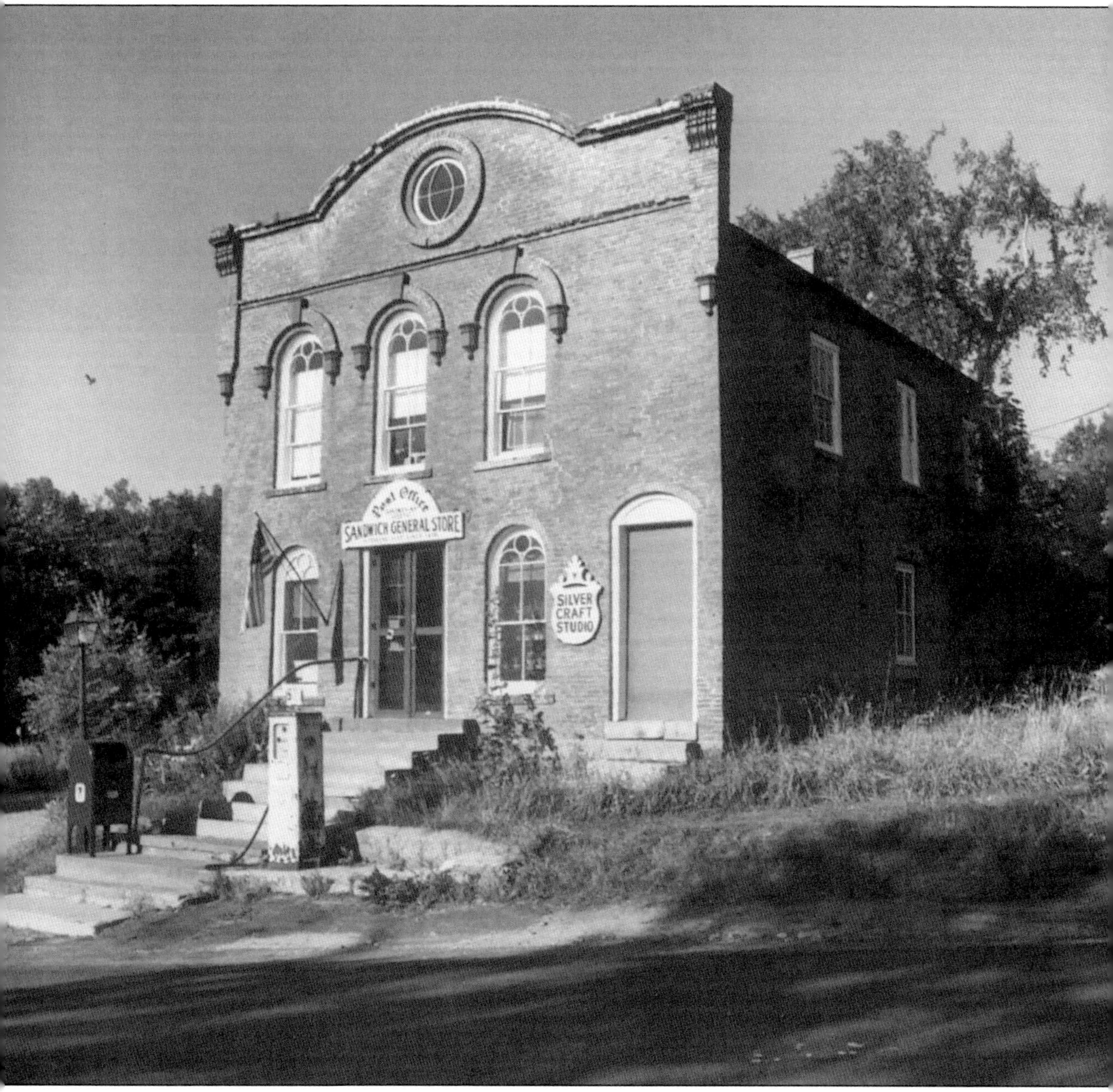

THE RED BRICK STORE, LOWER CORNER. Before Benjamin Burley opened his store at Lower Corner in 1785, men traveled to the lake on foot, crossed it by boat, and walked to Gilmanton, where they bought their supplies, which they carried home on their backs. The second owner of the store was Daniel Little, who ran it for 20 years. The third owner was Arven Blanchard, who ran it for 35 years, commencing in the 1840s. In recent years, it has been a grocery store and T.D. Gotshall's silver jewelry shop. The retirement home of actor Claude Raines was once directly across the street from the store.

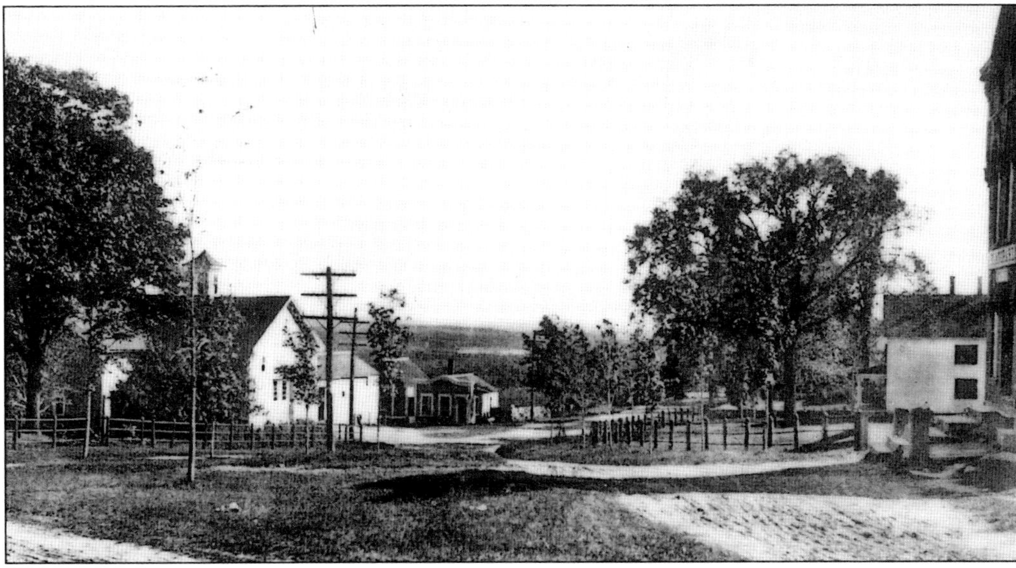

LOWER CORNER. The Lower Corner junction is a few yards south of the Wentworth Estate. Seen here are Red Brick Store, on the right, and the Ossipee Mountains, on the horizon. Straight ahead, the road comes to Moultonborough Corners where the Olde Country Store meets the Concord Stage. Turning left at the junction, the road leads to East Sandwich and Route 25.

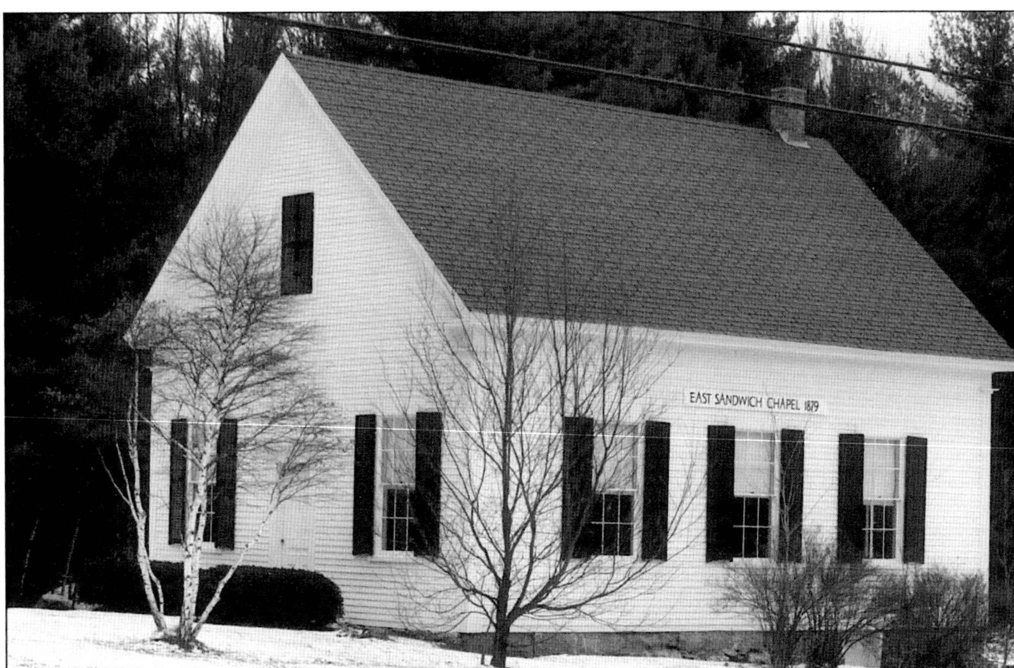

THE EAST SANDWICH CHAPEL, 1879. This chapel became the headquarters of the local temperance movement, where weekly meetings were held on Sunday evenings for 20 years. In January 1886, the Carroll County Temperance Convention was held at the chapel. The enthusiasm for the cause united men and women from all churches throughout the town and caused Sandwich to become a dry town in 1895.

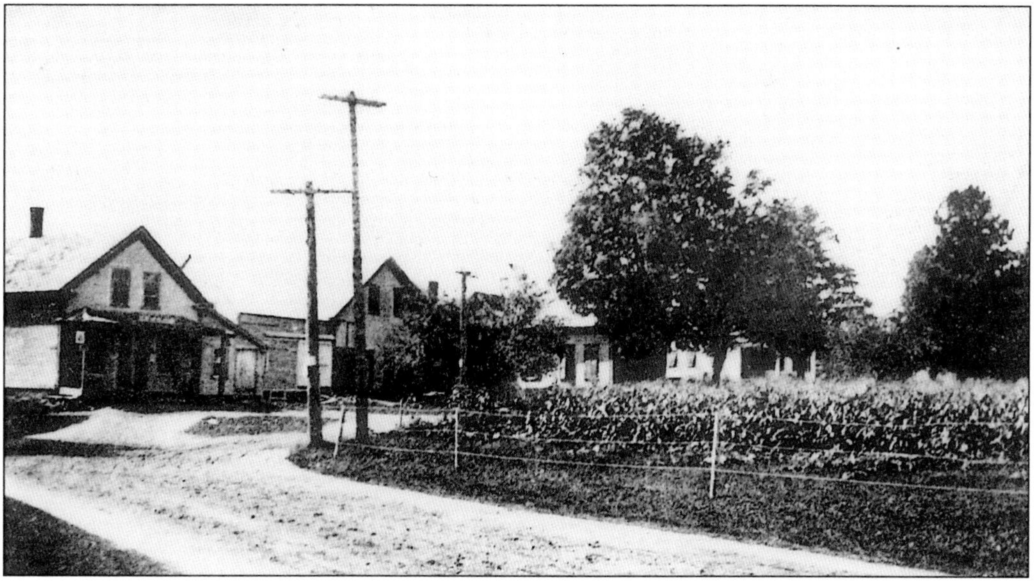

A VIEW OF NORTH SANDWICH AND THE GENERAL STORE (LEFT), 1920S. In North Sandwich and the Whiteface Intervale, some of the finest farms in the area may be found.

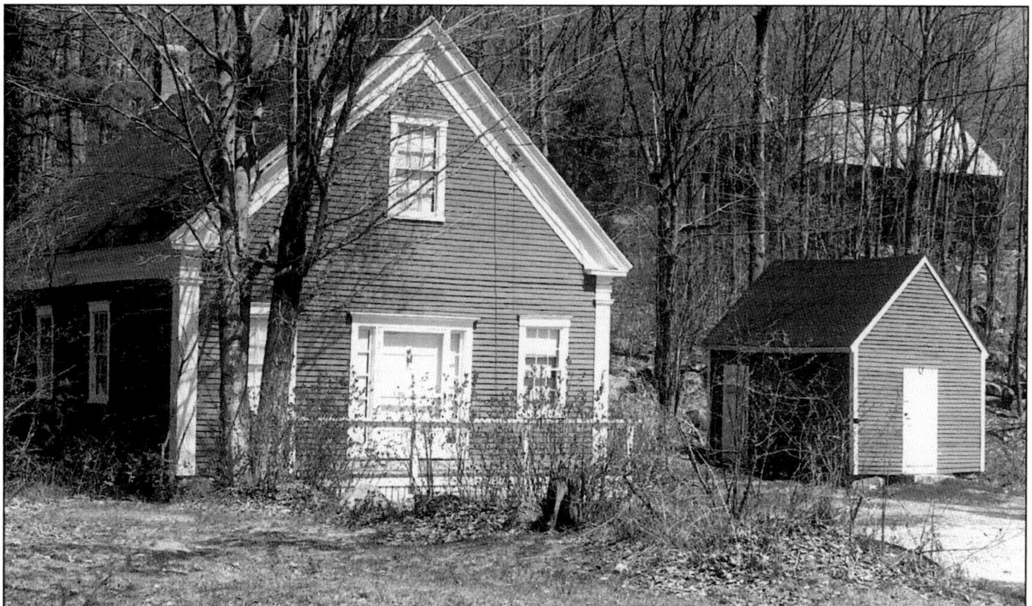

QUIMBY SCHOOLHOUSE NO. 11, NORTH SANDWICH. During the mid-1800s, there were as many as 25 district schools in Sandwich. These one-room schoolhouses were considered neighborhood schools. All the basic studies were taught: reading, writing, and arithmetic. In 1825, there were as many as 790 students attending the Sandwich district schools. Many of these schools were similar in design, with two doors on the front—one for the boys and one for the girls—and they often stood near an intersection of the roadway, such as the Quimby School in North Sandwich. The small building to the right was used as the outhouse.

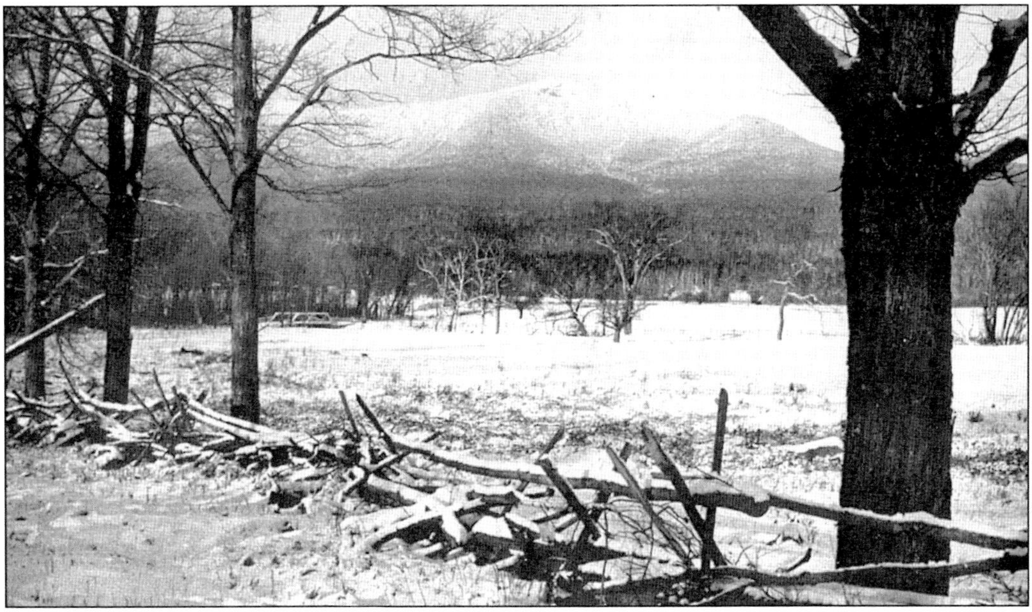

THE WHITEFACE INTERVALE. The largest farm in the Whiteface Intervale was first built by Henry McCrillis, who, with his wife, came to settle in 1780. His son Neal McCrillis (1792–1878) carried on the family farm. The Ambrose family also owned a large farm in the Whiteface Intervale. In 1868, Ambrose moved there from Sandwich Center and kept a large herd of cattle. Later, his son Langdon Ambrose (1855–1944) carried on the family farm, harvesting a large amount of maple sugar.

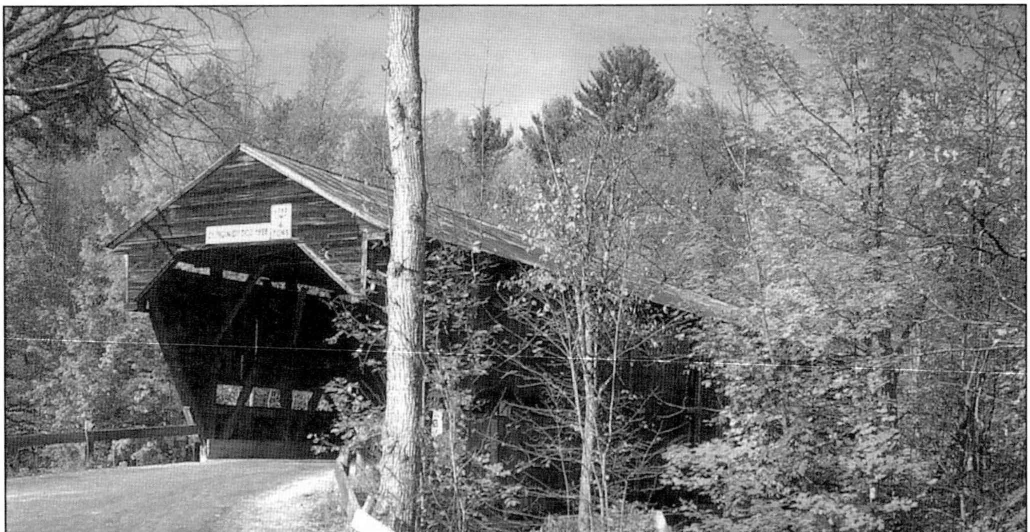

DURGIN BRIDGE NO. 45, NORTH SANDWICH. Originally built in 1826, the present bridge is the fifth built over the easily flooded Cold River. This structure was named for James Holmes Durgin (1815–1873), who operated a gristmill near this crossing, drove the stagecoach from Sandwich to Farmington, and was a link in the Underground Railroad. Durgin Bridge is one of the few remaining wooden Paddleford truss bridges in the state. It has an overall length of 110 feet and an outside width of 19 feet. The roadway within the bridge is 96 feet long and 14 feet wide. It was built by Jacob Berry.

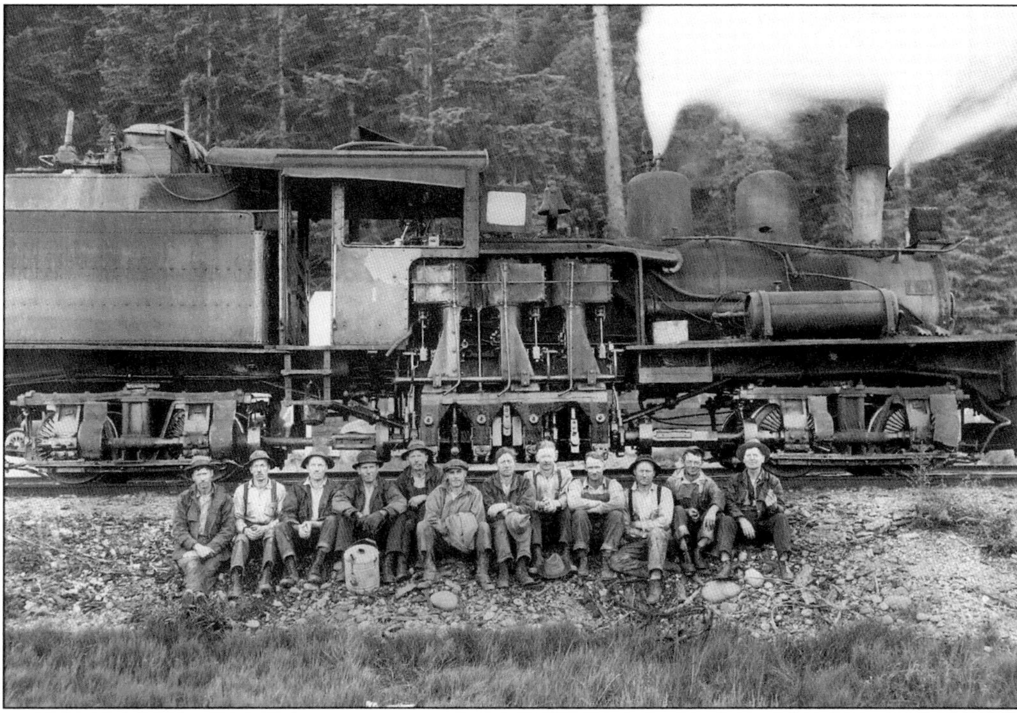

AN EARLY LOGGING LOCOMOTIVE, SANDWICH NOTCH, THE 1920S. The Sandwich Notch logging railroad was in full operation by 1920, with 12 camps and a huge imported labor force of 408 men. This manpower consisted mostly of the new immigrants—including 95 Russians and 65 French Canadians—who worked as choppers, teamsters, loaders, landing rollers, sled tenders, saw filers, blacksmiths, carpenters, and cooks.

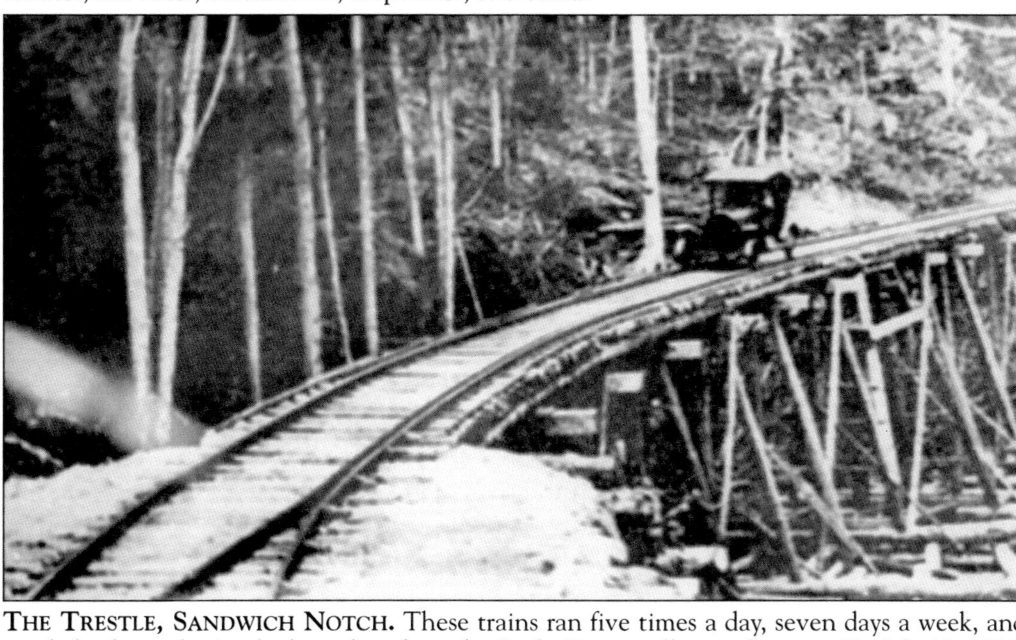

THE TRESTLE, SANDWICH NOTCH. These trains ran five times a day, seven days a week, and needed a dispatcher's telephone line from the Beebe River mill to each camp. On July 12, 1923, the entire operation came to a virtual halt.

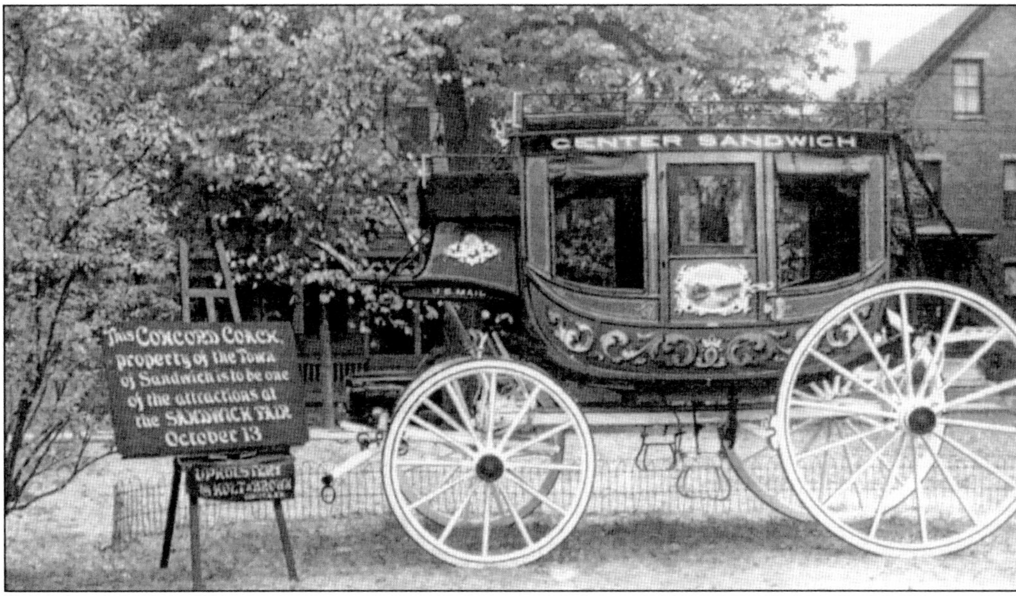

THE CONCORD COACH, CENTER SANDWICH. The original coach is the property of the Sandwich Historical Society, and it is generally used for the Sandwich Fair Parade that is held in early October each year. The origin of the Sandwich Fair dates back to October 4, 1892, when the Sandwich Grange encouraged agricultural fairs. The Sandwich Grange held the first Sandwich Fair and, in 1894, the Sandwich Town and Grange Fair Association was formed. Since its formation, the Sandwich Fair has become a very popular attraction, featuring cattle-pulling contests; vegetable, art, and crafts exhibits; and a grand midway. However, a major part of the fair has always been the parade.

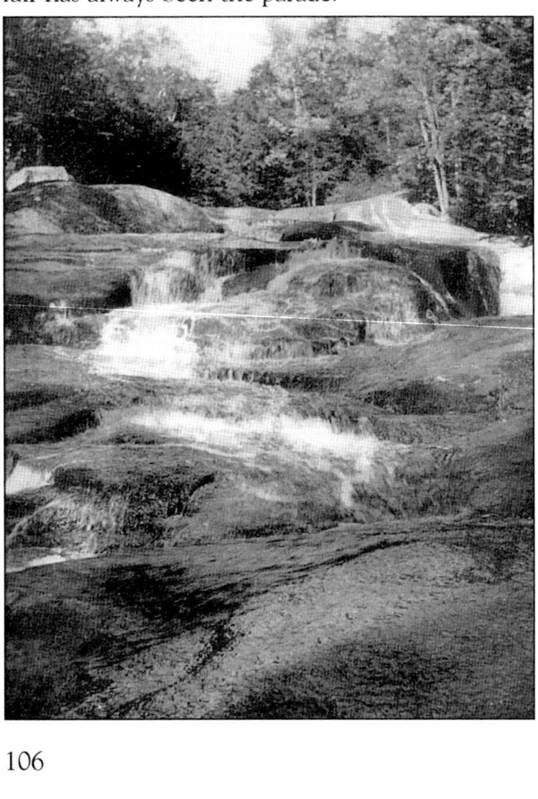

BEEDE FALLS (COW CAVE). This popular area was made into a park during the Great Depression, when the Civilian Conservation Corps (CCC) developed the Cow Cave-Beede Falls area into a public park. This beautifully secluded area is located on Sandwich Notch Road a few miles north of Sandwich Center.

Seven

Epilogue and Reflections

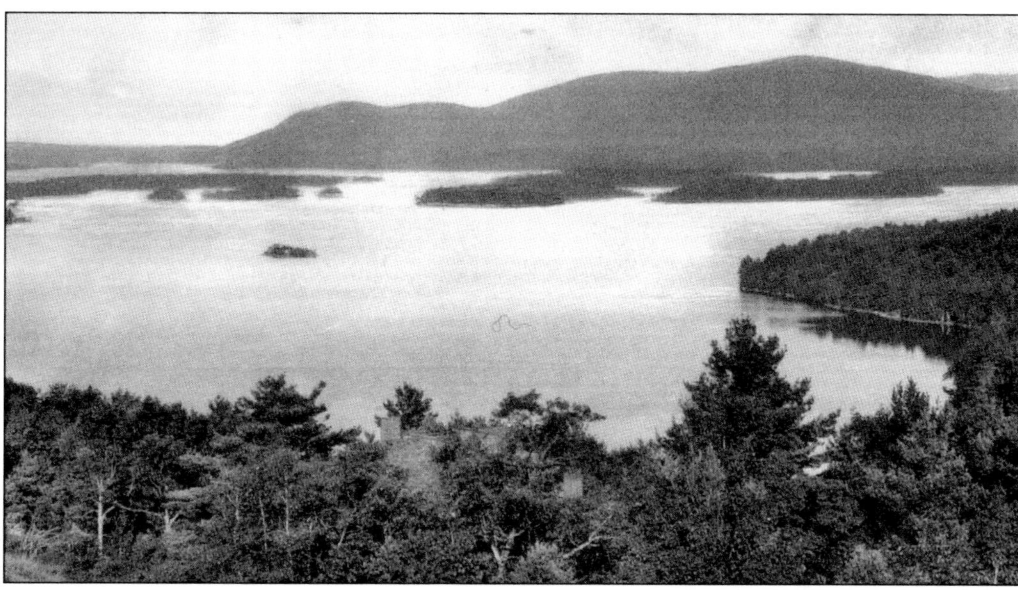

Squam Lake, from the Asquam Hotel, Looking Southeast to Red Hill. It is not a sense of seclusion amid the forest—of being shut in by untamed hills amid the heart of the wilderness—that Squam Lake inspires. The lake is not shut in by any abrupt mountain wall. Its shore and islands fringe the water with winding lines and long capes of green. But the mountains retreat, leaving large spaces of cheerful light and vistas of more sloping land.

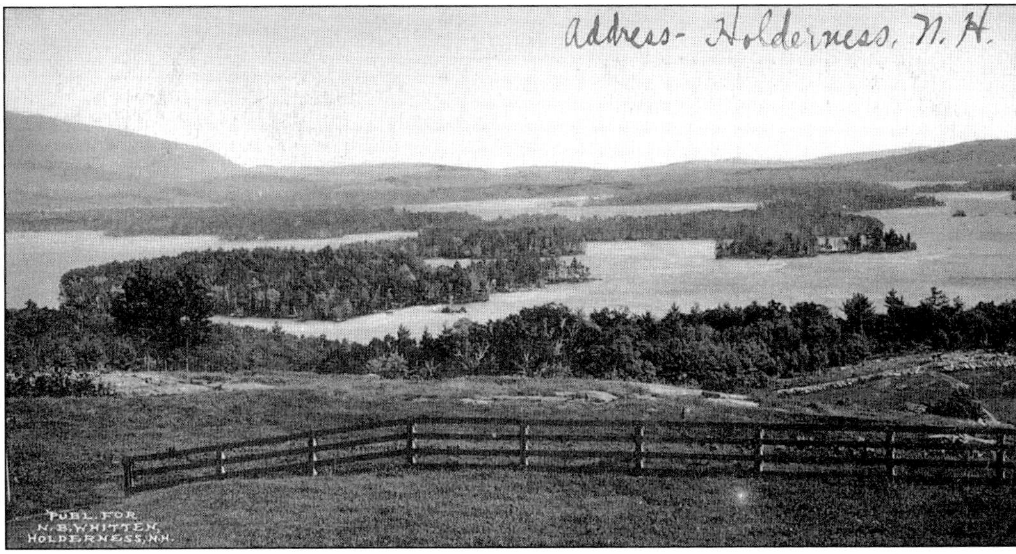

A View Looking Southwest toward Squam Lake. Taken in 1907 in a southwesterward direction from the Webster Estate, this breathtaking view reveals the open water with its many islands.

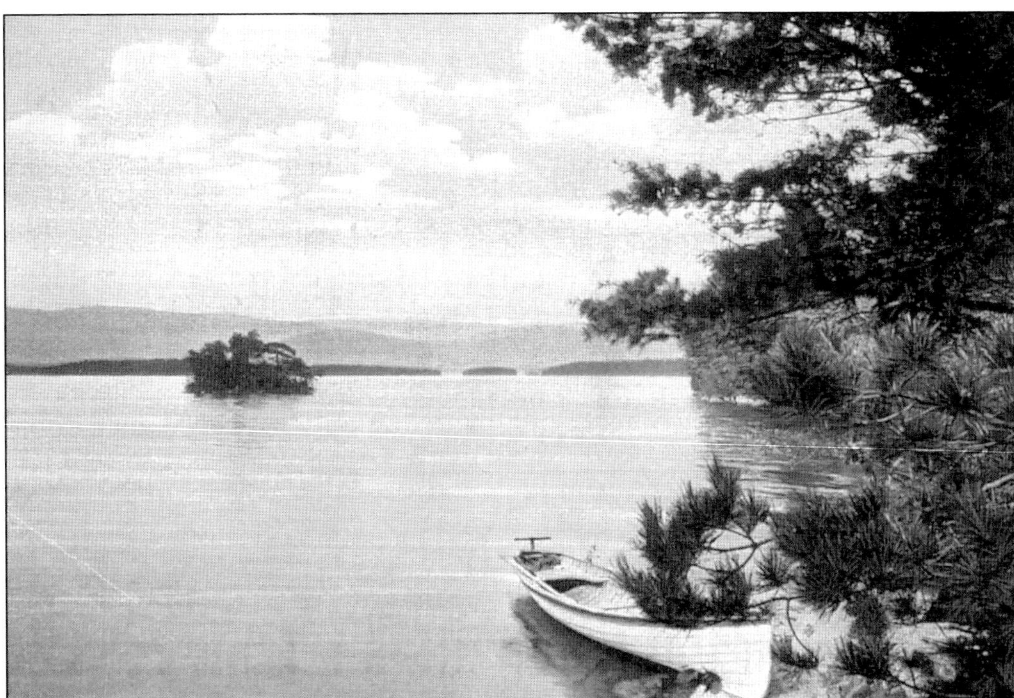

A Quiet Cove, Squam Lake, 1938. The sky is clear, the moment is peaceful. There are clouds enough to relieve the soft blue and fleck the sentinel hills in the far distance. The foliage gracefully shadows the shore with a dreamy haze, tinting the lone boat with the warmth of summer solitude.

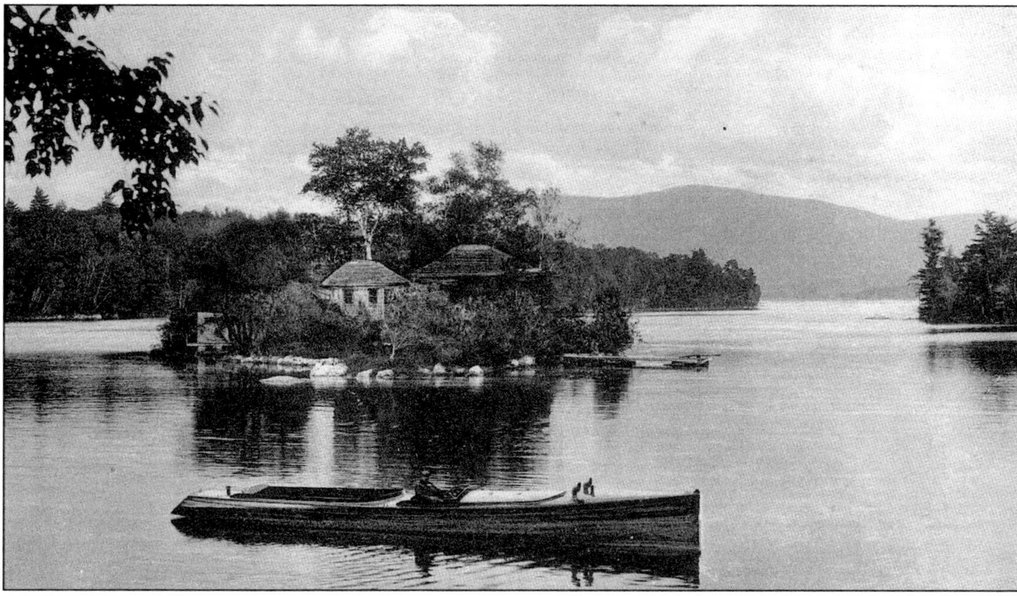

CAIRNS COVE, SQUAM LAKE. What a rare joy, when on a warm July afternoon, we may set afloat our craft and drift in some secluded cove, so as to celebrate the harvest of midday.

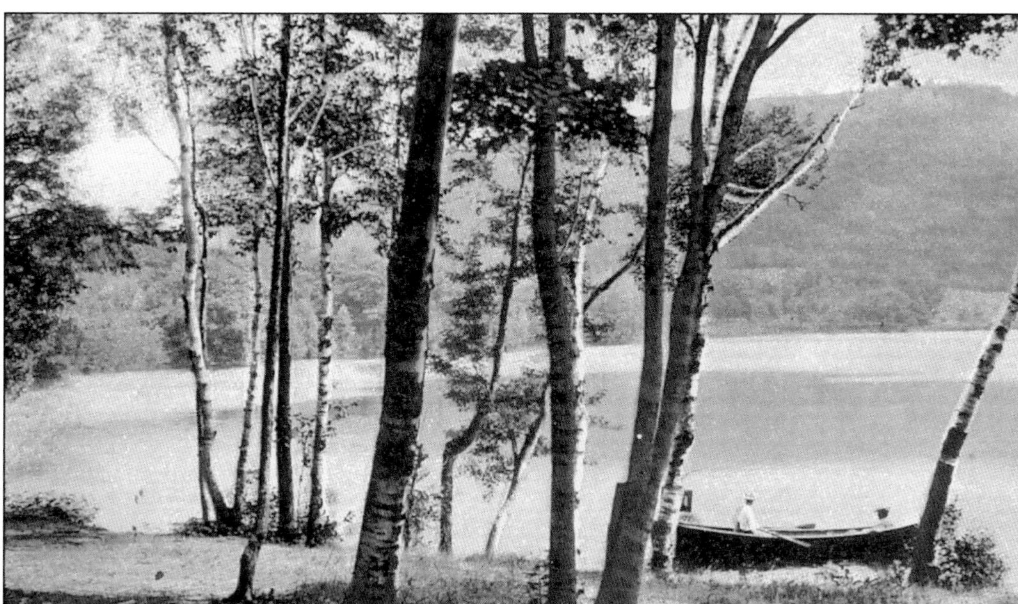

THE BIRCHES ON THE SHORELINE, SQUAM LAKE, 1907. Perhaps there is a faint breeze across the water; however, there is no ripple on its surface.

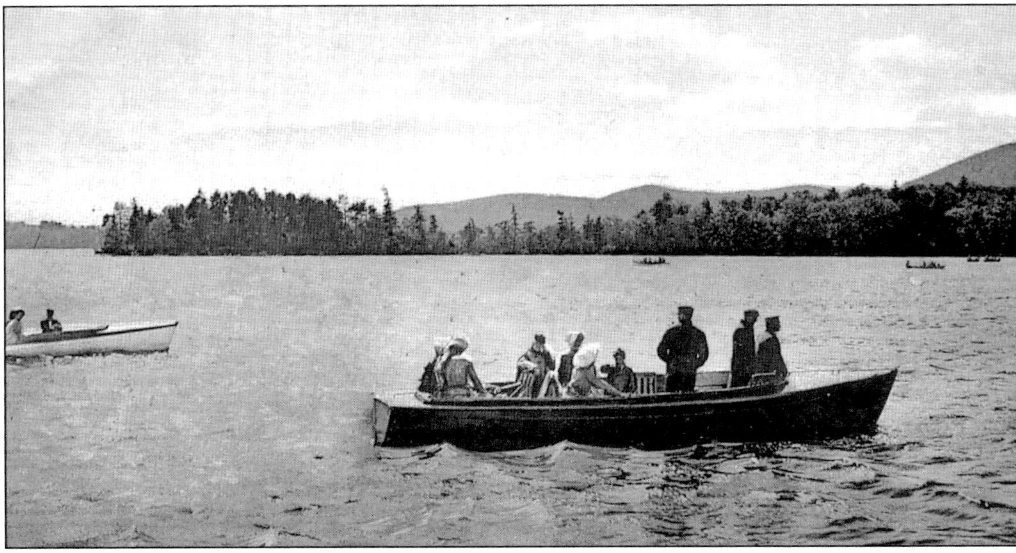

BOATING NEAR COITE'S POINT, SQUAM LAKE, C. THE 1930S. A midday excursion is often seen on Squam Lake, as visitors dressed in fine attire enjoy the summer breeze off the lake.

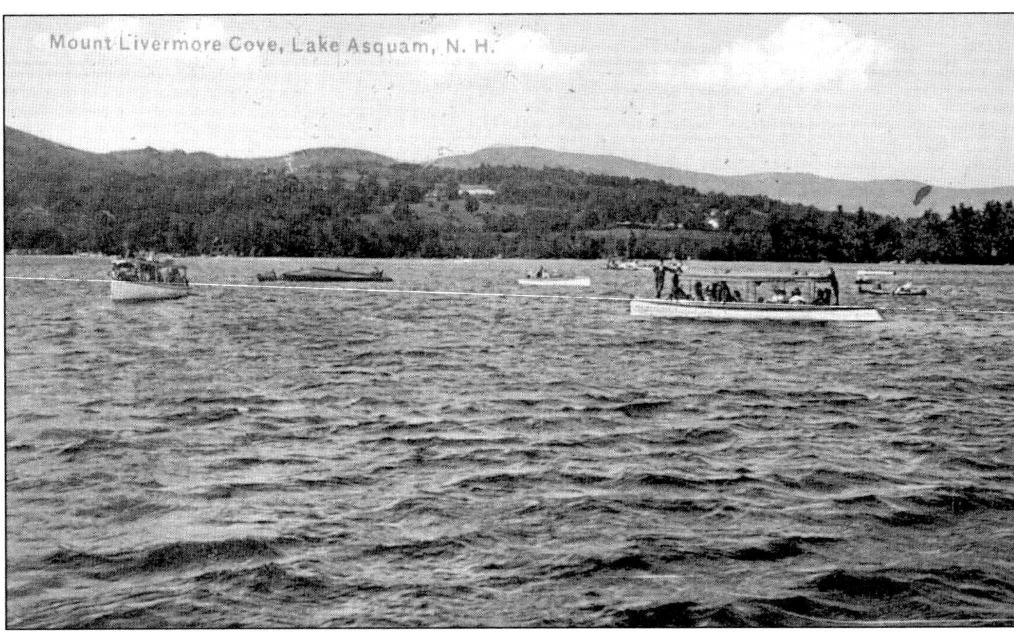

AN EARLY STEAMER, MOUNT LIVERMORE COVE, SQUAM LAKE. From the late 1800s to the late 1920s, private vessels joined in the parade of steamers.

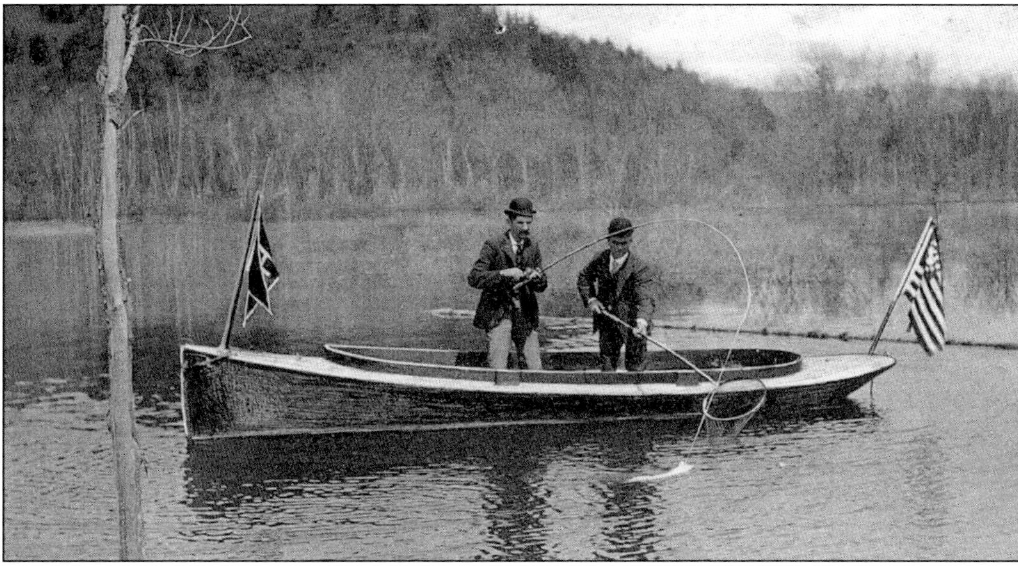

A QUIET MOMENT OF FISHING, THE SQUAM RIVER, ASHLAND. These two men, in their best suits and derby hats, are dressed for the special occasion of catching the one big lake trout of the season.

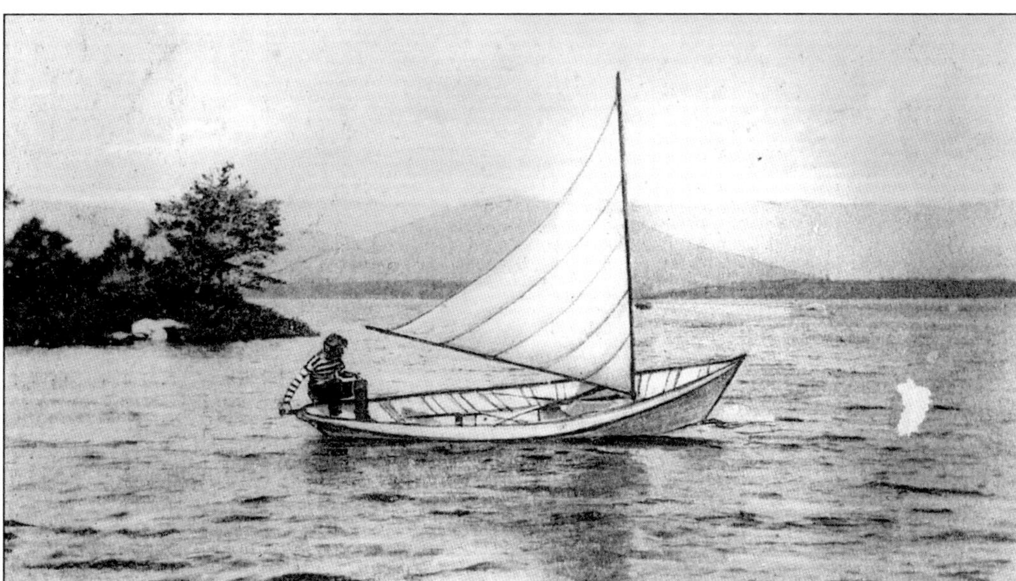

SAILING ON SQUAM LAKE NEAR ROCKYWOLD, SEPTEMBER 1908. This camper from Rockywold has found the perfect breeze on Squam Lake.

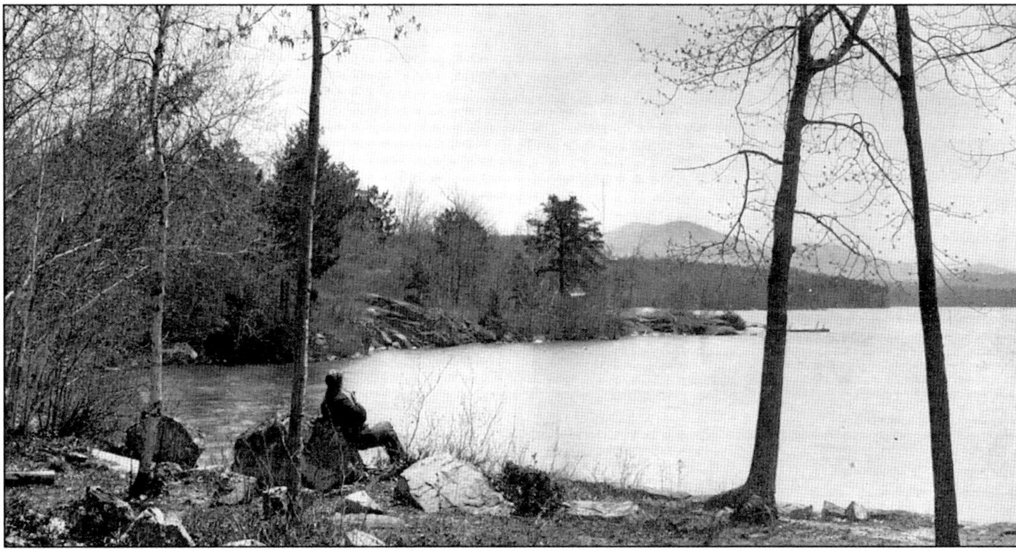

A Pipe Dream. A quiet moment of reflection may be had on the shore at this secluded inlet of Squam Lake. As early as the mid-1800s, when the Boston, Concord, and Montreal Railroad provided easy access to the Lakes Region, thousands of visitors flocked to enjoy the quietness of the lakes away from the city.

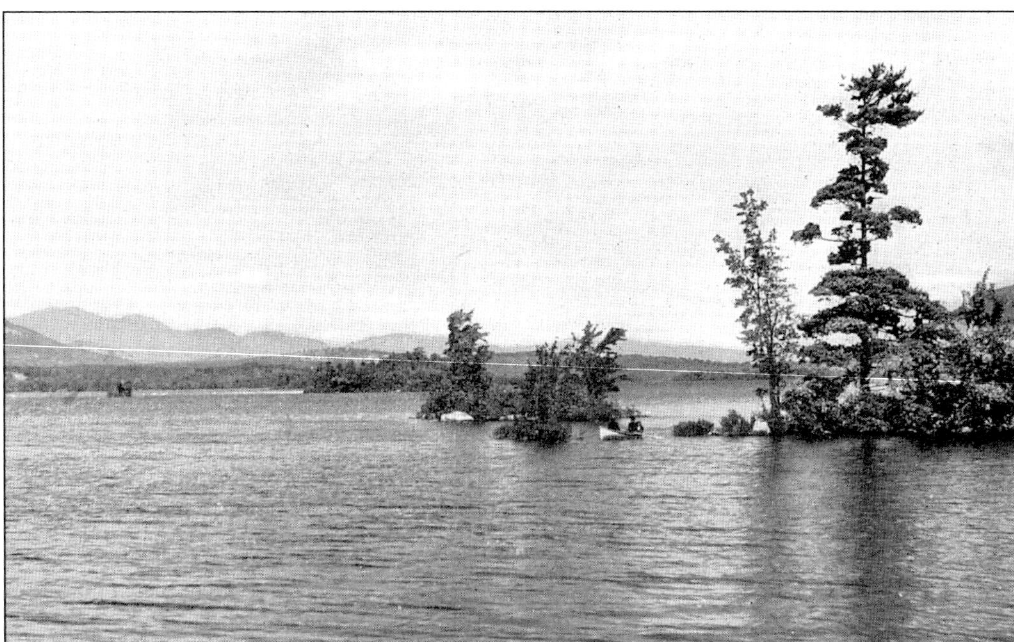

Canoeing among the Islands. There is no better feeling than to canoe alone among the islands on the lake. During the late 19th century and the early 20th century, many tourists rented or bought small affordable boats so that they could feel the restfulness of a quiet lake.

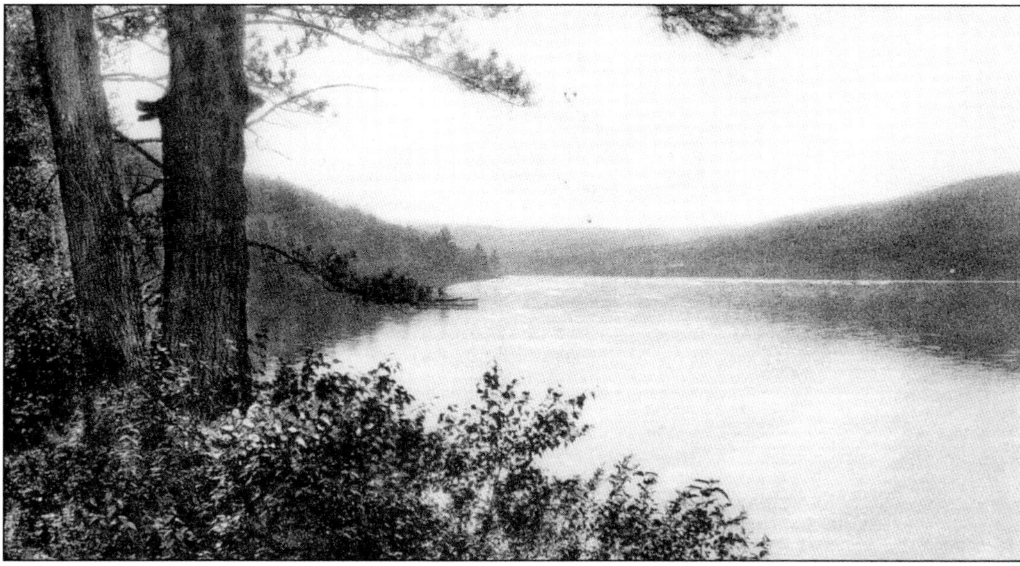

LITTLE SQUAM LAKE, HOLDERNESS, LOOKING WEST. The murmuring pines and hemlocks beckon us to spend a reflective moment alone in nature. Framing the shore of Squam Lake is an abundance of pine, spruce, hemlock, oak, maple, and birch, which add life and color to Mother Nature's beauty.

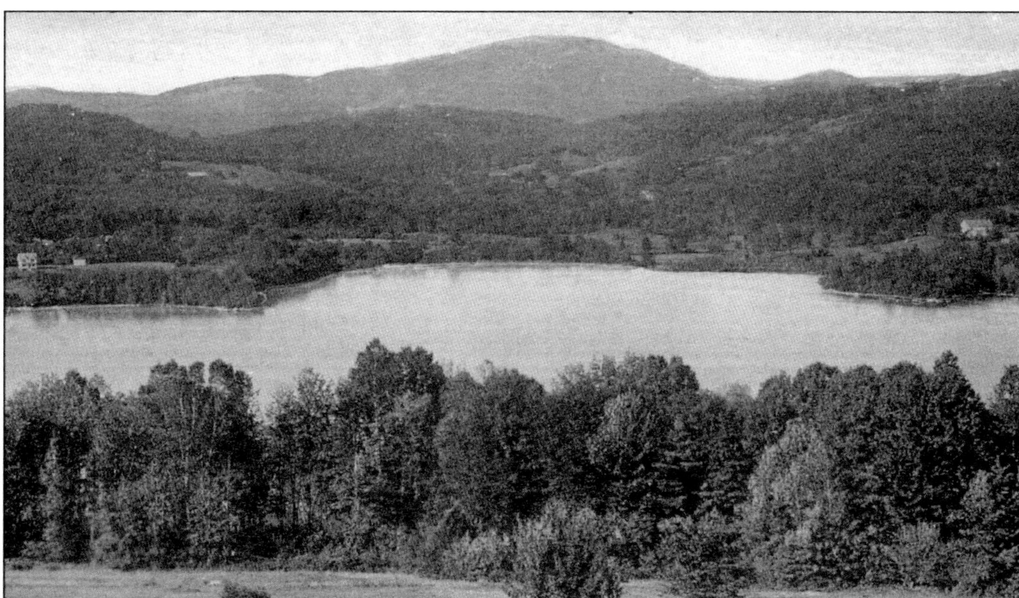

LITTLE SQUAM LAKE, FROM LAKE VIEW FARM, ASHLAND. From the rich green pastures that embrace the countryside, our vista of Little Squam Lake and the distant mountains draws us to a time primeval. The forest and farmland are richly displayed around the lake, adding to the original quality of life as once seen by our forefathers hundreds of years ago.

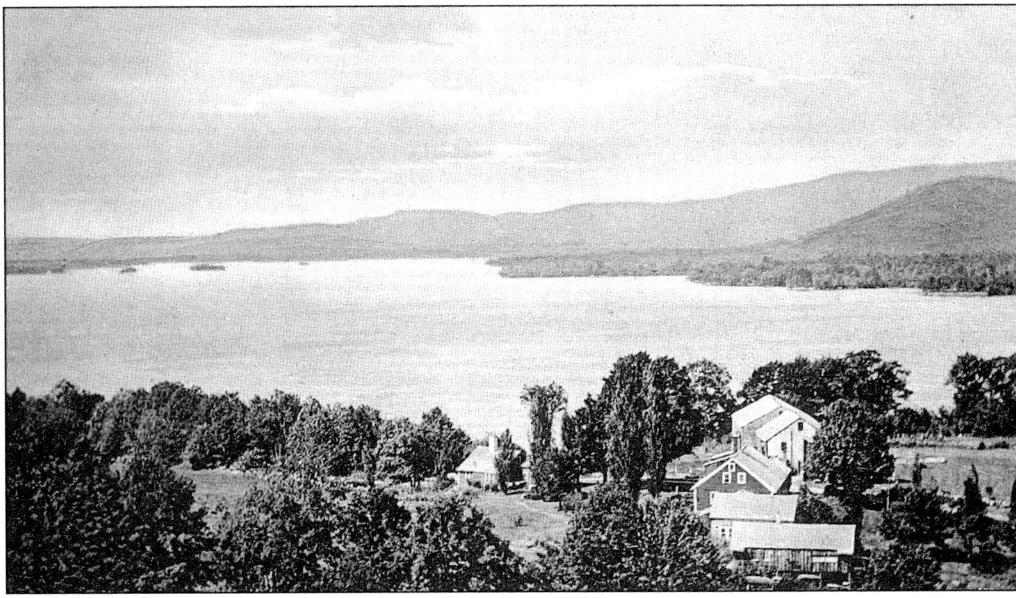

A PANORAMIC VIEW OF SQUAM LAKE FROM RED HILL, SANDWICH. The quiet of the water and the hills seems to have the quality of still ecstasy. There is a romantic enchantment in the air; this paradise seems to open wide its gates to our gaze. We stand silent and spellbound with a stranger. We feel a thrill when a voice from the forest breaks the solemn stillness of this almost supernatural vision. Our minds ramble over the most striking incidents of sculpture, when the sublimity of the scene is always in harmony with the grandeur of this moment. Besides a few summer cottages and farmhouses clustered about the shoreline and nearby hills, Squam Lakes remains as a Golden Pond with its charm and seclusion.

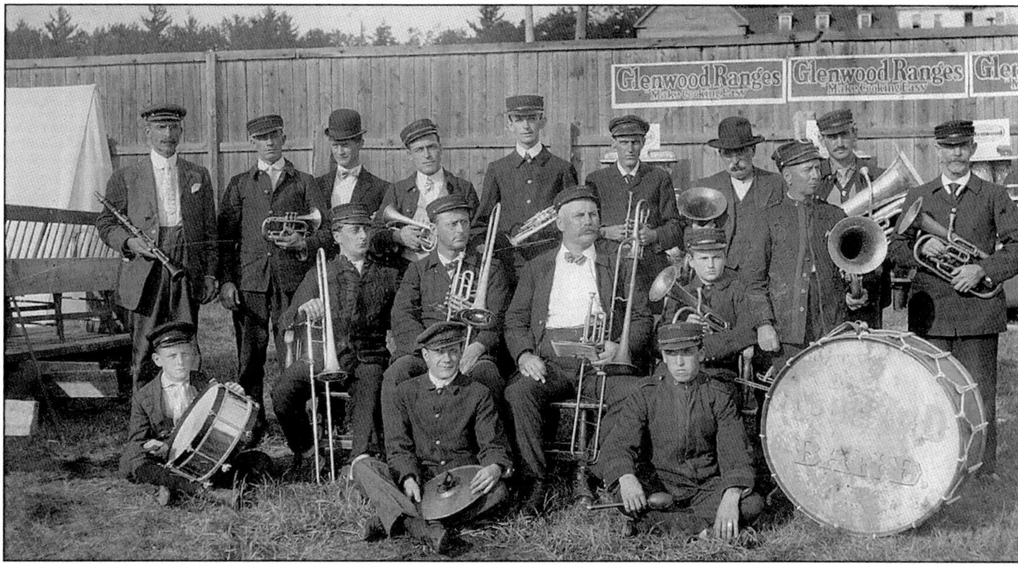

The Ashland Town Band, October 1, 1908. For many years, the pride of each community was the town band. During the summer months, it was not uncommon to hear and see the local band perform in the village square or at the bandstand each Saturday night. In some towns, this tradition has continued with weekly Saturday night concerts open to the public. Center Harbor is one such town. Seen here, from left to right, are the following: (front row) Leslie Wheeler, Lewis Tallier, and John Flanders; (middle row) Tom Smith, Curt Eastman, Charles Clough, Roy Clough, and Brooks Wheeler; (back row) Charles Shaw, Joe Rattan, Herbert Greenwood, Henry Peaslee, Harry Allard, Rodney Evans, Dan Bowen, Edgar Eastman, and James Welsh.

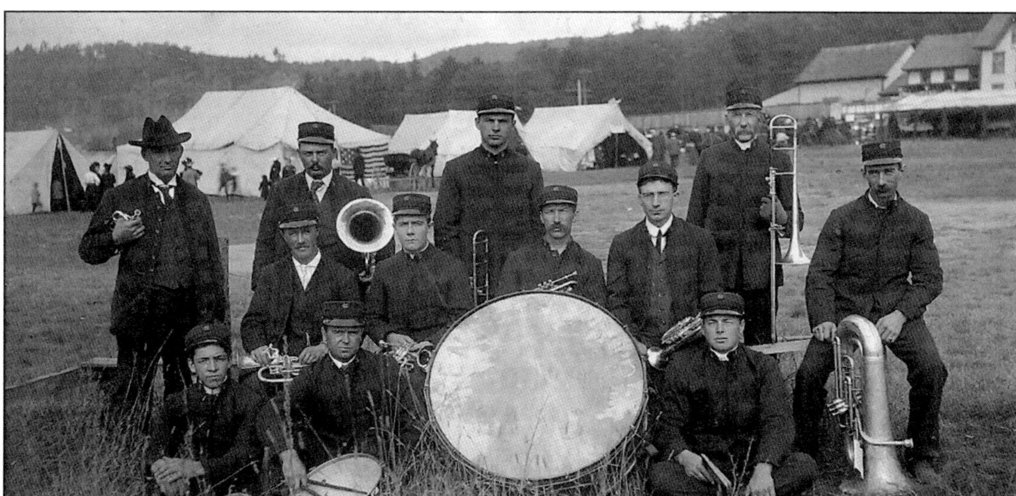

The Center Harbor Town Band at the Ashland Fair, 1904. The Center Harbor Band is considered the oldest town band in the state. Stephinus Kelley founded the band in November 1878. Since then, it has performed continuously during the summer for more than 123 years. Members seen here, from left to right, are as follows: (front row) Lester Blackey, Albert Kelley, and Charles Sanborn; (middle row) Minot Bickford, Perley Bryant, Edgar Smith, Henry Leighton, and John Perkins; (back row) Carl Paine, Louis Kelley, Percy Kelley, and Stephinus Kelley.

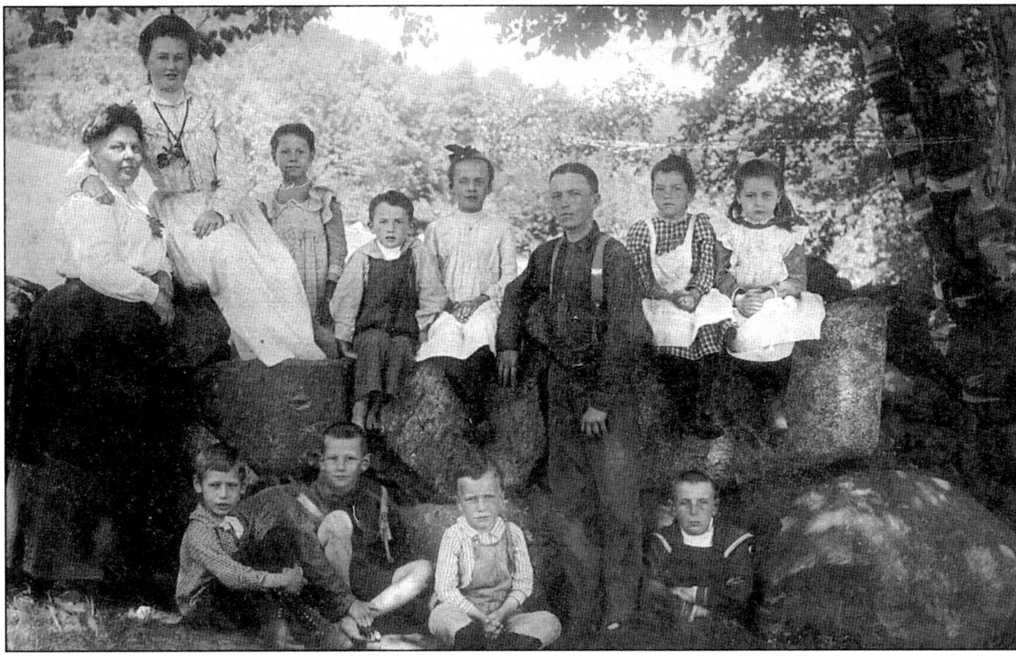

THE CRAM SCHOOL, WEST CENTER HARBOR. Seen here, from left to right, are teacher Delia Kelley, Blanch Boynton, Mary Webster, Edgar Davis, Hazel Davis, Leon Hawkins, Lavinia Lovett, May Bartlett, Paul H. Perkins, Edward Webster, Leon M. Huntress, and Otis Hawkins.

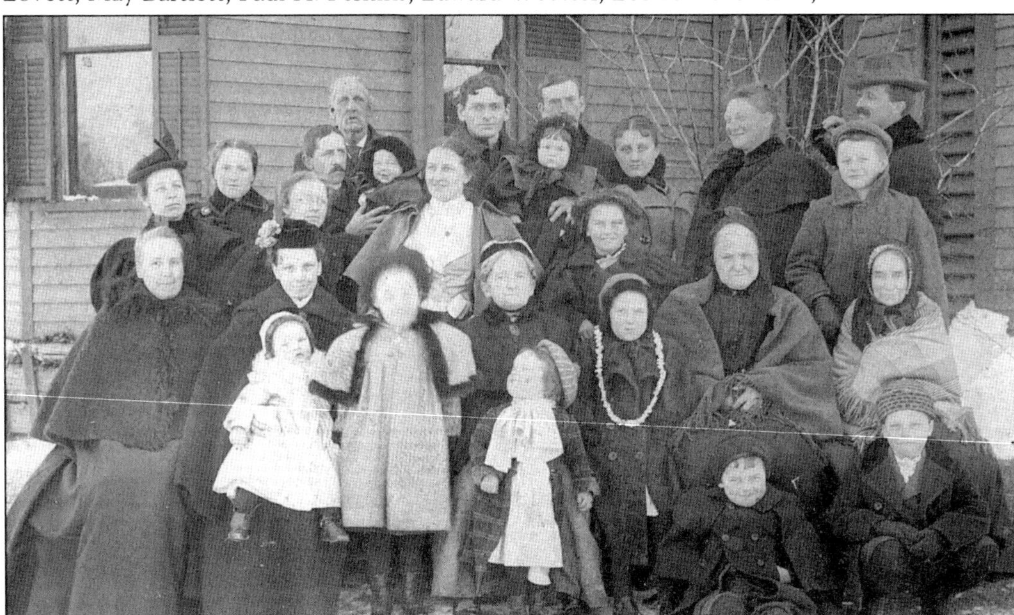

A CLASS PICTURE AT MOULTONBOROUGH CENTRAL SCHOOL, 1927. Seen here, from left to right, are the following: (front row) Katherine Smith, Gertrude Merrill, Mildred Davis, Frances George, Thomas Abbott, Robert Lamprey, and Burleigh Moulton; (middle row) Ruth Shaw, Mary Cram, Robert Shaw, Richard Moulton, Richard Hatfield, Richard Martin, Arthur Lamprey, Edwin Brouillard, and Robert Spafford (teacher); (back row) Richard David, Charles Whitehouse, Lee Porter, Edna Cram, Mildred Glidden, and Herbert Martin.

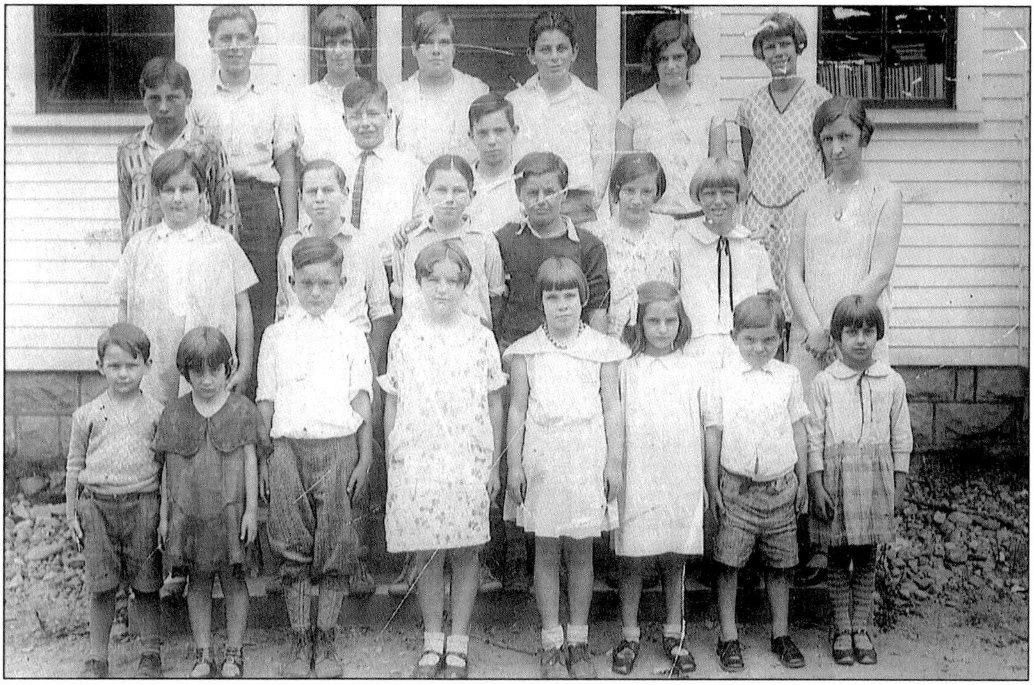

A CLASS PICTURE AT THE BRIDGE SCHOOL, HOLDERNESS, 1930. Seen here, from left to right, are the following: (first row) Lloyd Perkins, Dorothy Perkins, Harry Heath, Rita Sommers, Ester Marden, Arlene Davie, Cleston Davie, and Doris Perkins; (second row) Phyllis Sommers, Kenneth Hawkins, Clifton Hawkins, Louis Francisco, Barbara Forbes, Thelma Watts, and Ruth Prescott (teacher); (third row) Rocky Guyotte, Lester Heath, and Robert Marden; (fourth row) John Davison, Eleanor Downer, Marion Marden, Roger Hawkins, Corinne Welch, and Glenna Watts.

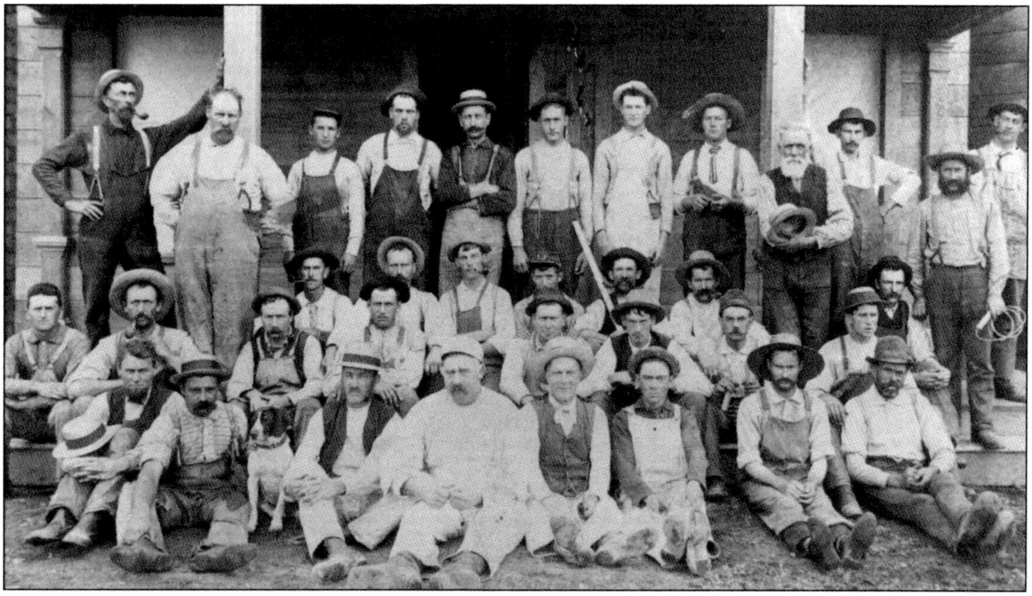

THE CONSTRUCTION CREW FOR ROXMONT, 1889. Several years were spent in constructing the castle called Roxmont, Dr, J. Alonzo Greene's unique home on Moultonborough Neck.

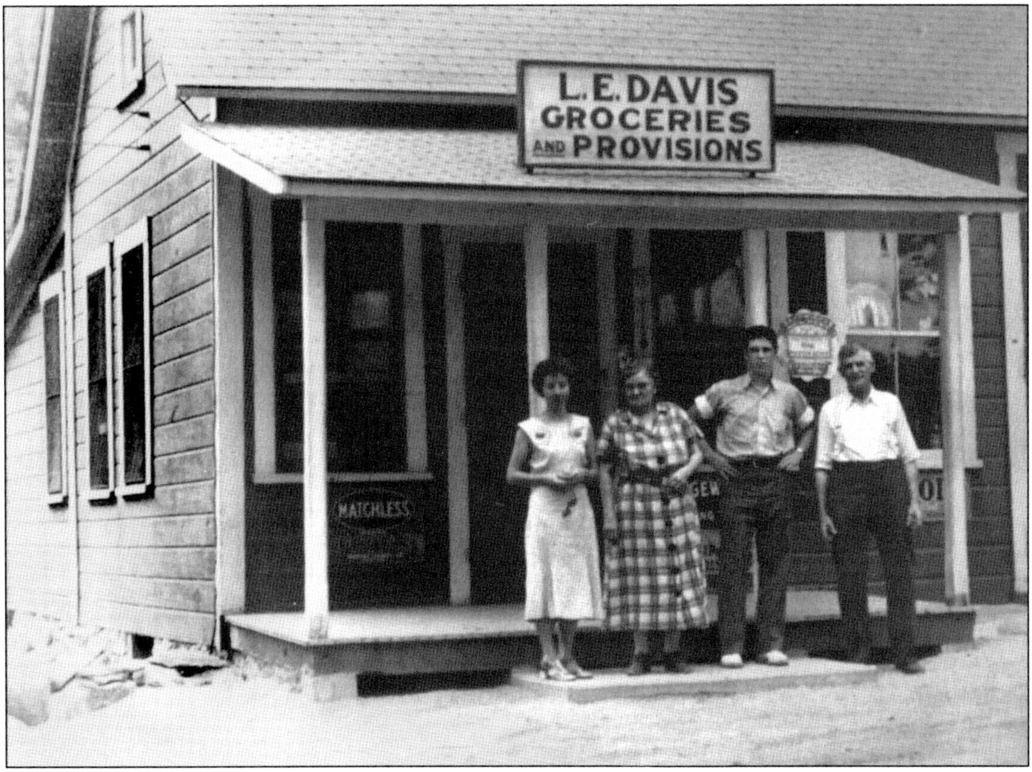

L.E. DAVIS GROCERIES AND PROVISIONS, 1938. This was the original General Store on Moultonborough Neck. Pictured are unidentified, Ada Davis, Richard McCormack, and Lynn Davis.

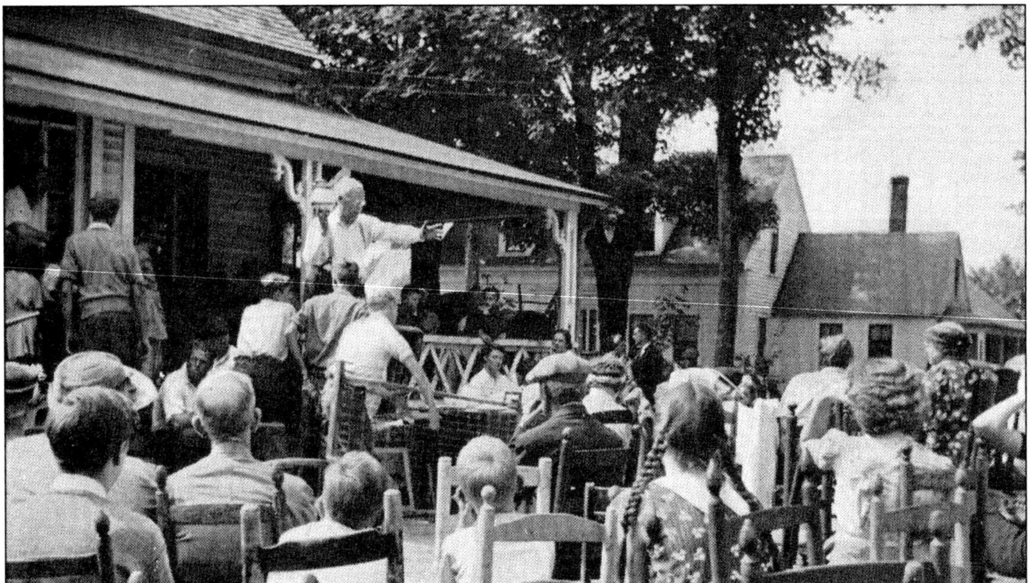

THE COUNTRY AUCTION, THE 1960S. A very popular summer activity is always the country auction. Here is a typical view of such an auction in progress in Sandwich.

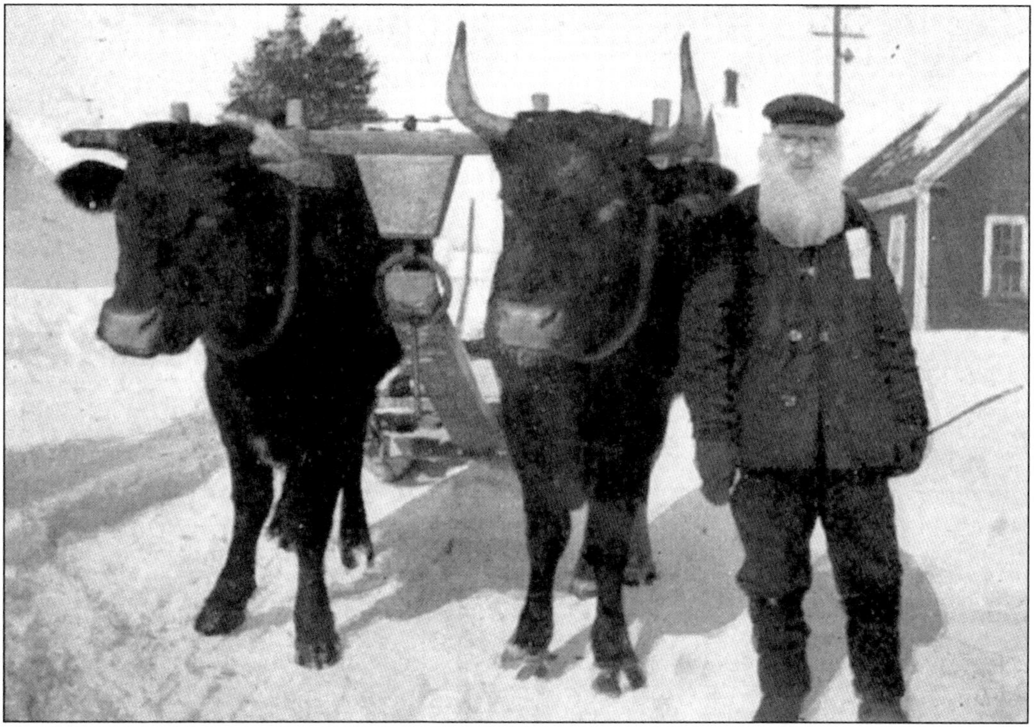

JULIUS KNOCKMAN AND HIS OXEN, ASHLAND. Many years ago, Julius Knockman, with his pair of oxen, was affectionately known as a very colorful character in Ashland.

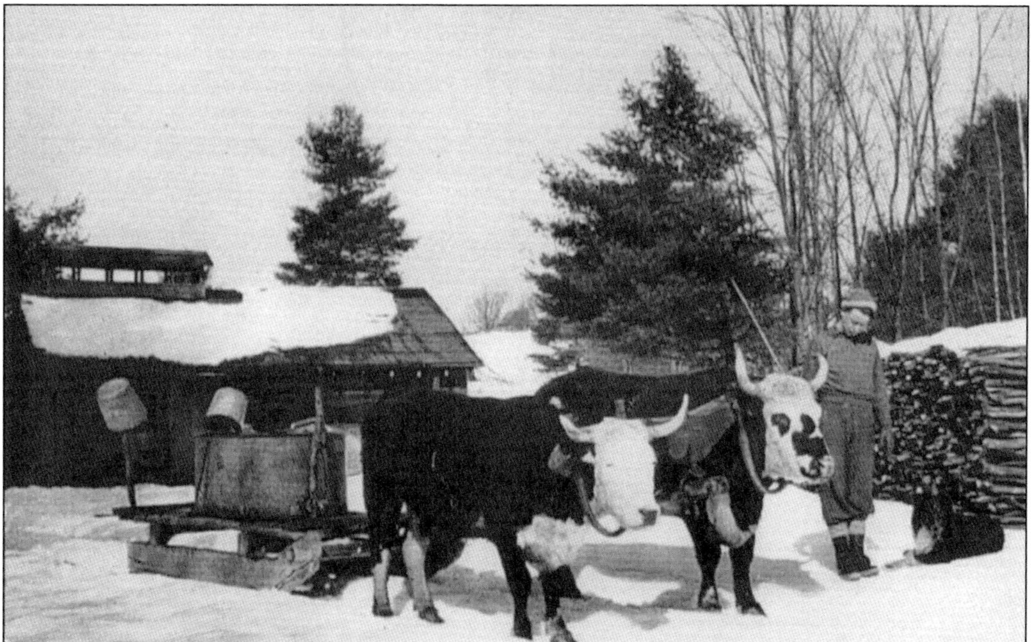

A YOUNG LAD WITH A DOUBLE-OX TEAM, C. THE 1930S. This team is very possibly from Wesley Tewksbury homestead in Sandwich.

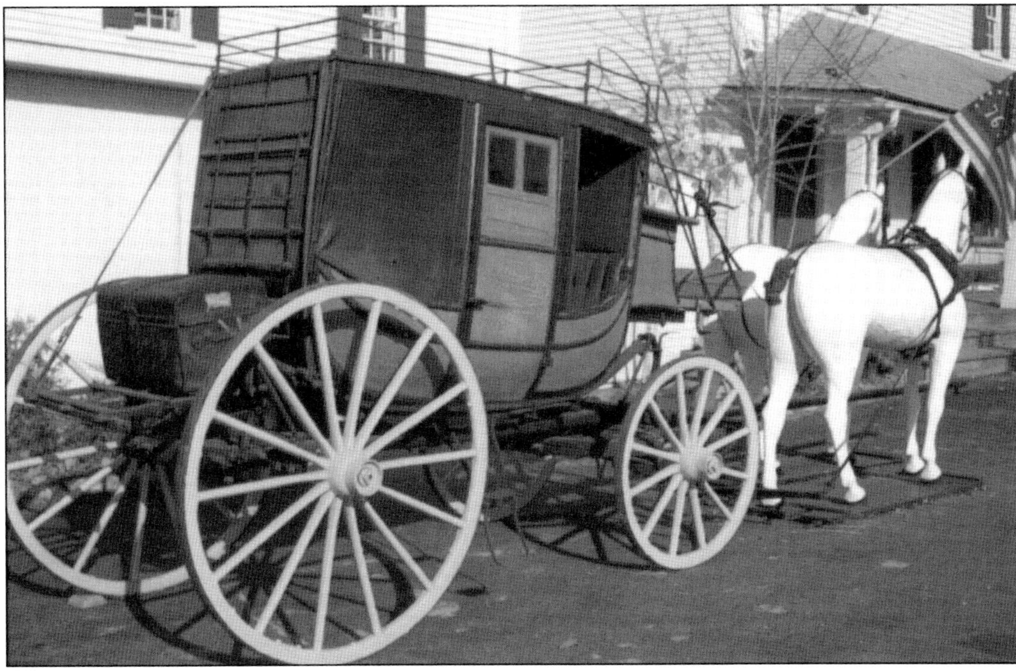

THE ORIGINAL CONCORD COACH NO. 22. This coach can be seen at the Olde Country Store in Moultonborough. It was built in 1847 and is the oldest existing stagecoach of the more than 3,000 manufactured in Concord. It was built for the Bellows family, founders of Bellows Falls, Vermont.

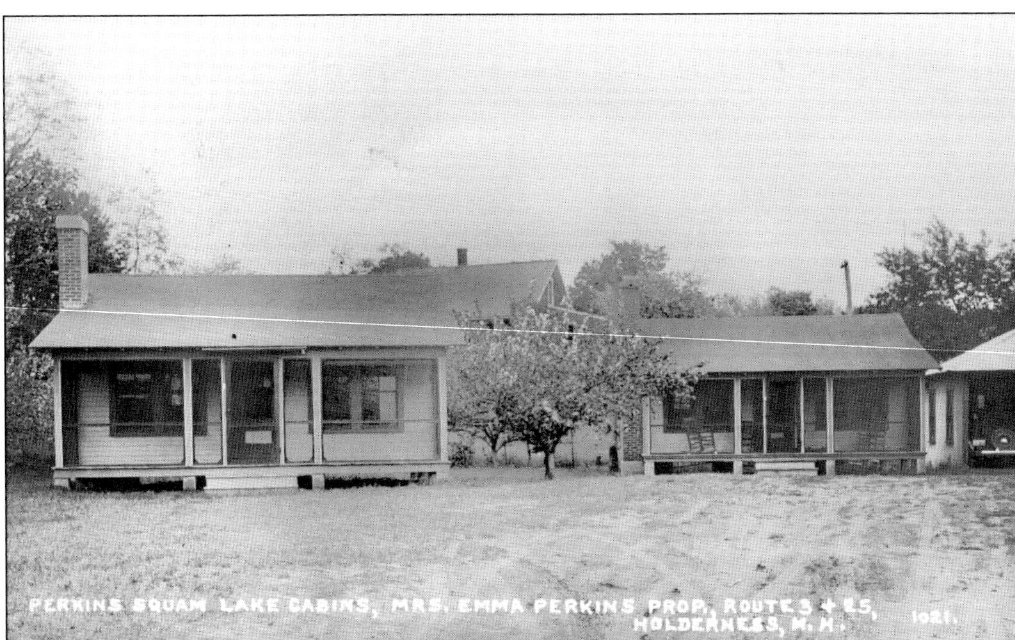

A CABIN COLONY, HOLDERNESS. This group of cabins was typical of tourist stops around the lake. It is Emma Perkins's Squam Lake Cabins, a popular vacation place on the lake.

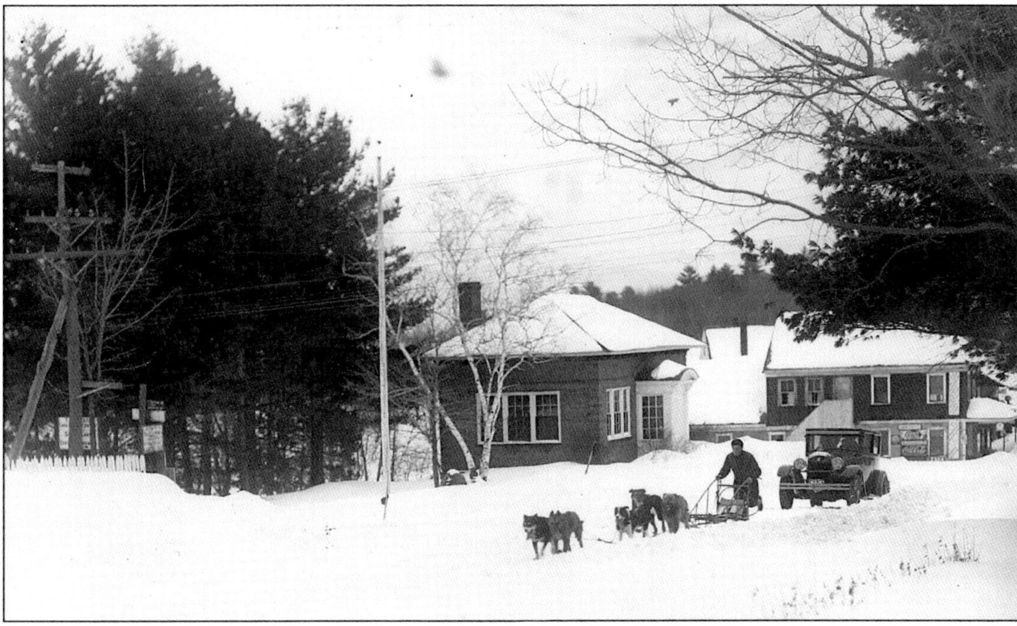

Dogsled Racing through Holderness, c. the 1930s. This annual race usually ran through Holderness as part of the winter carnival. On the left is the library.

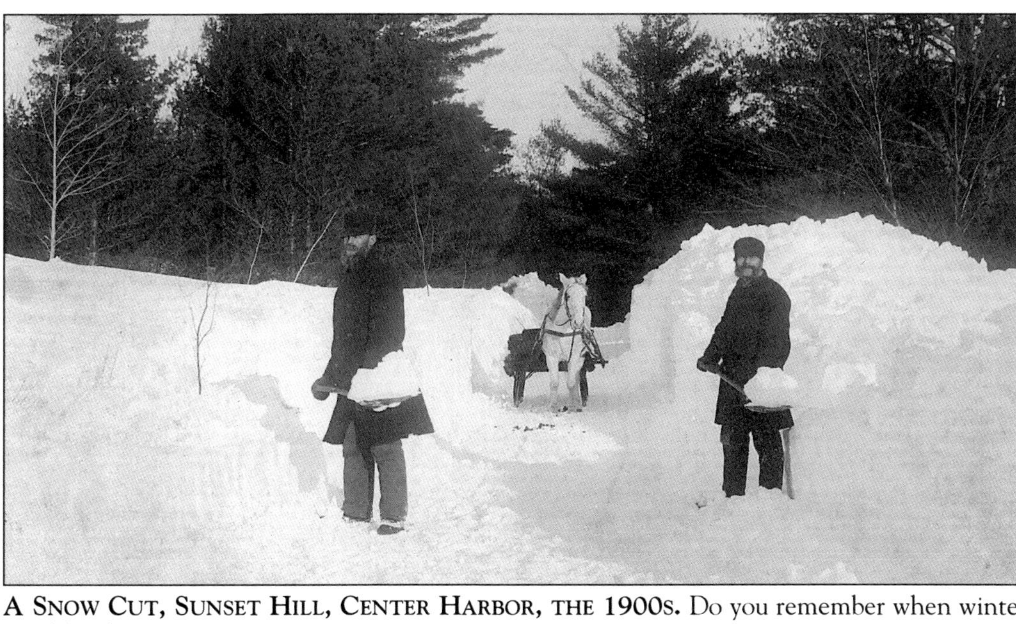

A Snow Cut, Sunset Hill, Center Harbor, the 1900s. Do you remember when winter was like this?

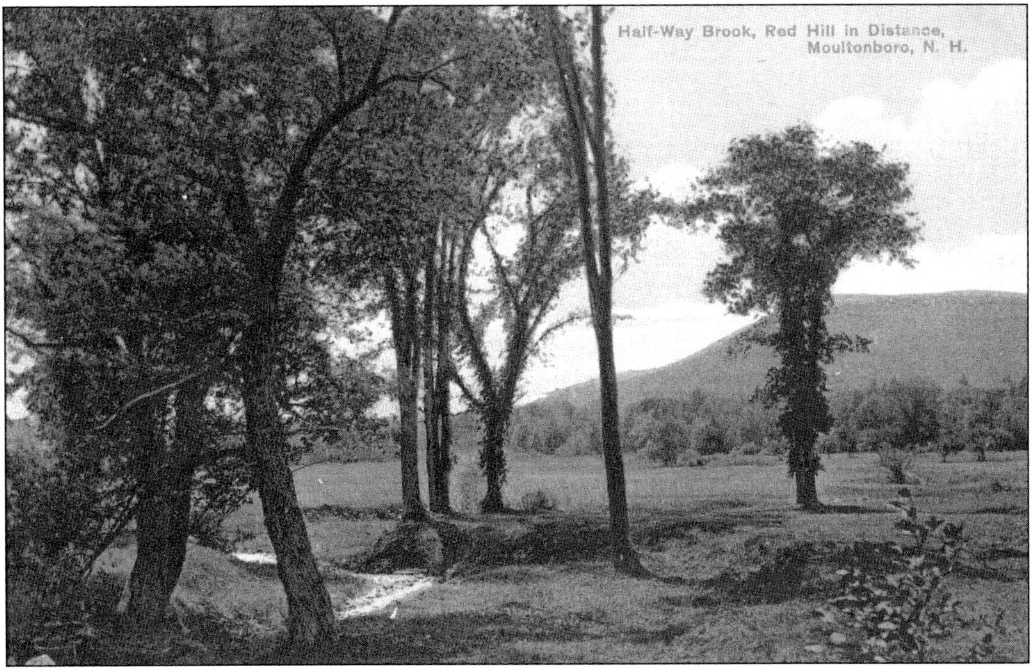

HALFWAY BROOK, MOULTONBOROUGH. What a pleasure: a plush pasture, a quiet country brook, and Red Hill in the distance.

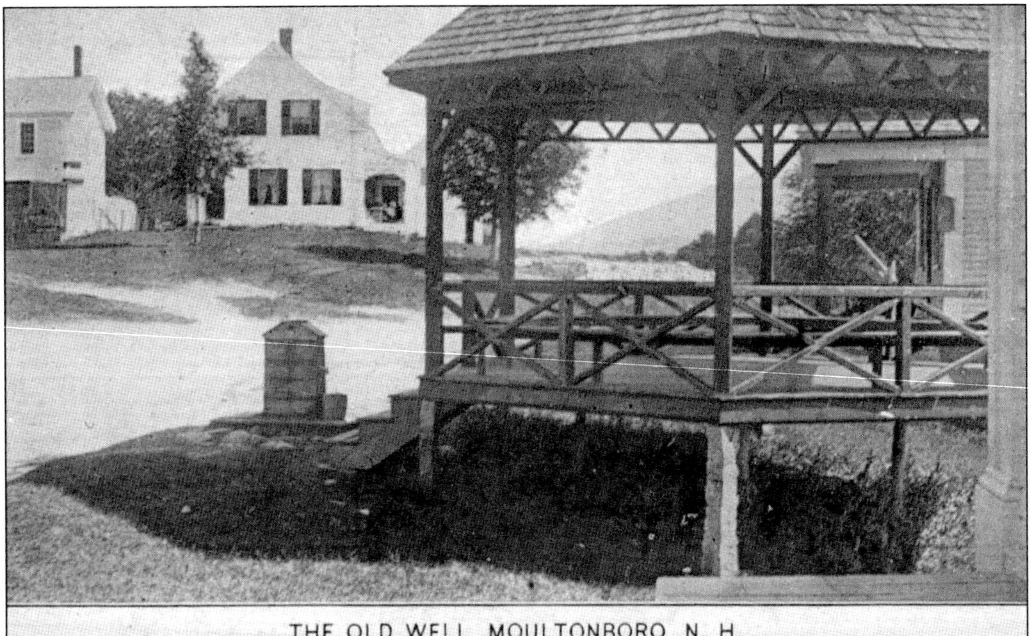

THE OLD WELL. Located at Moultonborough Corner, this was a popular resting place for travelers to and from the White Mountains. The building in back of the stand is the Methodist church.

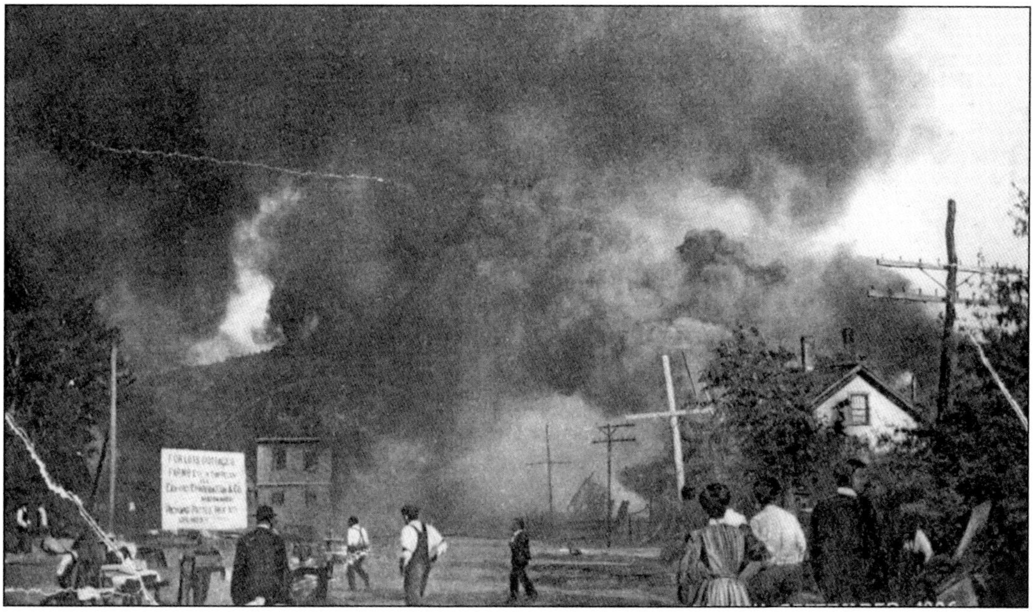

A Fire Scene, Holderness. On September 17, 1906, a major fire destroyed the center of Holderness village.

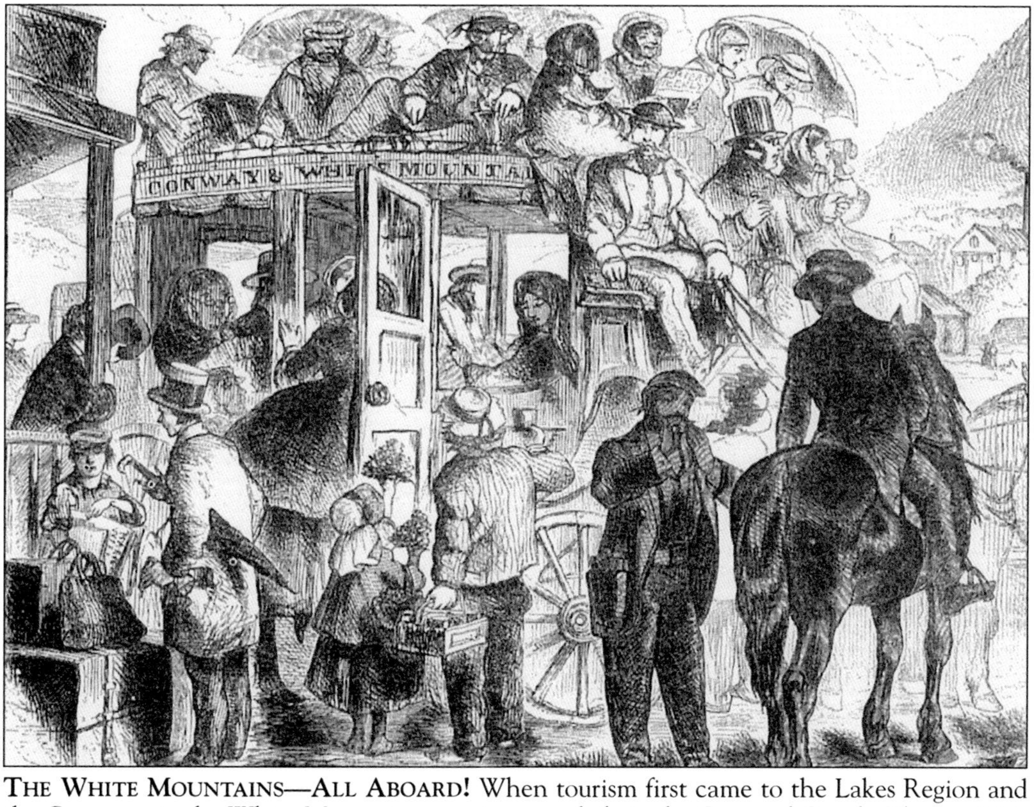

The White Mountains—All Aboard! When tourism first came to the Lakes Region and the Conways, in the White Mountains, tourists traveled via the Concord Coach. This *c.* 1800s scene may be of Center Harbor.

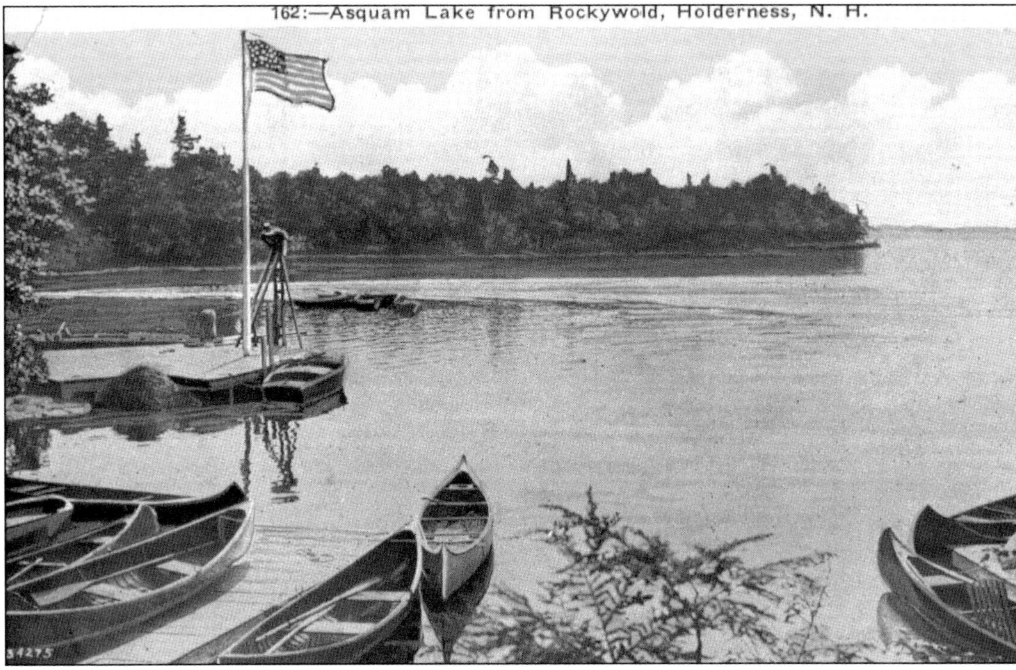

THE WATERFRONT, SQUAM LAKE. At the docks of Rockywold, this welcoming sight invites visitors to take a canoe excursion on Squam Lake.

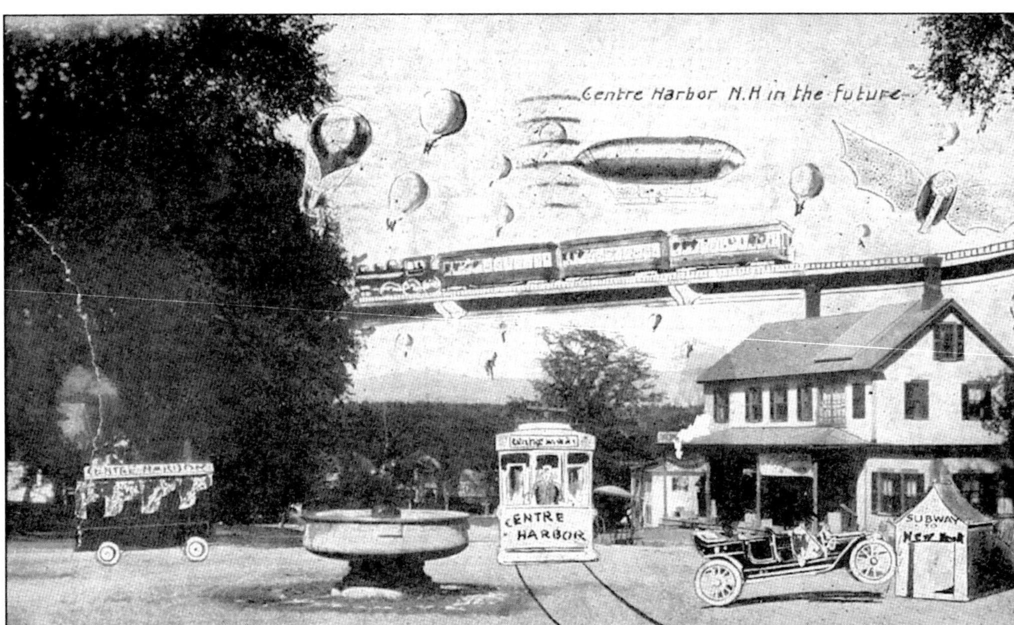

CENTER HARBOR IN THE FUTURE. This humorous old postcard signals what the 21st century will bring to the village.

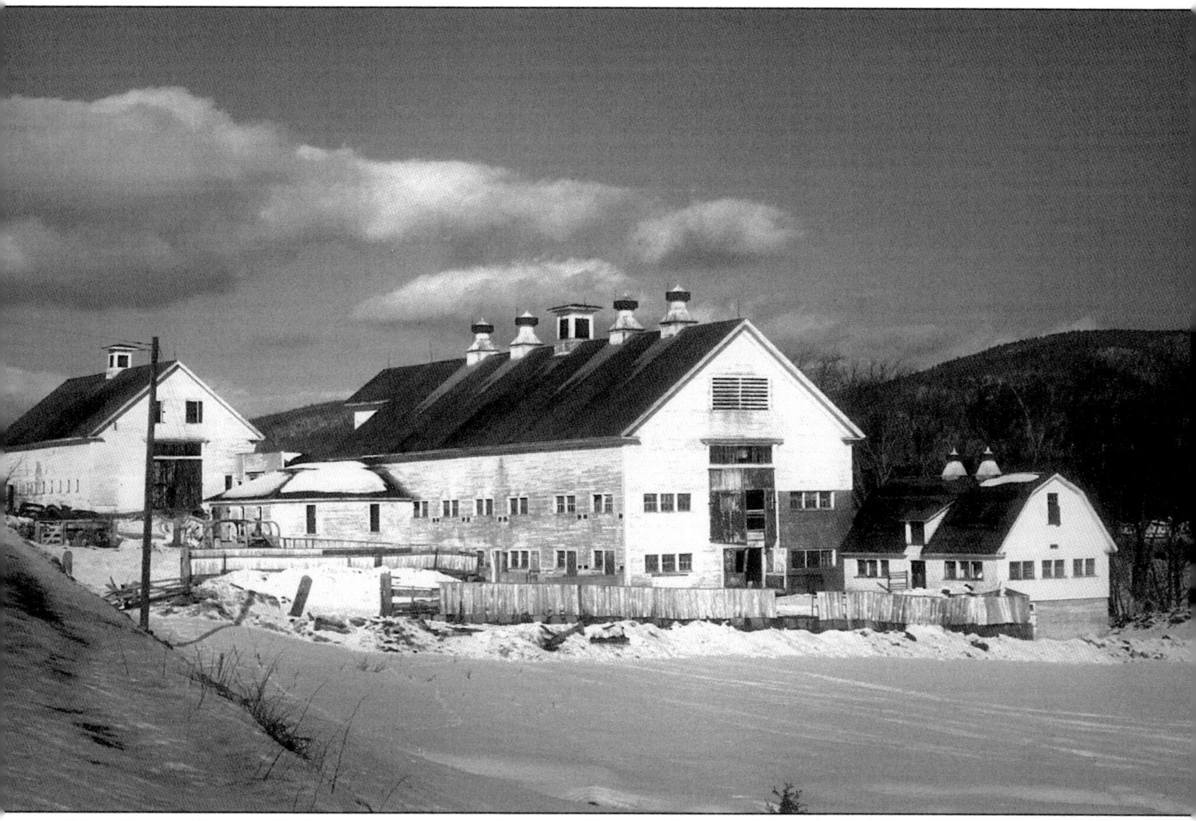

THE DANE FARM. Today, as we approach the village of Center Harbor on Route 25, this grand farm proudly stands as a landmark on the shore of Lake Winnipesaukee. Ernest B. Dane and family came to Center Harbor from Brookline, Massachusetts, and purchased most of the farms that came on the market during World War I, thus preserving Center Harbor country village. The Dane farm included many acres bordering Lake Winnipesaukee and was known as the Longwood Farm. The farm supplied feed for the prize Guernsey cattle in this barn.

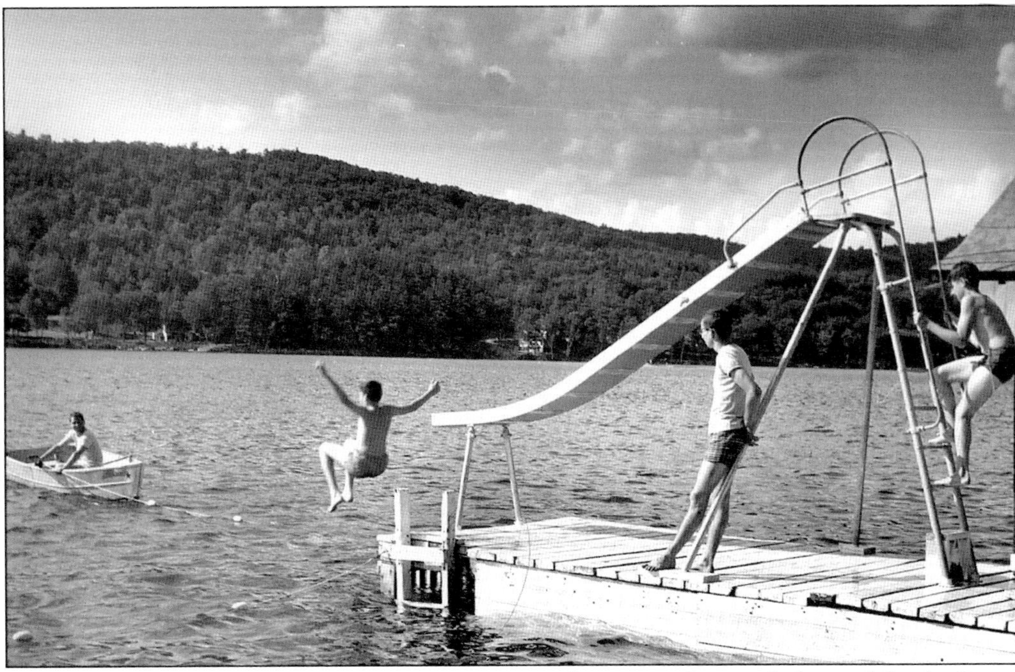

CAMP SQUAMASEE BATHING SCENE. Boys' camps began on Squam Lake and Little Squam Lake; thus, it is appropriate to include this image, a typical scene on the lakes today.

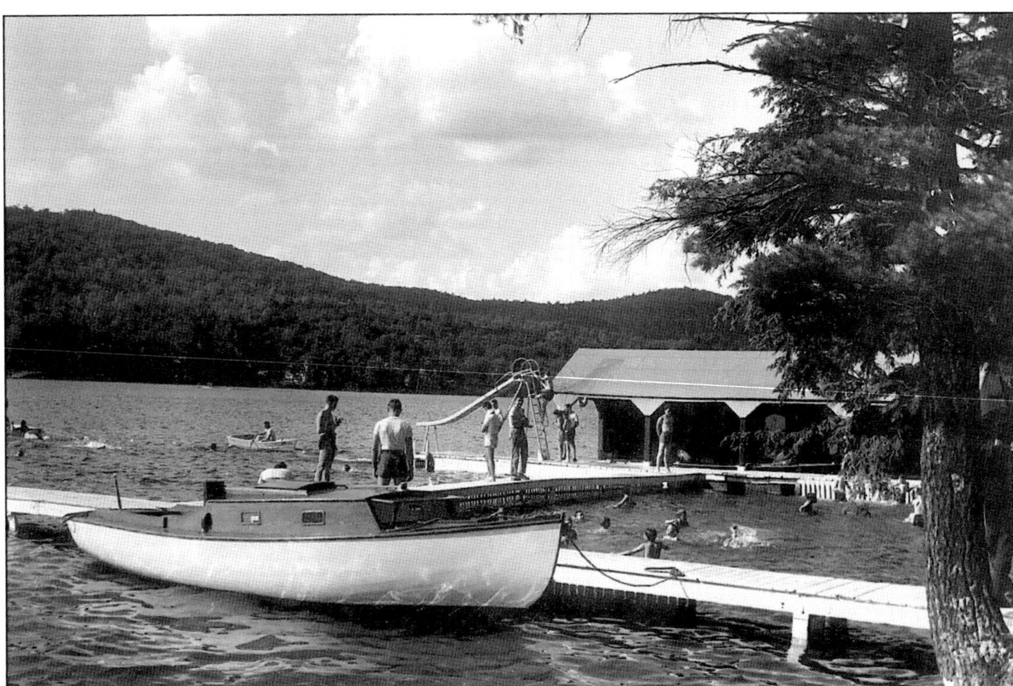

CAMP SQUAMASEE, LITTLE SQUAM LAKE, HOLDERNESS. The area is secured as the waterfront is closed down.

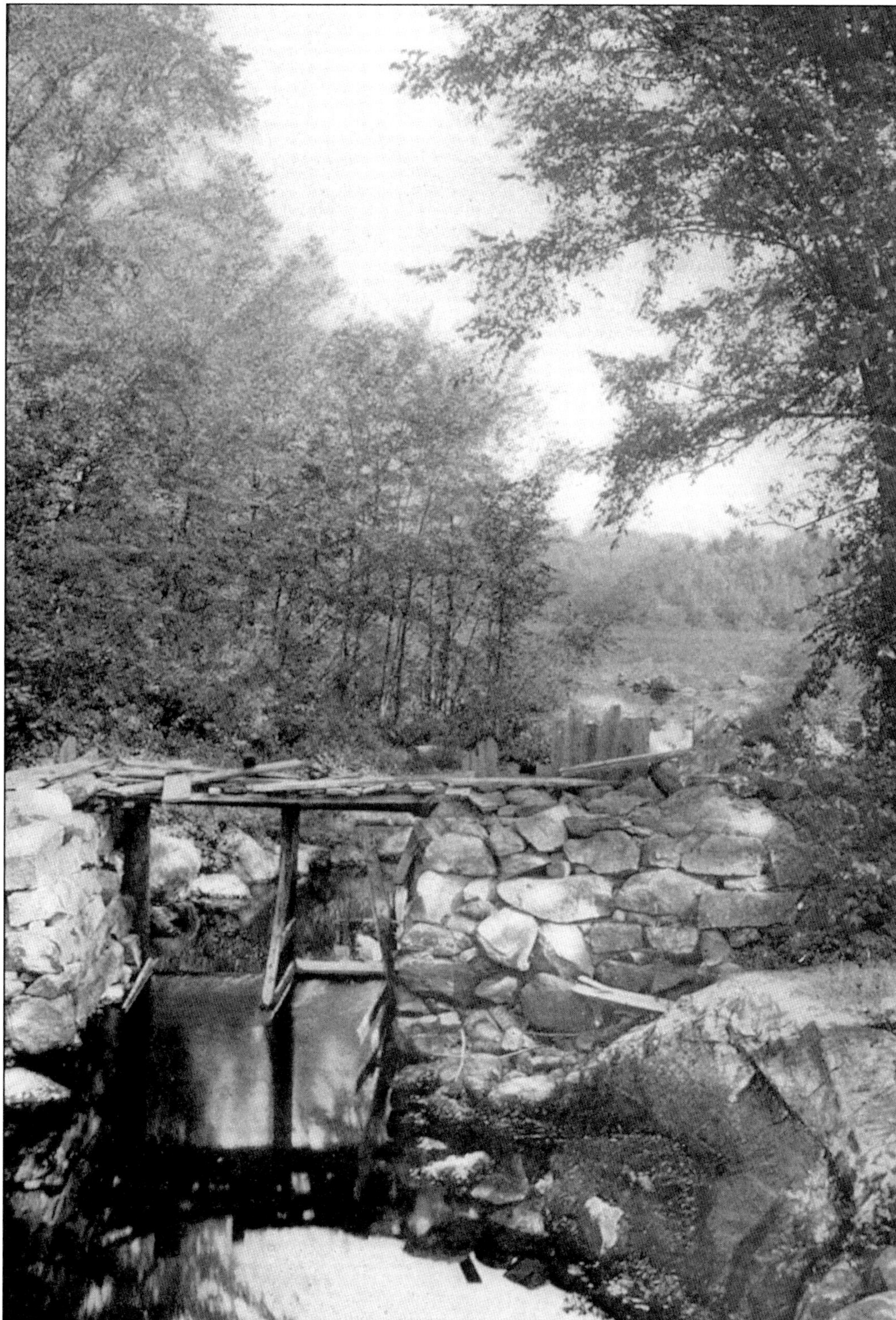

THE STREAM. Nature, at her best, invites the artist and photographer.

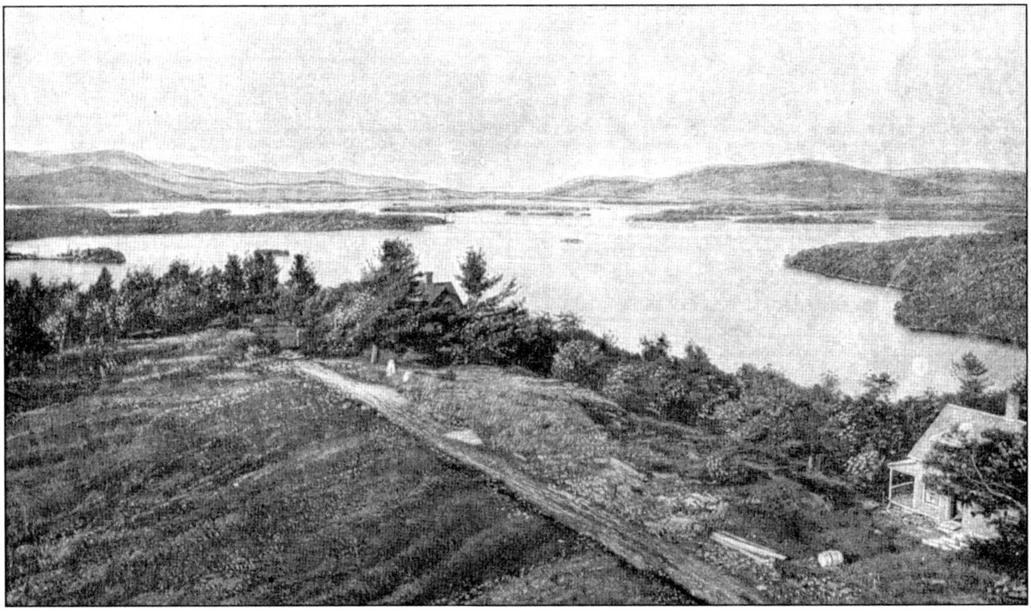

A Bird's-eye View of Squam Lake from Shepard Hill, Holderness, the 1930s. Very little has changed in terms of the charm and beauty of the broad expanse of Squam Lake.

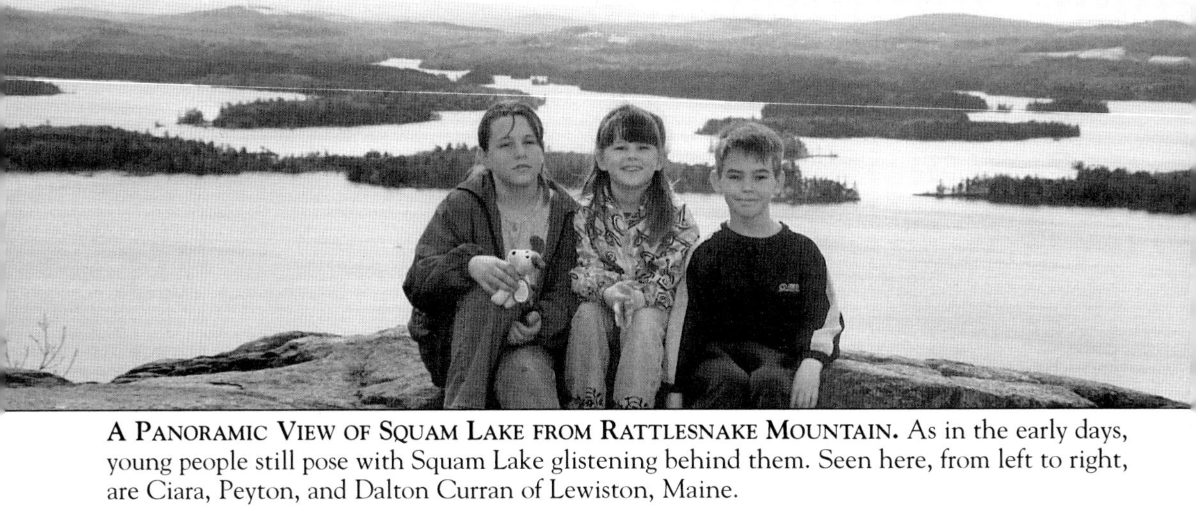

A Panoramic View of Squam Lake from Rattlesnake Mountain. As in the early days, young people still pose with Squam Lake glistening behind them. Seen here, from left to right, are Ciara, Peyton, and Dalton Curran of Lewiston, Maine.